Exploring Lacan's Encore Seminar XX

Exploring Lacan's Encore Seminar XX examines the themes presented in Encore, the seminar presented by Lacan between 1972 and 1975.

Raul Moncayo, Barri Belnap, and Greg Farr focus on Lacan's presentation of the theory of the Third Jouissance, clarifying the difference between jouissance as a concept and as a word. The authors argue that although there are many words that Lacan uses for jouissance, there are only five concepts of jouissance: the first is inconvenient, the second is convenient and inconvenient, while the last three are convenient and constructive.

Exploring Lacan's Encore Seminar XX will be essential reading for academics and scholars of Lacanian studies, Lacanian analysts, and readers interested in Lacan's theories of the 1970s.

Dr. Raul Moncayo has taught at many academic institutions in the Bay Area and abroad. As a retired training director of a large public psychiatric clinic in the Mission district or barrio of San Francisco, he formed and informed generations of clinicians. Dr. Moncayo was founding member of LSP (Lacanian School of Psychoanalysis). He is also the founder of the Chinese American Center for Freudian and Lacanian Analysis and Research. He has published 12 books with Karnac and Routledge. Among them are *Psychoanalysis and American Literature*; *Lacan and Chan Buddhism*; *The Practice of Lacanian Psychoanalysis*; and *Knowing, not-Knowing and Jouissance*.

Dr. Barri Belnap, MD, is a physician and psychoanalyst. A graduate of Geisel School of Medicine at Dartmouth, she completed residency and fellowship at The Austen Riggs Center in Stockbridge, Massachusetts, where she served as a senior clinician for 27 years. Now she is devoted to her private psychoanalytic practice, study of group relations, and leadership. Her speaking and writings span topics from psychoanalytic techniques of PTSD and psychosis and psychopharmacology to affect theory.

Greg Farr currently serves professionally as the Archivist of the Episcopal Church in Connecticut and was formally employed as the Archivist and Librarian at the Austen Riggs Center in Stockbridge, Massachusetts. Greg first developed his interest in Lacan's works during his doctorate studies in the Philosophy of Religion at Boston University. He earned his undergraduate degree in Religious Studies at the University of Montana and his Master's Degree of Theological Studies again at Boston University. Greg additionally completed two years of graduate study in Philosophical Theology at the University of Virginia and subsequently earned an MLIS degree at Drexel University in 2012.

Exploring Lacan's Encore Seminar XX

The Torus of Reason

Raul Moncayo, Barri Belnap
and Greg Farr

LONDON AND NEW YORK

Designed cover image: © Getty Images

First published 2024
by Routledge
4 Park Square, Milton Park, Abingdon, Oxon OX14 4RN

and by Routledge
605 Third Avenue, New York, NY 10158

Routledge is an imprint of the Taylor & Francis Group, an informa business

British Library Cataloguing-in-Publication Data
A catalogue record for this book is available from the British Library

ISBN: 9781032543789 (hbk)
ISBN: 9781032543772 (pbk)
ISBN: 9781003424581 (ebk)

DOI: 10.4324/9781003424581

Typeset in Times New Roman
by codeMantra

Contents

Preface

The origin of this book can be traced back to a seminar led by Raul Moncayo at the Austen Riggs Center between 2016 and 2018, which consisted of an in-depth study of Jacques Lacan's *Seminar XX, Encore: On Feminine Sexuality, The Limits of Love and Knowledge (1972–1973)*. The dialogue with Barri Ann Belnap, Greg Farr, and other participants was the framework for both the seminar and this book. Unlike other books on Lacan's *Seminar XX*, this book is structured differently as it does not rely on individual scholars' personal impressions of Lacan's *Seminar XX*. The participants engaged with Lacan's *Encore* in our publication and raised inquiries drawn from individual encounters, practical applications, and the principles that aid in clarifying both.

In his 1972–1973 seminar, Lacan developed his theory of the 'Third jouissance' based on feminine jouissance, the jouissance of the mystic, and the letter jouissance of meaning as an enigma and a riddle. Our text clarifies the difference between *jouissance* as a concept and as a word. In this book, we argue that although there are many words that Lacan uses for jouissance, there are essentially three forms of jouissance and three forms of the 'Third jouissance'. The first form of jouissance is inconvenient, the second is convenient and inconvenient, while the third, in its three formal expressions, are convenient and constructive.

Seminar XX represents Lacan's teaching on feminine sexuality. Given the importance that Lacan has attributed to the phallus, one would expect that he would confirm Freud's idea about feminine sexuality. For Freud, the libido was basically masculine and the same as phallic sexuality, or masculine sexuality. In this seminar, without explicitly saying so, however, Lacan responds to contemporary feminists. He declares to the world the two propositions that the woman does not exist and that there is a supplementary form of feminine sexuality available for women. Women are not lacking anything in the Real. Anatomical reality is Imaginary and Symbolic. Further, we demonstrate in this work that Lacan's interest in feminine sexuality is not only specialized, because, like Freud, Lacan used female hysteria to draw healing from the psyche, and, unlike Freud, he constructively used hysteria to derive mathematical and topological knowledge about the Mind and the psyche.

Acknowledgments

We would like to give thanks to other participants in our seminar, especially Dr. Elizabeth Weinberg, Dr. Megan Kolano, Dr. Françoise Davoine, Dr. Amy Taylor, Mr. John Prusinski, and Dr. Lisa M. Barksdale-Shaw. We would also like to express our appreciation for the Austen Riggs Center in Stockbridge, MA, and offer a special loving thanks to our respective family members, friends, and colleagues.

We want to thank each other for our help in writing this book as well. Barri brought her years of clinical experience as a psychiatrist, a psychotherapist, and a psychoanalyst, and her excellent skills as a scholar. Greg brought his knowledge of archives and his invaluable understanding of philosophy and religion to the project. We especially wish to thank Raul for sharing with us his extensive knowledge of psychoanalysis across its varied schools. He brings particular focus to the key clinical questions and can trace how different analytic schools answer them differently and why. This allows the conflicts between the schools to be a source of learning instead of confusion and highlights Lacan's own unique contribution to the field of psychoanalysis. Additionally, Raul is able to link such issues to complex developments in the fields of physics, mathematics, religion, literature, and philosophy, which makes learning with him especially valuable. We are grateful for Raul's personhood, teaching, and friendship.

This book represents years of study and discovery in good company.

Chapter 1

Writing, Love, and the Four Levels of the Signifier

Moncayo Seminar: November 10, 2016, *Encore, Seminar XX*, pg. 29, Section 2

TEXT: The written is in no way in the same register or made of the same stuff, if you allow me this expression, as the signifier. The signifier is a dimension that was introduced by linguistics. Linguistics is the field in which speech is produced, is not self-evident. A discourse sustains it, which is scientific discourse. Linguistics introduces into speech a dissociation, thanks to which the distinction between the signifier and the signified is grounded.

RM: Here Lacan is differentiating between speech and written language, or speech and linguistics. One thing is the spoken speech, and the other the linguistic structure, or the analysis of linguistics in terms of the signifier and the signified.

GF: What does he mean by 'scientific discourse'?

RM: Levi-Strauss was trying to use Saussure's linguistic theory as a model for scientific discourse for the social sciences. This has to do more with the analysis of language rather than speech. The practice of analysis is the practice of speech. Lacan is trying to use the theory of linguistics for psychoanalytic theory.

GF: Is Lacan more influenced by Saussure or Jakobson?

RM: He uses both, but the theory of the signifier follows from Saussure. Except that Lacan reverses it, because Saussure puts the signified on the top of the equation and the signifier on the bottom. Lacan reverses the order, putting the signifier above and the signified below. So, he changes the order of the elements. For Saussure, the signified was a mass of undifferentiated ideas and feelings and the signifier is a word – that's the vertical relationship. The horizontal relationship is that words can be substituted for other words. For Lacan, the relationship between the signifier and the signified is more important than the relationship between an undifferentiated mass of ideas and feelings and words. Later, Lacan will also wonder what the connection is between the signifier and the Real, which seems to indicate a difference to where the signified is simply another signifier.

MK: Can you say something about how this relates to metaphor and metonymy?

DOI: 10.4324/9781003424581-1

RM: Well, yes, because metaphor and metonymy describe the relationship between signifiers. Metaphor is the condensation between two signifiers and metonymy is the displacement of one signifier to the next. But metaphor is not just simply a condensation, because there is something about the signifier in metaphor that is concealed since the metaphor represents something but also conceals something else. What the metaphor is concealing is not so obvious.

TEXT: Distinguishing the dimension of the signifier only takes on importance when it is posited that what you hear, in the auditory sense of the term, bears no relation whatsoever to what it signifies. That is an act that is instituted only through a scientific discourse. And it is not self-evident. Indeed, it is so scarcely self-evident that a whole discourse – which does not flow from a bad pen since it is the *Cratylus* by none other than Plato – results from the endeavor to show that there must be a relationship and that the signifier in and of itself means something. To the contrary, a linguist as discerning as Ferdinand de Saussure speaks of arbitrariness. That is tantamount to slipping, slipping into another discourse, the master's discourse, to call a spade a spade. Arbitrariness is not a suitable term here.

BB: So, I am interested in that latter point as well as the previous …

RM: I think it is in the *Cratylus* where Plato talks about the relationship between an object and the signifier, and the signifier in and of itself means something, as if there was a pre-established connection between the word and the object. So, that's a non-arbitrary relationship between the signifier and the object world. And, usually people attribute that more with the language theory of Peirce, as if the signifier had a piece of the object in it, and that is what allows the signifier to represent the object. This was also Freud's view.

BB: Do you mean the Peirce that John Muller talks about?

RM: Yes, [Charles Sanders] Peirce, the American philosopher, linguist, and logician. And, that view is consistent with Plato, but Saussure argues about the arbitrariness of the signifier – meaning that it's arbitrary what word we use to represent what object … that the meaning of the object is internal to language rather than language reading something that is intrinsic to the object. Does that make sense?

BB: It does, although what you are saying about Peirce seems to me to contradict what John Muller is saying in his seminars. For him, it seems like it's the interpretant[1] that gives language its meaning. I believed that Lacan thought, along with Saussure, that the relationship between signifier and signified is arbitrary insofar as it is defined by the 'language game'. And the 'language game' can be played multiple ways but always in relation to its historical and cultural link.

RM: Well, it's the differential relationship to the other signifiers – that's where the meaning comes from. The link between the object and the signifier is arbitrary.

GF: From what I know about Peirce, he was very concerned about the fact that what we say in our language can somehow connect with reality, in one way or another.

RM: Right, so 'connect with reality' is the key term, as if there was a 'pre-established' reality there, right?

GF: That's right, and he doesn't necessarily claim that there is a link, but rather thought that the more one engages with the sign or the thing, one is going to land eventually on something real. What I understand about Peirce is that he was arguing with Kant concerning the nature of 'intuition' and the problematic of understanding something intuitively … that is, already 'built in' to your mind *a priori* … but with Peirce, there are only signs and their interpretation – and these different signs – the icon, the index (the index, in particular, has a direct link to its object and the icon 'looks like' the object), and the symbol – has some kind of connection or carryover to the object.

RM: Right, but in Lacan, even though the index … let's say letters that associate to some animal, like they say the letter 'A' is the iconic image of a bull … that connection for Lacan is suppressed under primary repression. So, the original connection to the object is lost, and meaning becomes internal to the structure of language. So, in Lacan, the object is defined – as in Saussure as well, although Saussure is a little more complicated – the object is defined by the concept. And, the concept is defined by the word, because you have no discernable concepts without discrete words. So, is thinking outside language? Well, there is an element of the signified that is this undifferentiated mass of ideas, but those are still of the subject – they are not intrinsic to the object itself. So, the object in Lacanian psychoanalysis is constructed by the Imaginary and the Symbolic.

In Peirce, there are four levels that we believe need to be organized in this way under the influence of Lacanian theory. The first level corresponds to some vague idea or quality of feeling, a quale,[2] otherwise known as the thing in itself. The second level is the icon or the visual representation. The third level is the index or the pointer where you use objects or fingers to point at images. The fourth level is the level of the signifier which itself has four units: letter, phoneme, morpheme, semanteme. Then the relationship between images and words is that between signifier and signified. Or the signifying relationship can be between words/signifiers. Finally, the signified for the signifier can also be in the Real of jouissance and the body. This level goes back to the first level where the experience of the body is some form of undefinable feeling defined as the thing in itself.

BB: Is that why, when he says in that last paragraph, that when Saussure speaks about arbitrariness it is wrong – he says, "That is tantamount to slipping, slipping into another discourse, the master's discourse, to call a spade a spade. Arbitrariness is not a suitable term here". Why is he saying that?

RM: Because meaning is internal to the structure of language and it's arbitrary in that sense. Language can be co-opted by the Imaginary … how 'the master' makes use of the language for purposes of political manipulation, expediency, or to use the signifier to secure a lack in the subject, and so forth. So, there's a 'slipping', because it's arbitrary, and the meaning of the object 'slips' within language. Then he adds that it doesn't have to be the 'master's discourse'. But, when he adds the 'master's discourse', then this is how the slippage falls into ideology or the imaginary use of language.

BB: So, is he playing with two definitions of 'arbitrary' – one being that the Imaginary isn't arbitrary because it is defined by all of these other interests … and the other kind of arbitrary is that the link between the signifier and the signified is a convention?

RM: Well, it's an arbitrary use. The 'master' is making arbitrary use of the structure of language and then the structure of language is arbitrary in relation to the object.

BB: Yes, that makes sense.

GF: Yes, it does … but how can we distinguish 'language' from culture and society?

RM: Well, what is society? It's a social link, right? And, the social link is constructed on the basis of language, which is an aspect of the Symbolic. But, in the Symbolic you also have 'myths', you have 'values', you have 'laws' … so language is one of the aspects, but it's a determining aspect of the Symbolic.

BB: I thought I might just read this footnote, no. 14…

TEXT: "… linguistics, in the field in which speech is produced, is not 'self-evident' (aller de soi)". The expression Lacan uses here, *aller de soi*, variants of which are repeated throughout the next few paragraphs, can generally be translated as to be self-evident, but more literally means to go at it alone; stand-alone requires no outside support. Here, linguistics is sustained by another discourse, scientific discourse.

RM: The scientific discourse, meaning that language is explained by a scientific discourse. In this sense, the scientific discourse refers to how Levi-Strauss (1967) wanted to use linguistics to give social science a structure. So, 'going it alone' means that language 'goes at it alone' in defining the objects of reality. It doesn't need reference to the object. So, let me read you something from Peirce … this, I quote him … "according to this, every sign has a precept of explanation according to which it is understood to be a sort of emanation, so to speak, of its object". You see [here] how the sign is an 'emanation' of the object? "If the sign be an icon, a scholastic might say that the species of the object emanating from it found its matter in the icon. If the sign be an 'index', we may think of it as a fragment torn away from the object". (So, here we could say it is like the letter 'a' being torn away from the image of a bull.) "The two in their existence being a whole or one part of such a whole". The sign, or the index in this case, could be a part of the whole. So, he is making the object a whole – or there being a 'hole' between the sign and the object. "If the sign is a symbol, we may think of it as embodying the ratio or 'reason' of the object that has emanated from it". That means Peirce is establishing a certain kind of rationality to the symbol, which I guess would make sense if we were to think of the symbol as a signifier (although not in other ways that people think about symbols). We may think of it as embodying the ratio or reason that has emanated from it so that the object has a ratio or a rational structure out of which emanates the symbol. "These of course are mere figures of speech, but that does not render them useless". So, you see Peirce is pretty clear in this, whether it is the sign (icon), the index, or the symbol – they are all emanations from or different aspects of the object. That seems to be in very strong contrast to the notion of the signifier as being arbitrary in Saussure, and it follows more in the theory of language that we find in Plato, in this dialogue that Lacan is quoting [*Cratylus*].

EW: I did not know that dialogue, so I just read a summary of it to help me out, and the summary said that there are two characters that Socrates is talking to in the dialogue. The first is said to represent the 'naturalist' point of view, which says the meaning of a word comes naturally from what the object is … and he [Socrates] spends some time convincing that person that that could not be completely true, which takes you more in the 'arbitrary' direction. Then, at the end, the person arguing for the arbitrary position – that there is no connection – he ends up demonstrating that there has to be some natural connection. So, he kind of argues both sides.

RM: Right, so the way I reconcile that is that there is an original connection between the letter and the object, but once the letter becomes a letter – meaning 'the bull' becomes a letter 'A' or the 'ox' becomes a letter 'A'– then the letter 'A' is used differentially in relationship to other letters to construct signification rather than by reference to the 'ox'. So, the letter has a connection to the object, but that is lost as the letter then functions as a basic unit of the signifier in relation to the other two units of the signifier, which are 'the word' as opposed to 'letter' and 'the sentence'. The word is a morpheme and the sentence is a semanteme. So, at the level of the word and the level of the sentence, the signifier functions differentially rather than in relationship to the object as the letter originally did. Does that make sense? [*Participants agree*]

TEXT: To say that the signifier is arbitrary does not have the same import as to simply say that it bears no relation to its meaning effect, for the former involves slipping into another reference.

RM: Yes, so that would be the other reference – the meaning effect (*signifiance*) – the effect that the signifier can have, for example, on the body as opposed to in relationship to another signifier. So, the signified can be another word, but the signified can be more than a word – and that's where he comes up with mathematical symbols (i.e., square root of –1, or a signifier without a signified).

This is also a reference to what Saussure talks about in terms of the plane of undifferentiated ideas and feelings, which is a way of talking about jouissance. So Lacan says that jouissance is a form of thinking that is not determined by language. That would be where the signifier is functioning at that level (body) rather than functioning at the level of another signifier.

BB: That is so helpful! Thank you!

RM: So, now what he says about discourse … I think he is making this reference there to be careful not to mix up different discourses and to stay within the consistency of a particular discourse, because although different discourses may use the same words, they are not necessarily the same concepts. In order to stay consistent to the concept, you have to stay within the internal logic of the discourse, and that's a common way of thinking about things. But it is also contradicted by the fact that neither Lacan nor Freud did that because Freud borrowed concepts from other fields – economics, anthropology, sociology, philosophy, biology, physics – and Lacan did the same with linguistics, anthropology, sociology, et cetera. So, they both borrowed from other discourses outside of psychoanalysis in order to construct psychoanalysis.

TEXT: The word, in this case, can only be situated on the basis of what discourse constitutes by way of a link (*lien*). The signifier as such refers to nothing if not to a discourse, in other words, a mode of functioning or a utilization of language qua link.

RM: An ambiguity in Lacan, in Lacanian theory, is that S_1 and S_2 can mean the relationship between two signifiers. Since a signifier is what represents a subject for another signifier, it can also represent the relationship between two subjects as they are speaking. It's both a link between representations and a social link between subjects.

BB: What's the connection between the phallus and the signifier? And how does the signifier kill the object?

RM: Well, because of sexuality. It's the problem that Freud came up with in *Beyond the Pleasure Principle* – he defined *Eros* as that which makes links or unities, [which] brings things together and links them up. But, at the same time, he had to deal with the fact that sexuality also breaks the links between subjects. What's paradoxical in the title is that you don't know if in *Beyond the Pleasure Principle* the definition of pleasure is one of seeking a kind of stability of excitations (that would be more under the constancy principle) or whether pleasure means trying to reduce excitation to 'level 0', which is something that is impossible to achieve and its tied to sexuality. So, sexuality is trying to go to zero, and that's what makes it traumatic. In that sense, sexuality is more the 'death drive' than love. But, then the problem with love is also that love can also break unions or create unions. This is because the two drives are intertwined, and that is why sexuality can involve both life and death. It can create new life, but it can also destroy life. People commit suicide and murder out of love. What is also paradoxical is that what we said about love and unity in *eros*, applies to the Greek *agape* [Platonic love]. *Eros* for the Greeks was always ambivalent – thus Nietzsche's *Birth of Tragedy*. *Eros* includes the phallus, but in agape the phallus is missing (i.e., the Symbolic phallus). Regarding 'the word' killing the object, the word kills the object, because as a system, the word refers to another word over the object. The killing of the object is the positive determination of the death drive in language.[3] The death drive helps the subject to be inscribed in the Symbolic. And that's the radical ambiguity in Freud's text between the life drive and death drive, and between *agape* and *eros*. But Lacan also talks about human beings being 'speaking' beings – that's the 'living speech'. Then, on the other hand, language also destroys the relationship to the object. That's what I was talking about before in terms of the link of the letter to the object being severed.

GF: So, the link of the subject is the primary link?

RM: It's a primary link within language.

TEXT: Already, by merely swimming with the tide of analytic discourse, we have made a jump known as a worldview (*conception du monde*), which to us must nevertheless be the funniest thing going. The term worldview supposes a discourse – that of philosophy that is entirely different from ours.

If we leave behind philosophical discourse, nothing is less certain than the existence of a world. One can only laugh when one hears people claim that analytic discourse involves something on the order of such a conception.

RM: Okay, so there he is following Freud, I forget exactly where it was in *Civilization and Its Discontents*, where he says, "psychoanalysis is not a philosophy because it's not a worldview". It's not something that explains everything … it is not like philosophy that is supposed to give you an entire view of the world. Lacan is just emphasizing that psychoanalysis is not philosophical discourse. This is the whole problem about what philosophy is, because, you know, a lot of people think that Lacan is very philosophical because he incorporates philosophical discourse into psychoanalysis. But, in no way does he try to claim that psychoanalysis explains everything. So, it's not philosophy because it's tied to direct experience, and it's tied to a specific practice. Although now he is going to talk about Marxism because Marxism tried to define philosophy in terms of a practice instead of just simply theory and worldview.

TEXT: Language proves to be a field much richer in resources than if it were merely the field in which philosophical discourse has inscribed itself over the course of time. But certain reference points have been enunciated by that discourse that are difficult to completely eliminate from any use of language.

That is why there is nothing easier than to fall back into what I ironically called a world-view, but which has a more moderate and more precise name: ontology. Ontology is what highlighted in language the use of the copula, isolating it as a signifier. To dwell on the verb "to be" – a verb that is not even, in the complete field of the diversity of languages, employed in a way we could qualify as universal – to produce it as such is a highly risky enterprise.

RM: The copula there is the copula in language between words – and the verb 'to be', as if 'being' could be designated by language. So, this refers to the problem of whether being is given by language or whether Being, referring to ontology (because in Heidegger you have the 'ontological' versus the 'ontic' dimension of objects), is a place in which language stops or fails to describe Being. This then refers to the question of the Real – but it is not like the Real exists on its own outside of the Borromean knot. So, there is no ontology, [as if] there were a ground, or even a groundless ground of Being that is independent from the signifier – they both arise together. You can't reduce Being to language either because all you get is the ontic dimension.

BB: So, what makes a gospel 'a gospel' when he is talking about Marx, because sometimes people speak about religion and whether psychoanalysis is a religion. I am just curious … what makes a gospel 'gospel'?

RM: Religion has been criticized for making promises but leaving the world unchanged. For example, Christianity was supposed to bring the redemption of the world, and although Christ arrived, the world remained unchanged. So, Marxism, which continues the tradition of the prophets, was strongly focused on social injustice, the oppression of the poor, and the helpless. Marxism continues that tradition in promising to fight injustice and agreeing with the statement that 'it is easier for a camel to go through the eye of the needle than a rich person to enter the kingdom of heaven'. The difference between religion and philosophy, because before Marx, what Marx called the 'poverty of philosophy', is to leave the world unchanged. So, he wants to ground philosophy in a revolutionary practice. Lacan here I think is making a little of fun of that, because they would not like it if people said that Marxism is a gospel or a religion in the same way that psychoanalysts don't like it when people refer to psychoanalysis as a religion. But the gospel refers to that belief that there's a link between the verb, or 'the Word', and an experience.

The Jewish book of Genesis in the Torah says that "In the beginning, the earth was void and unformed". And then God said, "Let there be light". In the Gospel of John, which is the Gospel and not the Torah, God spoke, and the world was created.

BB: I don't understand that exactly … aren't there many relationships between a word and an experience?

RM: Yeah, if you say, for instance, the 'living waters' of the gospel. The 'living waters' of the gospel – the waters of salvation – refers to an experience. So, that's why Lacan says that the gods are real. It refers to an experience and not just a philosophical or intellectual discourse. In religion, it refers to an experience, whereas in Marxism, it refers first to a practice. But, in either case, it is not a purely intellectual, philosophical discourse. Practice leads to experience.

BB: I see.

TEXT: In order to exorcise it, it might perhaps suffice to suggest that when we say about anything whatsoever that it is what it is, nothing in any way obliges us to isolate the verb that is pronounced; it is what it is (*est ce que c'est*), and it could just as well be written "idizwadidiz" (*seskecé*). In this use of the copula, we would see nothing at all. We would see nothing whatsoever in a discourse. The discourse of the master, m'être, emphasizes the verb to be (*être*).

RM: It is idizwadidiz! [*ALL laugh*] The thing is what is 'it'? And, if you describe 'it' as something, then you are within the level of the Symbolic. Lacan is always talking about the Symbolic in terms of 'the master', so I am not sure why he is collapsing the two, because the discourse of the master is more an imaginary use of the Symbolic – like to be 'someone', to become 'someone' – and the master wants to become 'someone'. Trump wants to become 'someone', wants to be 'the savior' of poorly educated white America. But most likely he will fall flat on his face. It's like when Schwarzenegger became governor of California – because the politicians don't know what they are doing, they are all subject of special interests, they are all corrupt, they are all full of shit, and so on and so forth – he became governor and he did not govern any better than any politician or any other governor, and, in fact, it took Jerry Brown to come and save him, you know, because Jerry Brown was a very skillful, experienced politician and then California thrived again. I believe that will be the same thing that happens with Trump – that Trump is going to fail as a politician because, like Freud said, politics and education in psychoanalysis are impossible discourses. And, because of that, they are impossible problems … so, to think, "oh, that's a bad politician because, look, they try to solve this problem and look what happened!" "But I'm the master! And, if I am given the same problem, of course I am going to solve it so much better!" So, he is going to fall flat on his face because he is not going to have any better chance at success in solving the problems that he blamed other politicians for not being able to solve. That's the effect of the Master's Discourse, and that, of course, is just a reference to how many felt after the election.

GF: You don't think Trump is going to be able to 'drain the swamp'?

RM: Only HE can do it! [*Laughing*] If anybody can do it, HE can! Going back, 'idizwadidiz' is like lalangue in the way he writes it in language. It's a homophony with "it is what it is", but he calls it 'idizwadidiz' because it is a reference to the 'thing in itself'. The 'thing in itself' doesn't have to do with the structure of (small 'b') 'being', because the structure of being is given by the signifier. And, yet, because the signifier has broken or lost its original connection to the object ... there was a connection to the object, right? ... from then on [after the loss], the object is defined within the signifying system. There is something about the thing in itself that retains a link, that retains a quality of the Real outside the Symbolic – and that link can only be established through lalangue rather than through language. So, here he says *idizwadidiz*!

Notes

1 The concept of "interpretant" is part of Charles Sanders Peirce's "triadic" theory of the sign. For Peirce, the interpretant is an element that allows taking a *representamen* for the sign of an *object* and is also the "effect" of the process of *semeiosis* or signification. Peirce delineates three types of interpretants: the immediate, the dynamical, and the final or normal. https://en.wikipedia.org/wiki/Interpretant.
2 A quality or property as perceived or experienced by a person; a property as it is experienced as distinct from any source it might have in a physical object (such as redness).
3 See Hegel's *Phenomenology of Spirit* (1807).

Supplemental References

Freud, Sigmund. (1920). *Beyond the Pleasure Principle*. SE 18, 7–64.
Freud, Sigmund. (1930). *Civilization and Its Discontents*. SE 21, 59–145.
Jakobson, R. (1990). *On Language*. Cambridge, MA: Harvard University Press.
Lacan, J. (1972–1973). *Encore. The Seminar of Jacques Lacan, XX*. New York: Norton, 1998.
Hegel, F. H. (1807). *The Phenomenology of the Spirit*. Cambridge: Cambridge University Press, 2018.
Heidegger, M. (1927). *Being and Time: A Translation of Sein und Zeit*. Albany: State University of New York Press, 1996.
Levi-Strauss, C. (1967). *The Elementary Structures of Kinship*. Boston, MA: Beacon Press.
Kant, I. (2004). *Critique of Practical Reason* (T. K. Abbott, Trans.). New York, NY. Dover Publications.
Marx, K. (1818). *The German Ideology*. New York: Prometheus Books, 1998.
Muller, J. P. (1996). *Beyond the Psychoanalytic Dyad. Developmental Semiotics in Freud, Peirce, and Lacan*. New York: Routledge.
Nietzsche, Friedrich Wilhelm. (1995). *The Birth of Tragedy*. New York: Dover Publications.
Peirce, Charles S. (1867, 2009). *The Essential Peirce: Selected Philosophical Writings. Volumes 1 and 2*. Peirce Edition Project (Ed.). Bloomington & Indianapolis: Indiana University.
Plato. *Cratylus*. Cambridge: Hackett Classics Plato. The Apology. In: Harvard Classics. CT: Grolier Enterprises, 1980.
Saussure, F. (1915). *Course in General Linguistics*. New York: Mc-Graw Hill, 1966.

Chapter 2

"Idizwadidiz"

Moncayo Seminar December 01, 2016, *Encore, Seminar XX*, pg. 36

RM: I have been reading a book Barri recently gave me, John Muller's *Beyond the Psychoanalytic Dyad* … it's a little different because he is thinking about the linguistic nonverbal still being verbal, but it's a code that is still not the signifier – and it doesn't seem to be related to the Father.

[AT joins seminar] MK: I mentioned that you [Amy] were a student of Bruce Fink.

AT: Yeah, I am so glad to be joining you all today. Thanks for letting me come in in the middle of things.

GF: We're always in the middle of things! [laughter]

MK: Barri just gave Raul John's book, and he's describing his take on John's ideas.[1]

RM: Right, I am reading it, so I'll have a better sense and can give you a little report at the end in terms of some of the similarities and differences, because basically he is using American developmental psychology and using Peirce's work … and Lacan … but, so far there is no relation [developed] to the Name of the Father with respect to the proto-linguistic code. So, that seems to be different. I am not saying it is wrong or anything. I am just pointing out some of the similarities and differences. I will have more to say, and maybe we can also look at the difference between 'the Three' or 'the Third' in Peirce – because Peirce has a notion of 'the Third' which is similar to 'the Other' in Lacanian theory. We can look at that later. I just wanted to let you know that I am reading that.

MK: Okay, we said that we were going to start at page 36, section 4? And, in the first page, Lacan is saying something about the difference between the letter and the signifier. So, let's read …

TEXT: The letter is, radically speaking, an effect of discourse. The first time, as far as I recall, that I spoke of the letter … I mentioned the fact that a certain Sir Flinders Petrie believed he had discovered that the letters of the Phoenician alphabet existed well before

DOI: 10.4324/9781003424581-2

the time of small Egyptian pottery, where they served as manufacturer's marks. That means that the letter first emerged from the market, which is typically an effect of discourse, before anyone dreamt of using letters to do what? Something that has nothing to do with the connotation of the signifier, but that elaborates and perfects it.

GF: Do we want to go on or do we want to talk about that?

RM: Sure, so he's talking about how letters arose. He doesn't say so much now, because he does that in *Seminar IX* on identification, but he traces the letter to the Phoenician alphabet and to the Chinese language, where you have a letter as an image – a pictogram. The earliest forms of letters were images of objects, which then became independent from the object. For Muller and Peirce, that would be the icon, which is the beginning of the code. In the Lacanian model, there's a repression of that link between the signifier, the letter, and the object. The connection to the object is lost and then the Symbolic becomes a kind of self-organizing system unto itself that is separate from the Imaginary. So, there is a conflict between images and words and that's the dynamic Freudian conflict of the psyche. But you don't see that conflict in the relationship for Peirce between icon, index, and sign/symbol – it's also unclear whether all those are the signifiers or whether the sign is something larger than the signifier. With Saussure and Lacan, the letter is the minimal unit of the signified. Then there is the phoneme, the word, and the sentence … those are the four levels of the signifier. So, the letter is still a unit of the signifier as distinct from thinking of all those things as the sign and the signifier as one of the levels of the sign. I am not sure how important that is, but that can be confusing because we think we are talking about the same thing, but we are not talking about the same thing. It's a slightly different way of thinking about the relationship of the letter, the icon, and the signifier. Does that make sense? Do you have any questions?

GF: How would you describe the 'manufacturer's marks'?

RM: I think he is talking about the materiality of the signifier (in French '*mot*' means 'word') or of language – how language or signifiers arose from practical situations as opposed to a more abstract process where you have an abstract system, like mathematics, that you applied to the reality of things. The 'mark of the manufacturer' … like 'Made in Japan' or an 'Apple product' … those are just words or sentences made of signifiers. I think when he mentions that in the text, he is referring to the meta-reality of the signifier and how it arose in practical conditions. Does that make sense? [*ALL agree*]

TEXT: We should approach things at the level of the history of each language. It is clear that the letters which upset us so much that we call them, God only knows why, by a different name to wit, Chinese letters, emerged from very ancient Chinese discourse in a way that was very different from the way in which our letters emerged. Emerging from analytic discourse, the letters I bring out here have a different value from those that can emerge from set theory.

The uses one makes of them differ, but nevertheless – and this is what is of interest – they are not without converging in some respect. Any effect of discourse is good, in the sense that it is constituted by the letter.

RM: Okay, so he is talking about the letters of the alphabet. He's not saying now how they originally evolved from objects, but rather how the letter is used [as a function] in mathematics or set theory, such as the letters he uses for the Symbolic phallus ($+\varphi$, $-\varphi$), the Imaginary phallus, the *objet a*, and so on ... and how he uses letters to describe his 'algebra'. Also, he is discussing what the relationship is between these letters that appear senseless ... like usually in mathematics, those letters in themselves are 'senseless' unless they are put into some kind of system. There is a similarity between that and how the letters arose, since the alphabetic letters arose in relation to objects, but they can only achieve structural efficacy with each other – meaning through a series of combinations with other letters to form words and sentences. That efficacy is only granted by this 'suture' or this repression of the link between the letter and the object, so that the letter by itself is left meaning nothing. And, somehow, that is similar to how letters function in mathematics and are used as mathemes.

GF: Could you say more about what he means by how these letters emerge from analytic discourse?

RM: Yes, which line is that ...?

GF: It's about halfway through the paragraph ... "Emerging from analytic discourse, the letters I bring out here have a different value from those that can emerge from set theory".

RM: The letters that are brought out, I think, are the letters in his mathemes that emerge out of analytic discourse, so that they have a reference in analytic discourse or are understood as letters within the context of analytic discourse as distinct from the mathematical symbols that are used within set theory.

GF: So, they get their meaning from the system that they are in?

RM: Exactly.

EW: When he says, "Any effect of discourse is good in the sense that it is constituted by the letter". ... I found that really mystifying.

RM: Yes, discourse ... there's a question of the relationship between discourse, speech, and writing. Discourse is also speech, but for Lacan, discourse is not speech. Discourse, let's say, is psychoanalytic theory in the same way Foucault uses the term 'discourse' as a theory but also as a social link and a practice. So, that's the way Lacan is speaking about psychoanalytic discourse ... but it's made up of letters! And so, I believe he is indicating that the effectiveness of any theoretical discourse is given by the use of the letter. The question of how that relates to writing is a further question because writing is what allows for the transformation of discourse. But, in Lacan's case, his discourse is an oral teaching – that's a further complication, because he wrote the *Écrits*. Yet, most of his teachings and all of his seminars were oral teaching.

AT: This seems already quite complicated, and that line in the last paragraph that EW just referenced seems to be saying the opposite of the first line we read today in the beginning of section 4, in that the last line seems to be saying discourse is constituted by the letter and the first line essentially saying the letter is constituted by discourse. This doesn't mean that it doesn't make sense, but it is complicated! I suppose the idea is that historically letters emerge out of discourse.

RM: Well, the letters … you know, the letter 'A', we have talked about this before, is the 'ox head' inverted. And the ox and the bull – the ox is a castrated bull – is associated with agriculture and work. So, we could say, the discourse was agriculture, work, and food, that in some way leads to the constitution of the letter as a representation of the ox. But then, when you invert it, it becomes an 'A' that has no reference to the ox. It's not a discourse in the sense of a written language, since we had speech before writing … people were already talking before they invented writing, so one can assume that people were already talking about agriculture and what to do with a cow or an ox. And then, through that form of speech, they then invented the letter. So, it all depends on how we define these terms, and I think part of the problem sometimes with Lacan is that he doesn't define the terms before he engages in a discussion about them. In fact, it is the reverse of turning the head upside down for letter A. The letter is an effect of discourse, and then he says discourse is organized by the letter.

AT: It seems like it is in two different senses.

RM: Right, so there is a dialectic there … and a contradiction.

GF: I thought it was interesting in the second paragraph there, where he says that 'the letter first emerged from the market', and, so, the market system. When I was first thinking about the 'manufacturer's marks', I did not interpret that so much in terms of a logo, but as some kind of scrawl or gibberish or the signature of some person that became the representative marks that would later become, in some way, the Phoenician alphabet.

RM: You mean that people were using some kind of system of marks?

GF: Exactly, like some sort of trace emerging from the market system.

RM: Right, so the unary trace in the numeral system – they would use lines and draw lines across them to indicate a set. Or, you have the marks also in the bones – the Ishango bones[2] – and all the marks there are prime numbers. So, that was the first system of marks. It was the unary numeral system, which is what it is called in mathematics. You have that in Lacan, where the unary trace is the basic elemental unit of the signifier – that is both a number and a letter. I guess the unary numeral system came before the system of letters. First came graphic images or silhouettes, then came markings, followed by numbers and letters. Language thus arose throughout the transitions between images, marks, and numbers.

TEXT: All of that is but a first sketch that I will have the opportunity to develop by distinguishing the use of letters in algebra from the use of letters in set theory. For the time being, I would simply like to point out the following – the world, the world is in [a state of] decomposition, thank God. We see that the world no longer stands up, because even in scientific discourse it is clear that there isn't the slightest world. As soon as you can add something called a quark to atoms and have that become the true thread of scientific discourse, you must realize that we are dealing with something other than a world.

RM: Okay, so first he distinguishes the use of letters in algebra from the use of letters in set theory. Then, he is getting to a distinction among the use of letters in mathematics, and algebra versus set theory – but he doesn't tell us much about that in typical Lacan fashion (which he could have!). He then goes onto this question of the world in a state of decomposition because there is no "world" there. Perhaps, he is saying that the subatomic is not a world … that the world only exists in the macro-level of the universe, which is explained by Einstein's theory, but that when it comes to the quantum theory, then the subatomic world is not a world. Although for scientists, the electrons and the particles that circle around the nucleus are not unlike the planets circling around the sun. So, there is a question whether there are worlds there or not.

EW: Is he saying something about, as we learn these things that the world becomes alien to us … becoming something that we can't really understand?

RM: Yes, so it's bizarre and uncanny, but most people now are making that association with the unconscious – that the logic of the unconscious is at a more subatomic, quantum level and that the logic of consciousness is more on the macro-level.

AT: It also seems that just literally dividing something up into smaller and smaller parts is a process of decomposition. You know, you are taking away the fully formed composition into smaller and smaller bits.

RM: Right, but, you know, the parallel universes that people are talking about now are happening at the micro-level. And they are literally other universes in which people say that whenever you make a choice between, let's say, this boyfriend and that boyfriend, or this girlfriend or that girlfriend, that you, in one world, you are with one person, and in the other world, you actually lived out the fantasy with the other person.

AT: Yeah, we are living the darkest timeline! [*ALL laugh*]

RM: Right, but in that sense, those are worlds even though they are very small. They exist at the quantum level, but there are other dimensions in which whole worlds take place.

TEXT: You must sit down and read a little work by writers, not of your era – you could read Joyce, for example. You will see therein how language is perfected when it knows how to play with writing. I can agree that Joyce's work is not readable – it is certainly not translatable into Chinese. What happens in Joyce's work? The signifier stuffs the signified.

It is because the signifiers fit together, combine, and concertina – read *Finnegans Wake* – that something is produced by way of meaning that may seem enigmatic, but is clearly what is closest to what we analysts, thanks to analytic discourse, have to read – slips of the tongue (*lapsus*). It is as slips that they signify something; in other words, they can be read in an infinite number of different ways. But it is precisely for that reason that they are difficult to read, are read awry, or not read at all. But doesn't this dimension of being read (*se lire*) suffice to show that we are in the register of analytic discourse?

RM: Okay, so he is talking about interpretation and reading different levels within language. Joyce explodes English language because in some way he includes the unconscious signifying chain link to the narrative or story, and he uses that as a compositional technique, where he is telling a story or narrating a narrative with certain characters doing something; and then he injects or he 'stuffs' the narrative with the unconscious signifying chain. Then it seems like it is hard to read or hard to interpret, or it's enigmatic, and that's what's similar with psychoanalysis. At the same time, with Joyce, it's a kind of reinvention of English, where he says we are at the end of English, and that's where the question begins, because where English ends, the unconscious begins – meaning the unconscious signifying chain. And, so, Joyce revolutionizes the use of the English language by making use of the unconscious and vulgar language.

TEXT: What is at stake in analytic discourse is always the following – you give a different reading to the signifiers that are enunciated than what they signify.

RM: So that's like the two levels of the signifying chain in the 'graph of desire'– one's the level of the narrative and the other one, the upper chain, is the level of the unconscious signifying chain. And, when people are speaking in analytic sessions, they start out with a narrative and then they may inject into the narrative various levels of the signifying chain. And some people do that work on their own, and they are more satisfying to work with. The other ones, you have to pull it like pulling teeth from the narrative in order to pull or to scan the narrative to select the signifiers that you then ask them to associate to, which then leads you to the signifying chain.

TEXT: Consider the flight of a bee. A bee goes from flower to flower gathering nectar. What you discover is that, at the tip of its feet, the bee transports pollen from one flower onto the pistil of another flower. That is what you read in the flight of the bee. In the flight of a bird that flies close to the ground – you call that a flight, but in reality, it is a group at a certain level – you read that there is going to be a storm. But do they read? Does the bee read that it serves a function in the reproduction of phanerogamic plants? Does the bird read the portent of fortune, as people used to say – in other words, a tempest? That is the whole question. It cannot be ruled out, after all, that a swallow reads the tempest, but it is not terribly certain either.

RM: That raises an interesting question, and that is one John Muller posits in his book where he is talking about what the relationship is between the code of signs in animals and the code of signifiers in humans and whether there are similarities between the two codes in the same way that there may be a similarity between how the code in the brain works internally and how the code in language works. And then, how those two codes come into interaction through the way language wires the neural chains and brain function. So, that's the link between the codes in the birds or in animals – the use of signs and codes – and the code of language and the signifier. Of course, that would also go into the question of the code in DNA. And, while Muller's thinking emphasizes that connection, other people, some Lacanians when you speak to them, say those things are totally unrelated (which is referring to how Lacan talks about the code in language) … they are not talking about how animals use the code in their use of signs. People like Colette Soler will make that statement. They don't want you to confuse the different orders, but they tend just to speak about Lacanian psychoanalysis only, whereas Muller is making the attempt to combine brain research and American developmental psychology with Lacanian theory. Here we see Lacan actually raising the question himself about the function of signs in animals and the question of the letter and the signifier.

AT: It seems like the question is something like what texts are available for the analyst to read – you know, should one be analytically reading these pollinating flowers? It seems what Lacan is saying is "go for it"!

RM: Right, that's our scientific field. Our scientific field is analytical, consisting of analytic observations, and that's what we limit our theory to – that's appropriate scientifically. But, on the other hand, there is also the question of how these different fields interact because they are not really separate in terms of how we experience our bodies and our minds. And, of course, when Lacan is talking about jouissance, he's talking about the body also. But, as far as analysts are concerned, we are just listening to the word. However, we know the word has effects on the body.

Do you remember that case I told you about where the young woman couldn't get pregnant? She had gone to every specialist in town, and they couldn't get her pregnant and they did not know why. She was married with a husband, and so, in South America, the doctors would tell them, "Well, we can't find anything [wrong with you] so you should go see a psychoanalyst". And, because her parents were South American, when all the medical options ran out, she went to see a psychoanalyst.

Through talking about her history – she wasn't particularly interested in the family dynamics or Oedipal dynamics – she just wanted to get pregnant. She didn't want an analysis really, but, in her narrative, I identified and used numbers – because, with Lacan, we also know with psychosomatic conditions, when they have no insight and no interest in using words to express emotions or thoughts and they only want a resolution of a physical symptom – then you can use numbers rather than letters. So I knew about that, and I started listening for the numbers, and the number '2' became the critical number. Later, she ended up getting pregnant with twins! [*ALL laugh*] And, of course, I have no proof – the proof is just that she came into analysis, there was a consistency in the logic of what the treatment consisted of, and a function of numbers … and then the fact that she became pregnant when she hadn't been able before! It's a psychoanalytic level of observation, but there is clearly an interaction between the mind and the body there. We see how there has to be some kind of interaction between these codes.

EW: So, the way I am reading this about the bird and the bees [*chuckles*] is that there are certain things that can have meaning but that it may be sort of ludicrous to expect the meaning to be available to reflection where the bee has its path, and it goes from flower to flower, but it's not in any sense conscious that its purpose is to pollinate flowers! You couldn't really say to the bee, "what do you think about your purpose in going around pollinating flowers?" In a way, it seems a little bit like a satirical comment on what we often try to do with analysis – that we say, you are "doing this" or "what do you think about this pattern", and what if people are just going around pollinating flowers and not having a particularly reflective sense of it? It seems like your example of working with numbers might be a way around that problem!

RM: Yes, in a way she did not know what happened to her. She was just happy that she got pregnant! And she did not want to know, frankly. And that's what people say Freud said about working with children. For example, Little Hans grew up and didn't have any memory or recollection of what had happened or the work that they had done, but it had its effectiveness. So, in a way, we don't need the 'becoming conscious' for a therapeutic effect, although this seems to contradict what Freud said about making the unconscious conscious as a necessary aspect of the therapeutic effect.

TEXT: In your analytic discourse, you assume that the subject of the unconscious knows how to read. And this business of the unconscious is nothing other than that. Not only do you assume that it knows how to read, but you assume that it can learn how to read. The only problem is that what you teach it to read has absolutely nothing to do, in any case, with what you can write of it.

RM: Here Lacan is referring to "the subject of the unconscious that knows how to read". That's an interesting statement, meaning that we are at the level of language with the subject of the unconscious, but we are not necessarily at the level of becoming aware or of consciousness. The subject of the unconscious is not a conscious ego. It could be, perhaps, the unconscious ego that Freud talks about in the Ego and the Id, but the unconscious ego is more the agent of unconscious repression, whereas the subject of the unconscious is both the agency of censorship and desire ... so, it's a little different. So, the subject of the unconscious knows how to read – there's a subject there and there is subjectivity – but not necessarily consciousness. So, I guess you can read unconsciously in that sense, and we could say that the dream is a kind of unconscious writing, isn't it? The dreamer is constructing the dream, but unconsciously – and there is a whole text and dialogue that goes on in dreams that bear a relationship to dream thoughts. And the dream thoughts are also words. So the dream is a kind of writing with words that is written and read by the subject of the unconscious.

MK: I think this is one of the most beautiful passages ...

RM: Yes, when he is thinking about it at that level, when he talks about the subject of the unconscious. This business of the unconscious is nothing other than that, this kind of ciphering. But, of course, he will later change that because then we have the Real unconscious, which is an unconscious of jouissance, and the main activity there is not ciphering. That's going to change eventually a little bit. And then he says, "the only problem is that what you teach it to read has nothing to do with what you can write of it". I guess that's the distinction between how people, you know, tell you about their dreams in a session, where the state of mind in which they tell you the dream is not the same state they were in when they had the dream. The hope is that the telling of the dream in analysis will trigger a regression that will make the subject regress to the familiar, usually rejected state of mind.

MK: I've thought about it too, and it's related to your case, that maybe you taught your patient how to read something, even though she could not speak about or articulate it, but she was able to read something that allowed her to get pregnant with twins.

RM: Right, she read it unconsciously, but the point is that there is a code there for reading that seems to interact with some kind of organic code that released whatever was blocking her body from being able to get pregnant.

MK: Yes, to me it's kind of what treatment is all about. Most of the patients cannot point to something in particular that they learned. It's not about learning a skill, but they just kind of wake up and notice that they are different than they were a year ago in various ways.

RM: Right, it's not like learning a skill. It's a different kind of learning. It's not the kind of learning you think of when you learn how to read or you are taught how to read, and you acquire that skill – that seems to be something different than the way the subject of the unconscious can learn to read something. Would you agree?

MK: I want to say that what he should have said is that the subject of the unconscious knows how to write, and it can also learn how to read. I mean, it writes the story all the time – it's writing all of these stories.

RM: Yes, but it has to read the dream thoughts, right? For Freud, the dream is constructed from the dream thoughts, so the subject of the unconscious has to read the dream thoughts and then write a dream which will hide – both reveal and conceal – the dream thoughts. That's why there is a need to decipher – it's because of censorship. And that censorship is unconscious.

MK: I feel very thrilled that we finished Chapter 3! [*ALL laugh*]

RM: Okay, very good! And then we go to love and the signifier. That should be interesting!

Notes

1 *Beyond the Psychoanalytic Dyad: Developmental Semiotics in Freud, Peirce and Lacan* by John P. Muller, 2014.

2 The **Ishango bone** is a bone tool dated to the Upper Paleolithic era, about 18,000–20,000 BC. It is a dark brown length of bone, with a sharp piece of quartz affixed to one end, perhaps for engraving or writing. It was first thought to be a tally stick, as it has a series of tally marks carved in three columns running the length of the tool, but some scientists have suggested that the groupings of notches indicate a mathematical understanding that goes beyond counting. Wikipedia (https://en.wikipedia.org/wiki/Ishango_bone).

Supplemental References

Freud, Sigmund. (1900). Interpretation of Dreams, *SE* 4.

Joyce, J. (1976, 1939). *Finnegan's Wake*. Centennial ed. New York, NY: Penguin Books.

Lacan, J. (2007). Écrits (B. Fink, Trans.). WW Norton.

Lacan, J. (1972–1973). *Encore. The Seminar of Jacques Lacan, XX*. New York: Norton, 1998.

Lacan, J. (1961–1962). *Identification. The Seminar of Jacques Lacan, IX*. New York: Norton.

Muller, J. P. (1996). *Beyond the Psychoanalytic Dyad. Developmental Semiotics in Freud, Peirce, and Lacan*. New York: Routledge.

Soler, Colette. (2018). *Lacan – The Unconscious Reinvented* (The Center for Freudian Analysis and Research Library (CFAR)). New York, NY: Routledge.

Chapter 3

The Metapsychology Past, Present, and Future

Moncayo Seminar November 17, 2016, *Encore, Seminar XX*, pg. 31

GF: I think we are midway through page 31, right after "idizwadidiz".
RM: There is the question of 'quiddity' – the 'whatness' of the object. He says …

TEXT: That is what Aristotle himself thinks about twice before propounding, since, to designate the being he juxtaposes to τὸ τί ἔστι, that is, to quiddity or what it is, he goes so far as to employ the following, τὸ τί ηv εἶναι – what would have happened if that which was to be bad simply come to be.

FOOTNOTE – This could also be rendered: would have been produced if that which should have been had come into Being.

RM: Yes, so there is a remainder of 'quidditas' that doesn't come into being, except that he put 'Being' there capitalized (or at least by the translator), and I think *être* in the French is 'being' rather than 'Being' … so there is a remainder of the quidditas or the 'thing in itself', or the 'no thing' that is subtracted from whatever it is we say about Being. But there is that point and the point about what 'could have come to be'. So, there's something that didn't come into being – in some ways it is the *objet a* that draws and stays out of the discourse of the master. And another way of saying it is that it is the Real unconscious [thing] that withdraws from speech and it remains 'what is it?'. That's the question of the quidditas. And 'the what' is in the Real.
MK: Can you say where the 'quidditas' word comes from?
RM: Well, he says it comes from Aristotle [as translated]. 'What it is', or the 'quiddity', I would say is the 'thing in itself' which, in Lacan, takes the form of the 'thing' or the 'no thing', and they 'ex-sist'. So, it's more in the Real than in the signifier or the Symbolic, and that relates, of course, to the jouissance of the mystic and feminine jouissance.[1]
MK: Could you also say, because I think I missed this last time, what the 'copula' is?
RM: The copula is the term 'to be', and Hebrew is one of the languages known not to have the term 'being'. Somebody could check that, but I believe that

DOI: 10.4324/9781003424581-3

to be the case. There is also something Lacan says in *Seminar XXIII* [*The Sinthome*] about the copula,[2] but I would have to look for it. I knew that at one time when I wrote my book ... you know things and then you forget! [*ALL laughing*]

MK: It's such a relief to hear you say that!

GF: This all stems from Heidegger's work most likely. Heidegger was interested in the copula as the 'place of investigation' – a place to capture 'Being' within language and he then examines the 'metaphysics of presence' in relation to this.

RM: For Heidegger, 'Being' appears within the 'house of language', so it's not an ontology that's independent from language. Yet, at the same time, language points to the limits of Being, because, for Heidegger, 'Being' is also [a] mystery. The mystery begins where language fails to say more about the quidditas, or about Being, so the copula of language is akin to the phallic signifier. The phallus in Sanskrit is the *lingam*, which relates to the link – the link between signifiers. But that is more associated with the Symbolic than the Real, because the Real is beyond the copula. I guess there is a play between the copula in 'copulation' and the copula between signifiers, and to what extent the copulation is determined and guided by signifiers as a form of social link. That is, the place where the social link and the sexual link interface. Also, the copula can produce a new being, a new signifier, and a new human being. But I think the point here is that the quidditas is more in the Real. The Real, of course – and people often take issue with this – is not outside the [Borromean] 'knot'. It is not a separate ontology that pre-existed the knot. So, the Real is inside the knot, but, at the same time, cannot be collapsed into the Symbolic. It is in the same way that femininity cannot be collapsed into the phallic signifier or the phallic order.

Shall we go reading? [*RM quotes from text, pg. 31 footnote*] "What would have been produced if that which should have been had come into Being". I am still not sure we have exhausted the meaning of that, because there is that 'what could have been' that wasn't, and whether that means some kind of aborted potential or project or whether that simply refers to the Real as that which is always abstracted from Being.

GF: Like a potential for Being that leaves traces just because it can become something.

RM: Well, there's a potential for 'being', like a project in the sense of Sartre that gets directed toward the future and which gets aborted. But that's more within the realm of Being. What didn't come 'to be' – what could have been but didn't come to be. That is in the historical, horizontal line. Whereas, what is subtracted or withdrawn from Being is not the potential of 'what could have been' but the potential of the Real.

GF: Do you believe, the Real, in this issue of 'coming to be', is it something the Real 'does' or is it something that only we can do in the experience of the

Real and only from the vantage of the Symbolic? As if the Real has its own repression just in 'making stuff'?

RM: Well, there's the true hole of the Real, which is a type of primary repression, but it is not like there is something repressed behind it, like in the 'false hole'. But in the Real, there's nothing behind it, although it looks like it is repressed simply because it's withdrawn from representation. And the withdrawal of representation is one of the mechanisms of repression that always produces a substitute within the Symbolic order. In the Real, there are no substitute representations to discriminate between. The Real is a form of experience, in the ontogenetic and phylogenetic scheme of things, that humans had before the onset of language. Later, the individual human being will re-experience the Real in the form of the innocence and absence of language in perception. What we mean by innocence is the absence of judgment and projection.

So not only the objects or the *objet a*(*s*) are lost, but also the sense of the 'unborn' if we assume that birth is really indicated by some kind of psychological birth as Mahler points out. The psychological birth is indicated by language – the birth of the subject into the signifier – and so what is of the Real remains outside. And there is a primary repression there in two senses: one is that there is a substitute produced which would be what is repressed behind primary repression. But there is also another type of primary repression which is simply that 'there's nothing there' and it's just that there is no way of representing it. The Real seems to remain outside or unavailable to us in some way even though it's part of our experience. Because the Real is always a part of our experience in the present, the present presence of the Real is what about our being in the moment that is outside representation. This could be a positive or a negative experience, the first or second Real in Lacan. The second Real only appears with the appearance of humans and a symbolic order. A human child in early childhood experiences both. And what happens to the Real when it is not present in the experience of the subject? It is present in the drive and longing for the Real within the Symbolic subject. This again is both a pleasant and unpleasant experience.

GF: That explanation is helpful, thank you.

RM: Should we read on? …

TEXT: It seems that the 'pedicle' is conserved here that allows us to situate from, whence this discourse on being is produced – it's quite simply being at someone's heel, being at someone's beck and call – what would have been you had understood what I ordered you to do.

RM: Okay, there he adds some more dimensions. There is the "what I order you to do". So, the not listening to the voice – I guess it could be the Symbolic voice of the Law or the voice of the Master (two things that are not the same thing). And what happens when you don't heed the Symbolic voice or the voice of the Master? The worst things happen to you.[3] But, the Symbolic voice here also means … 'heard' or 'understood', which is not the same as 'listening' because you may be listening, but you may not be hearing. And, if you don't hear what is coming from the Symbolic voice – in this case, meaning the subject of enunciation – then you miss out on something that doesn't come to be. So, this has a different meaning. But now we are talking about the Real manifesting within the Symbolic.

MK: Raul, can you say something more about the difference between the Symbolic voice of the Law and voice of the Master?

RM: I knew you were going to ask that! [*ALL laughing*]

MK: Is that obsessional, or what?

RM: No! No! Because I set it up! I set myself up! [*ALL laughing*] Well …

MK: I have a fantasy actually, which is that there is a difference between the "must do it" and the "must not do it".

RM: Yes, well, that's more the difference between the Ego Ideal and the Superego, right? The ego ideal is 'you must do this' and the superego is 'you must not do this'. So, the positive and negative commandments. But, the voice of the master, Lacan says in *The Sinthome, Seminar XXIII*, is one of the reasons the knot of three has to be undone, because it is put together by the master and it creates a false hole between the Imaginary and the Symbolic – the Real being is what links the two together, but it links them in a position of contradiction where words and images sort of supersede each other (where you have people arguing "words are the most important thing" and then you have other people saying "oh, that's just words"). You know, in art, painters usually privilege the image – like Picasso and Molinari [saying] what you call a painting doesn't matter because it is just words. And then, there are people who privilege the importance of poetic words, Shakespeare and what not. They [these positions] seem to have an antagonistic relationship, and so the master's discourse seems to impose an Imaginary meaning on the Symbolic which creates in the Symbolic a discourse of domination. In some ways people misidentify patriarchy with the Symbolic and often criticize Lacan for somehow reproducing the patriarchal system with his understanding of the Symbolic. But that's a mistaken overlay between the Imaginary and the Symbolic produced by the discourse of the master. So, in that case, we need to separate the dog from the bark!

So the voice of the master is kind of an imperative – that's what we don't like about tyrants or despots, Hitler or Mussolini, or Trump or Putin – that they cover over the true Symbolic with this overlay of ego, narcissism, and domination (the domination over women and people of color – the colonized or the servant, the slave, etc.). So the voice of the Symbolic would be more like the discourse of equality in the American constitution (which comes from the French Revolution). Anyway, that's my reading of it for better or worse.

TEXT: Every dimension of being is produced in the wake of the master's discourse – the discourse of he who, proffering the signifier, expects therefrom one of its link effects that must not be neglected, which is related to the fact that the signifier commands. The signifier is, first and foremost, imperative.

RM: So there, do you see the problem? There, Lacan is collapsing the distinction between the two. He seems to be saying the discourse of he who proffering the signifier – wouldn't you say 'professing'?

GF: 'Proffering' is offering something.

RM: Offering? I see. 'Offering' is what the signifier expects from you. When you use the signifier, the signifier emerges as an imperative. The thing is that in the master's discourse, the agent of the imposition is 'the master', while in the analyst's discourse the imperative comes from the Other. For example, we find anarchist analysands who are interested in analysis and queer theory. When it comes to the imposition of the NoF, they find it oppressive and patriarchal. So, they don't want to use the names given by their parents. They want to choose their own first name because the whole naming by the Other is reduced or collapsed into a kind of oppression or alienation.

In Lacanian theory, the particular alienation that the name provides is inevitable. Yet, they consider the naming to be socio-historical and oppressive and therefore that it could be undone – so they name themselves. But then, they are faced with a problem, for if they have children, what will they name their children? And how do they name their children without transmitting this imperative of the name? And then they run into this impossibility because it would be ... "okay, let's wait for the child to be of an age when he or she becomes an agent and then let's ask them, how would you like to be called? Would you like to name yourself?" ... because we don't want to be parents that give you a name that you don't like [for God's sake]! But, of course, that is utopian. It is impossible, because how could you have a six-month-old [child] without a name? Even if you consider registering the child in the symbolic register of the government, which happens at birth when you get a birth certificate – some people say, "oh, that's oppression ... that's becoming part of 'big brother' and the government is turning on us ... and we want to be free from that, and so on and so forth". Even if you do not register the child, how are you going to call the child? Is it possible for a child to be six months old or a year or two years old and not have a name to relate to other children or other adults, or teachers, or anything? No! It's impossible! And that is the proof that shows you that the so-called alienation of naming by the Other cannot be confounded with a kind of negative alienation or oppression.

However, Lacan says in *RSI, Seminar XXII* that he is interested in undoing the imperative aspect of the signifier, and this is what the process of nomination is for. The process of nomination is different from the naming of the child and somehow the process of nomination is how, within the wealth of your own experience, you may choose new signifiers for yourself or re-signify your own name. And this is an aspect of the emergence of the Name of the Father from the Real rather than from the Symbolic. Now, in this text, in *Encore, Seminar XX*, Lacan is still collapsing the two, meaning that the imperative of the word is the same as the imperative of the master – where the agency of the imposition comes from the master rather than coming from the structure of the Other (i.e., the structure of language). And those two need to be separated. But precisely, perhaps, the separation of these two and the re-knotting of the knot is what needs to happen in order to have the Name of the Father come from the Real and be able to separate the agency of the Other from the agency of the master.

GF: So, initially the Name of the Father comes from the Symbolic?

RM: Yes, it comes from the Symbolic, but it also has an Imaginary dimension in that the Name of the Father separates the child and the mother from this object of fantasy – which can be experienced as a kind of castration, something bad going down, something bad happening. But that's just the Imaginary aspect of it because the father has to momentarily occupy the place of the 'imaginary father', meaning the one who has the phallic attribute that the mother wants, even though the father himself is under the law of castration and is, in fact, castrated. For the child's sake, the father has to appear temporarily as having the phallic attribute that the mother wants so that the child is excluded from the parental dyad. That creates the subject, which is a form of subjection in some sense, as the child perceives (misinterprets) the mother's love for the father as a rejection of the child. However, there also is the reality that people are oppressed and subjected in society in ways that are detrimental to the individual ... but that's different – that's the imposition of the master on the Symbolic, or when the father remains in this position of the 'imaginary father', instead of moving on to be a 'symbolic father', and ultimately, a name that comes from the Real.

TEXT: How is one to return if not on the basis of a peculiar (special) discourse to a pre-discursive reality? That is the dream – the dream behind every conception of knowledge. But it is also what must be considered mythical. There is no such thing as a pre-discursive reality. Every reality is founded and defined by a discourse.

RM: There's nothing pre-discursive. The Real is not a pre-discursive reality before the Borromean knot, and yet, within the knot, it is beyond discourse ... so, that's the contradiction. And here is still the influence of the middle period of Lacan, the Lacan of the Symbolic and the signifier, where he is emphasizing the reality of discourse. It's like when people come to analysis wanting to discuss ideas with you ... this kind of a discourse analysis instead of analysis of speech is put together by the narcissism of the Ego, and the subject that is supposed to know, meaning that they want to teach you something with some kind of discourse that they have. This kind of discourse needs to be undone in analysis and transformed into just pure speech. A move from the ego of the statement to the ego of the subject of the enunciation. It's like when they are talking, but they are really trying to teach you something, or show you what they know, or something like that.

BB: So, which ego is that called?

RM: That's the 'ego of the statement'. That's the narrative. But that's distinct from the 'subject of enunciation', which has to do with just pure speech – which is where we are trying to go.

BB: Is 'pure' speech the same as 'full' speech?

RM: Yes, but Lacan changed from *Seminar II* to *Seminar XXIII*. In *Seminar II, The Ego in Freud's Theory and in the Technique of Psychoanalysis*, he makes the distinction between 'full speech' and 'empty speech' – 'empty' speech having a negative connotation. It's just a parrot talking or just repeating – but the 'parrot speech' even then is just a little bit more than just saying nothing (or saying silly things) because it also points to 'empty speech' in the sense that there is a connection to the Real and to significance rather than simply to another signifier. So, those terms are complex. In *Seminar XXIII* on the sinthome, he reverses it. He [Lacan] says that the 'full speech' is imaginary because it is trying to achieve some kind of comprehensive meaning, whereas the 'empty speech' is the speech of signification and significance (so, he reverses the meaning of those two).

BB: Thank you! [*Reading on*]

TEXT: That is why it is important for us to realize what analytic discourse is made of, and not to misrecognize the following, which no doubt has but a limited place therein, that we speak in analytic discourse about what the verb "to fuck" (*foutre*) enunciates perfectly well. We speak therein of 'fucking' and we say that it's not working out (*ça ne va pas*).

RM: So, I think we are talking about the difference between signifiers, and how signifiers constitute or develop the act of fucking or the sexual act – the copulation. And so when we say that 'it doesn't work out', meaning that the sexual relation doesn't work out between people, or between men and women, that this impasse is not at the level of the body, but that it is at the level of the signifier and signification. This means that the phallus, as an object of fantasy, is something that mediates the sexual relations. So, each partner has their own fantasy through which they relate to the other, and that fantasy is determined by the signifier (the phallic signifier). And, so, the fantasy never quite 'works out' because the other is not the object of the fantasy.

TEXT: That is an important part of what is confided in analytic discourse, but it is worth highlighting that analytic discourse does not have exclusivity in this regard. For that is also what is expressed in what I earlier referred to as "current discourse" (*discours courant*). Let us write that as "*disque–ou courant*" (pronounced the same way as *discours courant*, but *disque* means record or disk) – it goes around and around quite precisely. The disk is found in the very field on the basis of which all discourses are specified and where they all drown, where each and every one of them is just as capable of enunciating as much of the field as the others, but due to a concern with what I will call, for very good reasons, "decency" does so – well – as little as possible.

RM: Well, I am not sure what he means there other than there is something in discourse … 'current discourse', not the 'current of discourse'. There is within discourse "a disk that stays outside of the field or out of the game, or beyond the rules of all discourse. And it goes around and around for nothing, quite precisely". So, the discourse is going around this disk, and the disk that is outside discourse is representative of the Real. The words are going around it, trying to touch it, but they never quite do – thus, instead of getting a real meaning, we just get a proliferation of meanings that all drown there in the disk. They all drown – what are you trying to say? You are trying to say something, and your statement is going toward something, or your sentence is going toward something, and he says, "the last word occupies the place of Being" in *Seminar III, The Psychoses*. But it is always covered over by another signifier. So, this hole in the Symbolic, where speech is directed toward something beyond it also causes the Symbolic to close up into this infinity of meanings. I don't know if it's 'decent' or 'a decency' … I guess also when we try to be decent, when we speak, we miss the target precisely by trying to be 'decent'. And the clinical consequence of this is, how do we talk about sexuality in analysis since people are either cautious about speaking about it or they bring it out with all its vulgarity right off the top (which usually is not such a good indication). Anyway, just going through the process of breaking down the inhibitions to be able to speak openly about sexuality in analysis is something that is important, but it is not so easy. In that sense, you could say that it is the Real of sex that is difficult to talk about, both in the double sense of the literality of it, but also that there is something traumatic or something beyond words about it.

TEXT: What constitutes the basis of life, in effect, is that for everything having to do with the relations between men and women, what is called collectivity, it's not working out. It's not working out, and the whole world talks about it: and a large part of our activity is taken up with saying so.

RM: Alright, so what he is saying here is the whole point about 'there is no sexual relation', as opposed to the Freudian developmental phases, where the oral and the anal phase are integrated under the genital phase and the sexual object relation, and the love-based object relation were supposed to meet. So, in normal development, after adolescence, these two tendencies are supposed to be integrated in the choice of a partner (a marriage partner), and we know how that fails and that we can't have that as an ideal as it was present before in Freud's time. So, instead of analysis ending with a kind of happy ending of phallic jouissance, it ends more in the realization of the lack of a sexual relation and what do we do with that? And that is one of the aspects of the sinthome – how to make do with the lack of a sexual relation. This takes place in the context of how, in normative discourse, we still have marriage as an institution even though society doesn't expect marriage the way traditional societies expect marriage.

For instance, I was working with a student from China, and she was telling me how marriages are still arranged by the families. They consider the first year of marriage the most difficult one since the couple doesn't know one another and they were just brought together because of familial, social interests. In the first year, they get to find out whether they are a match or not! But, of course, in our society, and ever since the onset of modernity, romanticism became legitimized as a function of how people get together for marriage. And nowadays, even though, let's say, psychiatry expects social-occupational functioning as a criterion of normality, and social functioning includes relationships, everybody knows that relationships are in crisis and the divorce rate is as high as the marriage rate. And the fact that people stay married doesn't mean that there is a sexual relation. In the Lacanian sense, when the sexes are sexually excited by each other, they are instead really only excited by their own fantasy object. So the whole thing is more complicated in that sense – we could say that Lacan is addressing something that is more contemporary, distinct from Freud's time.

Notes

1 The French word jouissance means basically 'enjoyment', but it has a sexual connotation (i.e., 'orgasm') lacking in the English word 'enjoyment' and is therefore left untranslated in most English editions of Lacan. However, the concept of jouissance also means pain or suffering, a connotation contained in the meaning of the French word. The term does not appear in Lacan's work until 1953, but even then it is not particularly salient (E, 42, 87). The term seems to mean no more than the enjoyable sensation that accompanies the satisfaction of a biological need such as hunger (S4, 125). However, the sexual connotations of the term would become more apparent. In 1957, Lacan used the term to refer to the enjoyment of a sexual object (E, 453) and to the pleasures of masturbation (S4, 241), and in 1958, he makes explicit the sense of jouissance as orgasm (E, 727).

Against Freud's initial simplistic conception of the pleasure principle, the concept of jouissance develops the notion of the pleasure principle as a limit to enjoyment rather than as the drive for pleasure. The experience of satisfaction translates to a lowering of tension as well as the impossibility of returning to a mythical moment of union with the mother's breast. This eventually produces a connection between the search for pleasure and an increase of tension. Insofar as the pleasure principle functions as a limit to enjoyment, it is a law which commands the subject to 'enjoy as little as possible'.

The subject nonetheless constantly attempts to transgress the prohibitions imposed on his enjoyment, that is, to go 'beyond the pleasure principle'. However, the result of transgressing the pleasure principle is not more pleasure, but pain, since there is only a certain amount of pleasure that the subject can bear. Beyond this limit, pleasure becomes pain, and this 'painful pleasure' is what Lacan calls jouissance; 'jouissance is suffering' (S7, 184). The term jouissance thus nicely expresses the paradoxical satisfaction that the subject derives from his symptom, or to put it another way, the suffering that he derives from his own satisfaction (Freud's 'primary gain from illness').

In his lecture at the Catholic University of Louvain in the 1970s, Lacan asked his audience whether they could bear the life that they had. This question refers to jouissance by pointing to the impossible experience of bearing the unbearable. In this sense, jouissance is intrinsically related to suffering, and not just to pleasure or enjoyment or even sexuality, as the word commonly refers to in the French language. It is this paradoxical aspect of the drives and of pain and pleasure that is at the core of the definition of jouissance.

In the *Écrits*, Lacan introduces the concept of jouissance as something inconvenient, deadly, and traumatic that breaks the shield and barrier set up by the pleasure principle to protect the subject from unpleasant or painful experiences. When the protective barrier is breached or when tensions reach a certain magnitude or threshold, the subject experiences pain rather than pleasure.

At the same time, jouissance not only represents the point where pleasure turns into unpleasure. Jouissance is also used by Lacan to represent a form of phallic enjoyment as a form of pleasure or satisfaction. Lacan speaks of penile and clitoral masturbatory jouissance, for example, as a form of satisfaction involving having or not having the imaginary phallus. Phallic jouissance in this example can also be unpleasant due to the imaginary narcissistic identifications associated with 'having' or 'not having' the imaginary phallus.

The jouissance of the Other represents the fusion with the mother and the fantasy of the imaginary phallus. The fusion with the mother is initially necessary, but at some point it becomes inconvenient without the intervention of the Other that turns the jouissance of the Other into phallic jouissance. Phallic jouissance is pleasant and convenient, so long as it is ruled by symbolic castration. If the phallus remains in an imaginary fantasized position and becomes reified, this leads to an endless search for surplus phallic jouissance that eventually also becomes inconvenient or destructive (as seen in the examples of Don Juan or *la femme fatale*).

If the fantasy of the inexistent imaginary phallus drives the search for surplus jouissance, then revealing the inexistence of imaginary phallus allows the symbolic phallus to function as an organizing principle of the Symbolic. This, in turn, gives access to the Real as outside the signifier (lack of a signifier for the Real). The symbolic phallus is the signifier of a lack rather than a positive privilege. This is where we witness how Lacan begins to point out the benevolent aspects of the Third jouissance beyond the phallus. What generates this transformation is something internal to the phallic function of castration that both permits and forbids phallic jouissance and causes a movement beyond it.

In Lacan's early work, the inconvenient jouissance is presented in two ways. First, as a deadly excitation that overcomes the protective barriers set up by the pleasure principle and becomes a surplus or excess jouissance. And second, as the malevolent fusion of the mother and the child, when the child occupies the place of the mother's Imaginary phallus. The jouissance of the Other between the Real and the Imaginary is an inconvenient jouissance/pleasure because it is impossible to return to the fusion with the mother. The imaginary One with the mother is the Other that does not exist rather than the One that 'ex-sists' in the Real (*Il y a de l'Un* – There is something of the One). There is no Other of the Other because there is no ideal Other, only greater or lesser approximations. Lacan opens and reconceives this lack in the Other as the Real within the Symbolic. In *Encore, Seminar XX*, "...*Ou pire* (or worse)", Lacan (1971–1972) speaks of the primacy of the One in the register of the Real rather than the Imaginary.

If the first form of jouissance emerges between the Imaginary and the Symbolic as jouissance of the Other, the jouissance Lacan locates between the Symbolic and the Real is a second form referred to as phallic jouissance. Lacan links it to the *parlêtre* or the speaking being and a parasitic form of power. Phallic jouissance is also a surplus or excessive jouissance that, like a foreign organism, threatens to destroy the psychic body with a preoccupation with the bad infinity of the phi as an irrational number. In phallic jouissance, there is always a calculation with the power of who has or does not have the phallus. Thus, the function of castration and of nomination of the capital Phi as a Name rather than a number is required to put a stop to the parasitic bad infinity of the Imaginary phallus.

There must be a Third jouissance beyond the jouissance of the Other and phallic jouissance that would correspond to the new definition of the Real that Lacan advances in *Encore, Seminar XXIII*. Lacan began to formulate this Third jouissance in his very dense and abstruse paper *La Trosieme* (1975). However, he did not arrive at a clear formulation of the nature of this Third jouissance.

The relationship between *lalangue* and jouissance is ambiguous in Lacan. *Lalangue* produces what Lacan calls 'Other jouissance' or 'jouissance of the Other'. The use of the term Other jouissance is not clear in Lacan's work and often is found confused with the jouissance of the Other. Granted, Lacan, as Miller and others have pointed out, often was not clear himself about the six or eight names (rather than concepts) he used for the different types of jouissance. Compare, for example, the definitions given in *Encore, Seminar XX* and '*La troisième*'. In *Encore, Seminar XX*, there are two jouissances, although the concepts used there imply three jouissances.

La Troisième, as the title indicates, is dedicated to what we can refer to as the Third jouissance. Here, a third jouissance is developed from his concept of lalangue and the jouissance of meaning. While the second jouissance is generally recognizable as phallic jouissance, the first and the third are often confused. The jouissance of the Other or the first jouissance refers to the inconvenient drive to be an imaginary One with the mother. The Other jouissance or the Third jouissance instead refers to feminine jouissance and the jouissance of the mystic (of *Encore, Seminar XX*). The third jouissance presumes the existence of phallic jouissance and the intervention of the paternal and symbolic function.

2 Lacan says that feminine eroticism culminates in the wish to kill and castrate a man. The copula is represented by the symbolic phallus as something that is missing or does not exist. The phallic function is the function of castration, not of copulation, or the function of the copula of being is non-being or "dis-being". Castration for a man because the phallic function inhibits first before it facilitates phallic jouissance, and for a woman because copulation represents not having for a woman or the enjoyment of not having or of a cut that can also manifest in the form of a complaint (Moncayo, *Lalangue, Sinthome, Jouissance, and Nomination; A Reading Companion and Commentary on Lacan's Encore, Seminar XXIII on the Sinthome*, 2017).

3 A playful reference to Lacan's use of *s'oupirer* … 'it could only get worse'.

Supplemental References

Aristotle. (2009). *The Nicomachean Ethics*. Oxford World Classics. Cambridge: Oxford University Press.

Freud, Sigmund. (1920). *Beyond the Pleasure Principle*. SE 18, 7–64.

Lacan, J. (1954–1955). *The Ego in Freud's Theory and in the Technique of Psychoanalysis. The Seminar of Jacques Lacan, II*. New York: Norton, 1988.

Lacan, J. (1955–1956). *Psychoses. The Seminar of Jacques Lacan, III*. New York: Norton, 1995.

Lacan, J. (1960–1961). *Transference. The Seminar of Jacques Lacan, VIII.* New York: Norton, 2001.

Lacan, J. (1972–1973), *Encore. The Seminar of Jacques Lacan, XX.* New York: Norton, 1998.

Lacan, J. (1974–1975), *RSI. The Seminar of Jacques Lacan, XXII*, (Gallagher, C., Trans.). Retrieved from: http://hdl.handle.net/10788/179

Lacan, J. (1975–1976), *The Sinthome. The Seminar of Jacques Lacan. Encore, Seminar XXIII.* London: Polity Press, 2016.

Chapter 4

Listening to Signifiers and Hearing the Effect of Meaning

Moncayo Seminar December 15, 2016, *Encore, Seminar XX*, pg. 33

BB: What page are we on?
RM: Page 33, Section 3 [*ALL agree ... LB joins the seminar as a guest, a scholar in Law and Literature ... short welcome*]

TEXT: What we need to know is what, in a discourse, is produced by the effect of the written. Linguistics has not simply distinguished the signified from the signifier. If there is something that can introduce us to the dimension of the written as such, it is the realization that the signified has nothing to do with the ears, but only with reading – the reading of the signifiers we hear. The signified is not what you hear. What you hear is the signifier. The signified is the effect of the signifier.

RM: Maybe we can read one more paragraph and then discuss it?

TEXT: One can distinguish here something that is but the effect of discourse, of discourse as such – in other words, of something that already functions qua link. Let us take things at the level of a writing (*un écrit*) that is itself the effect of a discourse, scientific discourse, namely the writing (*l'écrit*) S, designed to connote the place of the signifier, and s with which the signified is connoted as a place. Place as a function is created only by discourse itself. "Places everyone!" – that functions only in discourse. Anyway, between the two, S and s, there is a bar, S/s.

BB: Raul, I was wondering, when he says that we are reading the signifiers that we hear, is that something about the priority of hearing over reading in our mind in such a way that when we are reading, we are actually sounding out something that we have heard. Is this a reference to lalangue, or something?
RM: Okay, so he is saying, "If there is something that can introduce us to the dimension of the written". He is talking about the difference between the written, as related to the letter, which is distinguished from speech. Speech has a stronger relationship to the signifier and sound than to the written and visual. So, he is trying to distinguish writing from language – that's one of

DOI: 10.4324/9781003424581-4

the things that is going on. Then, he is trying to distinguish the relationship between the signifier and the signified. In this, he says, "if there is something that can introduce us to the dimension of the written as such, it is the realization that the signified has nothing to do with the ears, but only with reading – the reading of the signifiers we hear". Thus, in what we hear, there may be something more than the signifier, meaning that the signified could be a sound and not necessarily another letter or another word. The signifier produces an effect of meaning at the level of the hearing. We may be listening to the signifiers, but we are not hearing the effect of meaning of the signifiers, and that's where the effect of the unconscious is located. Let's read footnote 23 …

TEXT: The French here is *La lecture de ce que entend de significant*, which can be translated literally as the reading of what one hears qua signifier (or qua signifying), the sentences that follow in the text are what allow for the translation I have provided there.

RM: Then he says that the signified has nothing to do with the ears and the signified is not what you hear. What you hear is the signifier, and the signified is the effect of the signifier. It's sort of like the distinction between listening and hearing, in some way, perhaps. What you listen to is the signifier, but … "the signified is the effect of the signifier". I would say that's the distinction between listening and hearing. You may be listening to the signifier, but you are not hearing the signified, which is not necessarily another signifier.

BB: I am hearing these two ways now. There's the 'something' that we are talking about, which is the signified …

RM: You heard the words that the patient was saying …

BB: Let's say there is something going on, and someone puts a word on it like 'look at that thing over there'. There is a 'thing' that is happening 'over there', and the words point out that thing 'over there'. There's the signified – that 'thing' happening – and then there is the signifier, or the words that I gave to describe it [the 'thing over there']. But isn't there another? Peirce would call it the interpretant – that is, the effect it has on me, or the particular meaning I make of hearing those words in this moment is another signifier, isn't it? It's different from the thing that we are describing. And I thought that was what Lacan was saying when he said the signifier was the effect of the signified... the interpretant?

RM: Okay, let's define the three for Peirce, would you define them?

GF: Icon, index, and symbol. And each has an 'interpretant' which is dynamic, feeling, and final.

RM: But is the interpretant the conscious interpretation that you give to something or is it the effect it is having on you?

GF: It is the effect of the sign on the person receiving (or interpreting) the sign.

RM: And that agency doesn't presume that it is consciousness.

BB: It doesn't, but it could be. [*GF agrees*]

RM: Right, so in the Lacanian sense, the interpretant would not necessarily be conscious, because you can receive a meaning from the words that are being spoken that is beyond the actual literal words that are being used. So, in Peirce's system, that would still be the interpretant.

GF: Yes, since there is a 'feeling' interpretant, which is more like the unconscious one. Then there is a dynamic interpretant, which is interactive, and then there is a 'final' or 'formal' interpretant in which conventional agreements [signs] are placed upon the action.

RM: Yes, that requires a conscious agreement ... something like a manifest discourse.

GF: Yes, and as a matter of symbolic registration, basically.

RM: Right, but there is unconscious registration. So, Lacan is always using these terms with an orientation toward psychoanalysis and the unconscious – which, I do not think, was there as an intent with Peirce. And, in addition, Lacan is going to talk about the arbitrariness of the signifier, because there is no intrinsic link between the object and the signifier. So, he is going to attribute the function of the written to describe something of the object that is not necessarily the same way the signifier would describe an object. Because the object is always given by the signifier, there is no intrinsic link between words and the objects they represent. He is going to talk here more about that, so we can continue after we read a little bit more. The other thing he is saying in the formula he offers is that the signified is also the place of the Other. So, he says, "one can distinguish here something that is but the effect of discourse, of discourse as such – in other words, of something that already functions as a link". Then he introduces the level of writing, scientific discourse, and notes the place of the signifier – linguistics there is another form of scientific discourse – and then the signifier is connoted as 'a place'. This is the place of signification, so the signified is also in the place of signification locating what meaning will be attributed to the signifiers being used and what the meaning of those signifiers will be in the place of the Other.

TEXT: It doesn't look like anything when you write a bar in order to explain things. This word is of the utmost importance because there is not anything you can understand in a bar, even when it is reserved for signifying negation. It is very difficult to understand what negation means. If you look at it a bit closely, you realize in particular that there is a wide variety of negations that it is quite impossible to cover with the same concept. The negation of existence, for example, is not at all the same as the negation of totality.

RM: Well, the judgment of existence is 'does this exist or does it not exist'. Whereas to say that something exists or that something doesn't exist is not the same as saying nothing exists. And there are different types of negation, like privation, frustration, castration. Those are all different forms of the negative. Although they are related, they are all forms of the negative – of a necessary negative, though not a negative in the negative sense! You know, it's a positive negative! Usually, when we say something is negative, we think of it as bad. But, here, the negative is being used more in the sense of electricity. You would not say the negative pole of an electric current is negative in that sense, right? So, negation, here, has that similar function, and he is relating the bar between signifier and signified as related to this [type of] negation. So, on the plane of the numerator, which is the signifier – you know, one signifier in metonymy is connected to another signifier. On the plane of the signified, the signifier could be more than a signifier in language. The question is what does that link between signifiers mean? It could mean one thing or it could mean something else, and that 'something else' that it could mean is at the level of the place of the Other of the unconscious and the signified. Those two planes don't always overlap or directly interact. They are like geological layers passing each other like two boats passing each other in the night, meaning the subject is not consistent with himself or in the use of his words, and the subject is not consistent with his communication with the Other, because you don't know what you are saying until you hear the response back from the Other. ("*Oh, that's what I was saying*" … *I thought I was saying 'this'*, but this person heard me say something entirely different). That has something to do with [the fact] that the level of the signified was not moving in the same plane at the level of the signifier.

GF: To highlight that, could you say that if you looked up a word in a dictionary and identified the metonymic association with that word or even just a definition (with another definition, et cetera) that the definition may not be connected to the 'meaning' of the word in its use context?

RM: Right, for each subject, in terms of their own constitutive speech. The way we constitute ourselves as a subject through speech is not moving at the same level as the level of the signified. So, the signified and the signifier may be different for different subjects – somebody used the same words … somebody liked it, somebody got offended … everybody took it in a different way in reference to their own history and their own use of speech. And, so, the bar is the bar of repression. This bar – the *S* (signifier) over the *s* (signified) – equals 'divided subject' because the bar divides the subject into two. The bar is actually diagonal because it allows for the subject to become the 'eight of infinity', as signified by the Mobius strip. And this comes from the theory of repression in Freud that we have talked about before... remember the three levels of censorship – primary repression, secondary repression, and suppression as a conscious formation. You know, when you are speaking, you are selecting words and deselecting others. It's not as if you are repressing them, but … 'when you said this, I was thinking this other thing' … but I am not going to tell you that because it would be socially inappropriate or inappropriate to this conversation. So, that then becomes kind of your own 'signified' – the place of the Other within you – that is where the signifiers are having an impact on meaning on you that you are not going to verbalize. That's suppression. Now, you may remember, and you may go talk to your friend or analyst and say, 'when I was having this conversation with so-and-so, I had these other thoughts and feelings that I didn't communicate, but I am now letting you know about them'. So, then you [the individual] overcame this first barrier by communicating to someone else. Now, that thing that you did not say while communicating may also fall under repression, and you may not even remember that you thought that or felt that. That's also possible, because then the suppression is taken over by the secondary repression and then it becomes unconscious in the repressed sense. Until then, it was unconscious in a descriptive sense, because you were aware of those signified, but you are choosing who you will talk to about them – that is the first bar. But they are there, in your mind, in a preconscious state … The preconscious in Freud, you will remember, is an unconscious in a descriptive sense (see Freud's *Metapsychology* – there is a descriptive unconscious and a repressed unconscious).

BB: I am not familiar with the term 'descriptive', what does this mean?

RM: The descriptive unconscious is like... you just said some words, right? Now you are listening to me. [*BB agrees*] What's in your mind, other than listening to me?

BB: I don't know! [*ALL laugh*] Just listening to you! [*More laughter*]

GF: Don't tell him!

BB: At the moment, a blank!

RM: A blank! Right! That 'blank' is the unconscious in the descriptive sense because it is not like you forgot how to speak. You're just silent for a moment, you are just listening, and you don't have anything particular in mind at that moment. Where did your mind go at that moment? It's all in the unconscious in a descriptive sense. The unconscious in a dynamic sense is the repressed unconscious. The repressed unconscious are those things in your mind that even if you try to communicate or to remember, you can't. It's like, 'I can't remember this dream'. Someone comes to a session, and they say, 'I remembered it, but now I forgot it again, for God's sake!' And, then, you start talking about whatever in the session and you hit upon something that reminds you of the dream, and then, all of the sudden you have recall of it again. That's an example of the dynamic unconscious, meaning it falls back into repression, which is where the dream stems from to begin with. From those repressed thoughts or words, the dream transforms those dream thoughts into dream images and represents them. But there is always something concealed about the dream thoughts that led to the dream, and that is where you try to get through the associations. But then, the whole dream is forgotten since the dream was made out of repressed elements, and the repressed elements in the dream are sucked into the repressed unconscious (then, you cannot remember it anymore).

That's the bar … and then there is the 'original bar', which is the 'Big Bang' theory of Freud – that the psyche, in the beginning, is created through this primary repression that creates the structure of the psyche. There is something under primary repression that will never be made conscious. Now what that is, is it the Imaginary phallus or the object of fantasy that the child was for the mother? 'I was just this narcissistic fantasy for you', and often people may have an experience of that to their great horror when they discover the mother that they thought loved them so much or whom they love so much was not really seeing them as a subject but they were only being seen as an object of the mother. Everybody has had that encounter – it's a kind of existential experience. That alludes to what is under primary repression. There is another way of understanding primary repression, which is that there is nothing repressed there – it's just that whatever is there is outside of signification. So, it is a barrier of primary repression in a sense that there is a dimension of experience that you will never be able to entirely capture in language. The Real, in that sense, is under primary repression. So, those are the two modes of primary repression – there is something about the object that remains under primary repression and that helps to generate the structure of the psyche, and at the same time, what is under primary repression is what simply signifies the Real, which is outside signification (that is not necessarily repressed).

BB: Is the experience of being an object for the mother in some ways different from the idea of the object that one registers and which then becomes a part of a fantasy?

RM: You thought your relationship with your mother was your kind of '*Madonna col bambino*' relationship. The 'good mother' loving her child, with maternal tenderness and all that … that's what you thought. But, at some point, the child has the realization that there is more than that – that the child is also functioning as some sort of fantasy object for the mother and [the feelings] are about the mother and not about the child. That's a residue of the second type of primary repression. The first type is when there is no 'there' there. The repressed material does not exist. And, then there will be a series of substitutions to that primary signifier that will function within the repressed unconscious, which is what is within the repressed unconscious. These are substitutions for the original object repressed under primary repression, and then the primary unconscious works with those substitutions. There are also substitutions to the substitutions, which is the preconscious.

GF: Is it possible to say something about jouissance in that formulation of primary repression?

RM: Yes, so, there are three jouissances: the 'jouissance of the Other', 'phallic jouissance', and the 'Other jouissance' – and the first and the third often get confused, the same way that people confused feminine sexuality with the early relationship to the mother before the intervention of the father, as if that was the properly feminine (as when Lacan says that the feminine comes

> after the phallic function in relationship to this Third jouissance, which is the feminine jouissance). The 'jouissance of the Other' has to do with the jouissance that the mother and the child experience through this fantasy ... *oh, you are my beautiful baby! I feel complete with you! I just needed to be a mother!* ... And, you know how people say that it is good for a woman to have a child to structure and stabilize her life, to give meaning to her life, and all of that. That's an aspect of it. Then there is the child, of course, being totally raptured by being at union with this mother and being at the breast and being in relationship with the breast and all that (or the bottle as it may be). So, that is the 'jouissance of the Other' which is just this fusion with the fantasy object. The one that we all try to get back to through our tender feelings in relationships, where we want to love and be loved in the model of this maternal dyad – it always fails! That fusion with the 'other' always fails – so, it requires the 'third'. Then, the 'third' turns it into something different that becomes something unpleasant about this person not being the person you thought that they were, and so leading to the absence of a sexual relation. With the 'jouissance of the Other', since the one and the third can be confused, there is something about the Third jouissance that is also there in the first, which is that whole question about maternal tenderness that Freud raised that he thought was a separate drive from the relationship to the object and the sexual drive.

There seems to be something about the third that is already there because the mother also had accessed feminine jouissance before in her own trajectory. Depending on how well the mother has been able to cross her fantasy she will no longer see her child as her own object. By the same token, the relationship to her own father will determine how she will relate to her partner. Human beings cannot do without a paternal metaphor. The paternal function is independent of gender and could be occupied by a man or a woman. If the function is rejected, the individual and the society will fall into either psychoses or perversion. There is something of the first jouissance of the Other and of phallic jouissance that are experienced early on, and that's why they can be confused. In *Seminar XXIII*, Lacan moves the Symbolic Third to the '*La troisieme*' of the Third jouissance, which itself has three meanings. That first jouissance is always trying to look for that fusion with the object, like with an addiction. An addiction is an example of trying to return to that fusion with the mother, whether the mother was good or bad. With addicts, you see those who have been deprived of maternal care, and therefore they remain fixated to that. You also see it in children that were completely loved and cared for, but maybe given too much. And because they were given too much, the rest of the world doesn't feel as good as that [maternal love] was and so they keep on trying to go back to it through an addiction.

GF, BB: Thank you! [Continues reading]

TEXT: There is something that is even more certain: adding a bar to the notation S and s is already a bit superfluous and even futile, insofar as what it brings out is already indicated by the distance of what is written.

RM: Do you want to read the note?

TEXT: (footnote 27) – Presumably, the distance between the S and s in the notation S/s.

RM: *So, there is a separation already between the signifier and the signified, so there can be some kind of relationship. It is the 'written' that brings out this distance. I am not sure how helpful that is in terms of defining the written language, but ...*

BB: So, if I were reading this out loud as a Lacanian, how would I say this [formula] S/s? ... Would I say 'big S' over 'small s' or signified?

RM: You want the 'church rules'? [*ALL laughter*]

BB: Yes, the 'church rules'! [*Laughing*]

RM: There are no real Lacanians! [*More extended laughter*]

BB: No! Don't tell me that! Who will I fight against?!

RM: In Spanish we say, 'so*mos Lacanianos pero no Lacanistas*'. In English it doesn't quite work – 'we are Lacanian but we are not part of Lacanianism'. We were talking about 'Lacanism' ... what's the proper way to speak in this church? ... I don't think that is very Lacanian.

BB: How would you say it? Do you say 'large S', 'small s' when reading it?

RM: Yes, the upper case, lower case ... big, small ...

TEXT: The bar, like everything involving what is written, is based only on the following – what is written is not to be understood. It is the same with the bar. The bar is precisely the point at which, in every use of language, writing may be produced. If, in Saussure's work itself, S is above s, that is, over the bar, it is because the effects of the unconscious have no basis without this bar.

RM: Okay, so we went over how the effects of the unconscious have no basis without this bar, because there is no repressed unconscious without the signifier. There is no repressed unconscious without the law, and also, there is no real unconscious without language indicating its failure to represent something beyond language.

BB: What does 'real unconscious' refer to?

RM: The real unconscious? Colette Soler wrote a book called *The Unconscious Reinvented*, where she refers to Lacan's understanding of the unconscious as the 'real unconscious'. Then, the question for us becomes what's the relationship between the 'repressed unconscious' and the 'real unconscious'. The 'real unconscious' is outside signification. It's not that there is something [necessarily] repressed there, it is just that whatever is there of the Real is beyond signification. So, it looks like it is similar to the repressed [unconscious], but it is not repressed. Now, the other thing that Lacan is pointing to here is 'writing', and he is going to talk about how the writing acquires this kind of quality of writing in mathematics where you are using symbols to designate certain things that are beyond language, as if mathematics was trying to access the Real outside language through writing – through these letters that are being used and of which he made use. And, in his writing he is using language, but at the same time he is using a different type of writing than ordinary language as a kind of cipher to represent something of the Real of experience. That's what is associated with writing here, and not being able to understand 'the writing' because writing is being written as if when you read a mathematical paper or a paper on logic, and it has all these formulas, and the physicists or logicians write this and that [in formula] and the reader is like, what?! and you can't understand a word of it. But that's because all the terms in the formula assume prior formulas that were demonstrated through this experiment or that experiment, and they all know these, and then they just use a letter to symbolize that. For them it has meaning, but for us, it has no meaning whatsoever. Lacan's writing, he is saying, is a little bit like that.

GF: Is he also talking about the fact that with the mathematical symbol, the meaning is concrete, whereas with written language, the space between the signified and the signifier is always going to be there?

RM: Let's say if you have an 'x'. An 'x' is an indeterminate variable, but as a result of the formula, you are going to achieve a concrete number for the 'x'. But, before you reach that concrete number, the 'x' is simply a placeholder for something that could be different things until you use the letters in such a way that the formula produces a result based on arithmetical functions. So, in a way, it is like trying to find the 'x' of the repressed unconscious. Since we do not know, we are using this formula to try to get to what may be the repressed signifier – the 'x' for this particular person as it relates to their relationships and their symptoms, and so on and so forth. Then, there is the 'x' that just represents the difference between the indeterminate and the undetermined.

GF: The known and the unknown knowns and that kind of thing?

RM: The unknown and the unknowable, which is a mystery yet to be known. The 'x' was a mystery until we worked the formula, and now it is no longer a mystery – now we have a complete value. Then there is the 'x' of something that will remain unknowable, and that is more like the Real unconscious. The repressed unconscious is like an 'x' arriving at a specific figure.

TEXT: Indeed, were it not for this bar, nothing about language could be explained by linguistics. Were it not for this bar above which there are signifiers that pass, you could not see that signifiers are injected into the signified.

RM: Okay, so if somebody was talking about one word – it is like this morning, in one session, where a patient used the word 'cloud' instead of 'clown'.

She intended to say 'clown' but instead she used the word 'cloud' through a slip. So, we could say that the word 'clown' is injected into the word 'cloud', which is functioning as a repressed signifier. She intended to say 'clown', but instead she said 'cloud'. So, I guess the similarity with 'clown' and 'cloud' is that they have three letters in common. There's a segmentation with the first part of the word and the last part of the word, and then the segmentation is used to draw a link between 'clown' and 'cloud' – and this is all happening unconsciously. So, it is a hermeneutic device being used by the unconscious to inject one signifier into another signified.

TEXT: Were there no analytic discourse, you would continue to speak like birdbrains, singing the (*disque–ourcourant*), making the disk go around, that disk that turns because there is no such thing as a sexual relationship – a formulation that can only be articulated thanks to the entire edifice of analytic discourse, and that I have been drumming into you for quite some time.

RM: This is a little dense … so the birdbrain singing the current disc, just going around – the disc that turns because there is no sexual relationship. The melody of a bird is repeated 'x number' of times. Ironically, Lacan says that to keep it very simple, that there is no sexual relationship because the object and the other are not the same. What does that mean? Well, the songs are seduction songs to stimulate and signal reproduction. The bird just sings as a tool of biological life and nature. The other that we are relating [to] in sex, we think it is the other, but we are actually enjoying our own object. That covers over the differences between the subject and the other and it creates this fusion through this fantasy object. But then, eventually, there is a gap that grows between the object and the other, and that leads to the lack of sexual rapport between the sexes (or merely rapport between the sexes) and this friction between the object and the other. And it's like, you know... you don't see me as I really am! You think that I am somebody that I am not! … which is the way it devolves in relationships. The person has a fantasy of who [or what] the other person is that fits into their own desire, but eventually it will come out that the other person, who may go along with that fantasy as part of the sexual enjoyment, is not the object. So, that's the 'there is no sexual relationship' – and the disc that turns in that formulation would be the disc of the object. It's sort of like the disc of thinking that is going around in our head all the time … like those cartoons that have a little circle of birds going around! [*ALL laugh*] Those birds are like the chain links of this disc of thinking that we have which leads us to interpret the world in our own particular way. Sometimes it works, but more often than not, it doesn't. So, that's the 'birdbrain', and it is sort of similar to 'idle speech'. This kind of thinking that is going on in our head, which is how we are interpreting the world – this could be a form of the interpretant in the other system we have been talking about – the way we are running through what we are hearing in our own head?

BB [And others in agreement]: Absolutely!

RM: And it does not cease from being written.

BB: Right! That's why the interpretant is unique in that formulation.

RM: Right, but it does not cease from being written because it's never actually being said. Lacan always contraposes. "It does not cease from being written" from "it cannot be written". But, because it cannot be written, we keep writing about it but missing the boat, nonetheless. We are talking and talking, but we are not saying anything. We are thinking and thinking, and this thinking is not helpful.

GF: So, when he is using this pun, *disque-ourcourant*, meaning the current discourse, the current discourse is what he uses to refer to that constant thinking that is not approaching the real thing?

RM: Right, exactly, making the disc go around. So, he speaks in metaphors like this, and they are hard to decipher. Another present consideration is how Americans view the English crown that they fought a war of independence against. The monarchy is not about power or wealth (there are many rich individuals born from the middle class), but about keeping the peace of King Arthur and pacifying the warring political parties. The royals are not educated on purpose. Intellectuals and prime ministers come from the educated middle class. The crown is supposed to keep the peace between the Tory and the Labor parties. Prime ministers have an obligation to meet with the King to give him a regular report of the condition of the State. The King cannot judge or show preference and should listen and be educated by the prime ministers. The role of the King is not to be rich, but to maintain the peace of the country and the institution. This is the purely formal function of so-called 'bird speech'. This differs from how men misunderstand the parallel speech and sociability of women in a group. Here, the parrot's speech signals interaction, humor, and intimacy.

Supplemental References

Lacan, J. (1975–1976). *The Sinthome. The Seminar of Jacques Lacan. Encore, Seminar XXIII.* London: Polity Press, 2016.

Lacan, J. (1972–1973). *Encore. The Seminar of Jacques Lacan, XX.* New York: Norton, 1998.

Peirce, Charles S. (1867, 2009). *The Essential Peirce: Selected Philosophical Writings. Volumes 1 and 2.* Peirce Edition Project (Ed.). Bloomington & Indianapolis: Indiana University.

Soler, Colette. (2018). *Lacan – The Unconscious Reinvented* (The Center for Freudian Analysis and Research Library (CFAR)). Routledge.

Chapter 5

Clarity and Conceptual Uncertainty (The Universe as a Flower of Rhetoric)

Moncayo Seminar, January 12, 2017, *Encore, Seminar XX*, pg. 54

TEXT: Just as the discourse I am trying to bring to light is not immediately accessible to your understanding, similarly, from where we stand, it is not very easy to understand Aristotle's discourse. But is that a reason why it should no longer be thinkable? It is quite clear that it is thinkable. It is only when we imagine that Aristotle means something that we worry about what he is encompassing. What is he catching in his net, in his network? What is he drawing out of it? What is he handling? What is he dealing with? What is he struggling with? What is he maintaining? What is he working on? What is he pursuing?

Obviously, in the first four lines [of Aristotle's *Ethics*] that I read to you, you hear words and you assume they mean something, but naturally you don't know what. "All art, all research, all-action" – what does all of that mean? It's because Aristotle threw in a lot of stuff after that and because it comes down to us in printed form after having been copied and recopied for a long time that we assume there must be something there that grabs one. That is when we raise the question, the only question – at what level did such things satisfy them? It makes little difference what use was made of them at the time. We know that they were passed down and that there were volumes of Aristotle's work. That disconcerts us, and it does so precisely because the question "At what level did such things satisfy them?" is translatable only as follows: "At what level might a certain jouissance have been to blame?" In other words, why did he get so worked up (*se tracassait*)?

RM: Yes, in other words, what pleasure, what enjoyment, what pain is driving Aristotle to write his work? What's the jouissance at stake in his questions?

EW: The way I understood this was referring back to the Aristotle quote, the four lines that Lacan talks about earlier, "all art, and all research, like all action" and "all reflected deliberation" … and Aristotle goes on, "tends toward some good". Thus, the idea … I think, to help us out, they will give us a more complete translation … "every practice, every investigation, likewise every action and decision, seems to pivot on the good, hence the good has been well described as that at which everything aims". However, there is an apparent difference among the ends aimed at. So, the question about how to

DOI: 10.4324/9781003424581-5

be satisfied by them, I understand that satisfaction to be achieved through different aims.

RM: Yes, so it's the good of truth, the pleasure of truth, and the pursuit of the ethical good. These questions always involve for Lacan the good of pleasure and the pleasure of the good, which are kind of collapsed together. The pleasure of a good being the satisfaction that comes from this pursuit of truth, the pursuit of the good, but also the pain, the frustration, and the disappointment that comes along as well with the pursuit of truth.

TEXT: You heard me right – failing, deficiency (*faute, défaut*), something that isn't working out (*qui ne va pas*). Something skids off track in what is manifestly aimed at and then it immediately starts up with the good and happiness. The good, the bad, and the oafish! (*Du bi, du bien, du benêt!*)

RM: What is "oafish" in English?

BB: Like a big clumsy, stumbling, troll-like creature ... like the Big Friendly Giant (BFG), the children's book written by Raold Dahl. It's like these big giants in these children's stories that are silly and stupid. So, is he saying this because people do not want to accept "the lack", and they end up covering it over with the good and happiness and is that just how it works? Lacan's not speaking for it, but just describing what happens ... the kind of foolishness of people?

RM: Well, but also that the good is bound up with failing, and deficiency, and things not working out.

BB: I see. If things just worked out, we wouldn't need good and bad. They would just work out.

RM: In the process of things working out, they also have to not work out. We have to tolerate that ambiguity, whether it's working out or not working out. There's always that uncertainty.

EW: He seems to be asking that question of why is Aristotle making such a big deal about this – that is, what's the point in this observation about the good?

RM: Well, it's because Lacan is trying to link it with jouissance. Jouissance brings a different perspective on the good.

GF: There is also this sense that there is a clear, unambiguous access to the good that we would like to imbue Aristotle with. As if they [the ancient Greeks] somehow knew what 'the good' ultimately is. But they have the same translation problem that we do today. [*RM agrees*]

TEXT: Reality is approached with apparatuses of jouissance.

RM: Let me say something about that. So, he's handling different ways of thinking about the pleasure principle. Because the way Lacan takes the pleasure principle, the way he talks about it, it's as a limitation on jouissance. As if the pleasure principle was more of a defense rather than a principle also regulating the drives themselves in terms of the pursuit of pleasure. So, Freud said that the pleasure principle seeks satisfaction and avoids pain. So, the seeking of satisfaction is the aspect of the drives, and the avoiding pain is the aspect of the defenses. They are both in one single principle. Do you see? And, usually when we think of the pleasure principle, in general, in the culture, we think of the pursuit of pleasure, right? But Lacan means it in the opposite way.

Freud used it in both ways. The way the pleasure principle is related to the defenses, Freud developed that through the concept of the reality principle, where the reality principle is the same as the pleasure principle except where the reality principle has to tolerate postponements of satisfaction. The ultimate aim is still the same as the pleasure principle. The other thing is how we usually use the term "hedonism". Like nowadays we think of hedonism as the unbridled pursuit of pleasure. Whereas for the Greeks, hedonism was related to the permissible pursuit of pleasure within society – it is a kind of rational pursuit that doesn't really constitute a threat to relationships or to society. So we seem to have inverted the meaning around the same problem that Freud and Lacan were grappling with in terms of the pleasure principle. Does that make sense?

TEXT: I push further ahead, at the point at which it can now be done, by saying that the unconscious is structured like a language. On that basis, language is clarified no doubt by being posited as the apparatus of jouissance.

BB: Seems like we could talk about that forever! [*All laugh*] ... should I keep going?

RM: Sure! But inversely, perhaps jouissance shows that in itself it is deficient (*en défaut*), for in order for it to be that way, something about it must not be working. Reality is approached with apparatuses of jouissance. That doesn't mean that jouissance is prior to reality. Freud left the door open to misunderstanding on that score – you can find his discussion on this in French as *Essais de Psychanalyse*. There is, says Freud, a Lust-Ich before a Real-Ich. That is tantamount to slipping back into the rut, the rut I call development, which is merely a hypothesis of mastery. It suggests that a baby has nothing to do with the Real-Ich (poor tot!) and is incapable of having the slightest notion of the Real. That is reserved for people we know, adults concerning whom, moreover, it is expressly stated that they never manage to wake up when something happens in their dreams that threatens to cross over into the Real. It distresses them so much that they immediately awaken – in other words, they go on dreaming. It suffices to read, be with them a little bit, see them live, and listen to them in analysis to realize what it means.

I did a little work recently on the question of the real ego and on the sequence of the reality ego before the pleasure ego and before the reality principle, which is the way Freud thought about it (although it is not very well-known). And this is what Lacan is bringing up here. Basically, the idea that real ego comes before the pleasure ego, I think, refers to how he talked about the drive for self-preservation as the ego drive in his early work. He talked about the self-preservation drive as an ego drive, which doesn't make a lot of sense because there is no real ego as such as we know it. But because of this connection with the self-preservation drive, he seems to assume that when the child is seeking nutrition with the breast, that action is the reality ego seeking nourishment or food. And in the course of seeking nourishment in food, an experience of satisfaction is produced. The experience of satisfaction here refers not so much to nutrients or the milk, but to the experience of being loved by the mother that produces a sense of union with the mother at the breast that then they try to re-find again – and yet they can't. And what happens during the period of satisfaction is that there were some mnemonic traces that were laid down. Then it becomes a question of the desire to re-cathect the image of the experience of satisfaction, and this is what's used as a test that the experience of satisfaction is happening in the next feeding encounter with the mother. And somehow, because that experience of satisfaction created some kind of ideal that is never found again in the experience at the breast of the mother, from then on, the experience of the breast of the mother is marked by both satisfaction and the frustration that the satisfaction doesn't seem to be the same that was originally experienced.

BB: You know this is like my favorite restaurant! Yes, this is a repeated experience! You get that favorite restaurant, that perfect croissant … but then it is not the same!

RM: Then you can try to go back and it's not the same! [*ALL agree*] So once that experience of satisfaction proves to be frustrating or disappointing, then the reality ego as we know it comes in terms of being able to postpone that impulse or short-circuit that impulse back to the original satisfaction. So, those are the three terms – the real ego before the pleasure ego, the pleasure ego, and the reality ego after the pleasure ego.

BB: Can we go back to the unconscious being structured like a language? For me, the unconscious being structured like a language has been meaningful, in that it allows me to focus on metonymy and metaphor. It also allows me to think about the making of meaning that is about the movement of signs in relationship to each other according to some sort of grammar that isn't necessarily the one I know as a waking person – but that it has a grammar, and that has a structure. It may not make sense necessarily … it is not just one source of information … but it's just like the language. There are so many things one could do with it. But it has its logic. It's not everything, but it's something itself, in that you make things of it again and again, and that thing you make of it has a certain meaning or certain force. But what does it really mean?

RM: That is correct, and with the following caveats. One is, there is the question of why that wouldn't be the unconscious in the descriptive sense, which is how Freud meant it. I mean the way Freud talked about the unconscious in a descriptive sense is the unconscious that is not repressed. So, in that sense, language functions unconsciously in a way, but it is not repressed. And yet, within the descriptive unconscious there are also signifiers of speech that are repressed. So, then you have the two levels of the unconscious in the descriptive sense and in the dynamic sense, both working within language. Does that make sense?

BB: It does, but when the unconscious is structured like a language … it's 'like' a language. It doesn't mean 'like' as 'equal' … it means similar but not equal to, doesn't it? Or does it mean like as equal?

RM: The reason that it is not equal is that we have to give it all these qualifications ….

BB: … which would include in the unconscious, there are things that there are still no words for. But, there are still icons, and senses that are made of rhythms and smells … they are not actually words.

RM: Okay, but that raises another question of a protolanguage before language. Some people use the semiotic for that, including John Mueller and Julia Kristeva. The question of images is more complicated, because, in Freud, language, the word for representations, is part of the descriptive unconscious, not the dynamic unconscious. And images were part of the repressed unconscious. So, from Freud's point of view, the unconscious is structured according to images rather than language … except, that what Freud says is that the image representation, the reason the unconscious is represented in images more than words, for example, in dreams, is because the words have been censored. In order to hide the words that have been censored, they are transformed into images. So that transformation into images has a defensive purpose in order to disguise the repressed speech. So that is why you ask for association to the images, to go back to the repressed speech that the images themselves won't give you. So that is one thing. The other thing is, Freud also says that the primary process – and now, he's going to talk about primary and secondary process – sucks the logic of language into this other logic of images where in a primary process there is unlimited displacement and condensation. Whereas, in language because it is a discrete structure, you have a limited condensation and displacement. Unless you are delusional or in the grip of a thought disorder, in which case the language would be used in the same way with unlimited displacement and condensation. And then, if this wasn't enough, there is the question of lalangue.

BB: Oh! Let's go there!

RM: Well, lalangue is a form of protolanguage, if you wish, because the associations are based on the similarities between sounds. And the sound relates also prior to language, because with a baby, you have sounds – *bah-bah, wah-wah* – you have all that, and *ma-ma*, you know. But it's almost like the *da-da-da* is more important than the signifier itself in some way, even though it is the beginning of signification. The sound has priority. And then, there's a question also [of] lalangue being the language of the desire of the mother as distinct from the structured language, the grammatical language, being more of the language of the father. And yet you cannot separate these two. That's the problem with people who try to separate the semiotic from the linguistic, as if you could have lalangue separate from language, which can't occur – but you cannot collapse them either. So that is the full ambiguity of the problem.

BB: Can you say something about what is at stake in the desire of the mother that is linked to lalangue? How is the desire of the mother represented in that link?

RM: The mother, let's say playing with the *bah-bah wah-wah*, the *da-da-da* …

BB: But could you put into a concept what you think she is doing?

RM: Yes, she's doing, "oh you're my beautiful object of desire, my precious agalma![1]"

BB: Is she not saying, "Let's join in this together" … "you are someone and I am someone, and I am inviting you into something together", and it's marked by the similarities, marked by the "you say it, I say it" … you mimic me and I mimic you … we do it in rhythm, et cetera?

RM: The mimicking phenomenon is how the ego becomes someone defined by both the object and by the other, the object is more the object of fantasy because it is the mother's narcissistic object.

BB: But isn't that actually there – a step beyond the immediacy of looking at a child and that mimicry back-and-forth – that iconic mirroring constitutes an early social link? I am wondering if it is not like that initial 'yes' to the child that invites the child into language. The child's beginning effort to make language happens in those early interactions with the mother.

RM: Right, but the thing is … don't be fooled because we have two lines of analysis. One is the developmental line, where you can say there is a beginning from an embryo to a fully developed human being, and the things that unfold in order: what comes before, what comes after in development. And then, the other line of analysis is that all those things that unfold in development are part of a structure that occurs simultaneously. The developmental line happens in diachronic time and the structural line happens in synchronic time. And, so, when you talk about the point of view from the structure, the desire of the mother has an intrinsic relationship to the Name of her own father and to her partner. So, that's why you cannot separate the two languages, because they are interconnected. When the mother is playing with the baby, the baby is addressed both as an object and as other. The object has to give way to the other, because if it stays just at the level of the object that the child is for the mother, the child gets trapped in the narcissistic investment of the mother as her own fantasy object, and then, the child needs to be in that place in order to be fully recognized. But, at the same time, that becomes something deadly if it is not transformed – if the child is not transformed from object to 'other'. And the other involves other people, right – it involves the father, the father being the paternal function (and the larger society).

BB: It's funny, because part of why I am pushing on this is that if we think about the trouble in psychosis and schizophrenia, both say something about difficulty in the maternal development, the development of the child and the maternal relation – and why this makes sense to me is that the mother who responds to the child without that beginning reciprocity of an invitation into language and instead treats the child as an object – it's as if it's an "other" but it's not really another but it is still within her fantasy, something goes wrong there. But I feel like a similar phenomenon happens in the beginning of every new session and maybe every new analytic relationship, that willingness to learn the language of the other comes up as an issue – it's a specific thing within a paternal structure. It's like *ga-ga, goo-goo*, you know … you're learning each other's private language. But I am trying to give a status to that and have a way to talk about that openness.

RM: But remember, that that positioning of the child in the mother's fantasy object is not pathological. That's necessary … even though, if it just stays there, it creates all kinds of problems further on. But it's not just like we can have a mother relating to an early infant purely as an 'other'.

BB: Right, maybe I was trying to say the mother relates to her child as an object, as if it's 'other', but it's not other. The child just remains an object. The kid never gets that recognition of "*look at me*". It's always, "*oh, look at this aspect of mom*" – they're always trying to find [themselves] in the mother's eyes, again and again, to get that reaction.

RM: What you need there is the intervention of the paternal function.

BB: I just don't want to say that! I just want to fight with that!

RM: But that is the problem with the culture and with our field – that it wants to stay mother-centric.

BB: I want to define the mother in a way that doesn't have to be 'mother equals merger with the child'. Rather, the mother, with the intervention of the father coming later, being the mother in her role as someone representing the couple and holding a differentiated responsibility for the unique development of their child.

MK: As long as the father is in the mother's mind.

BB: That's what I am trying to say.

RM: Wait! Wait! That's what Lacan calls the 'symbolic mother'. So, there's an Imaginary mother and a Symbolic mother. The mother that can hold the couple and can hold the relationship to the other as the Symbolic mother, who can also monitor her own urges to be an Imaginary mother.

BB: Exactly!

RM: But the Symbolic mother requires the relationship with the paternal function …

BB: The problem is, you see, it's these generations of clinical meetings where analysts act as if everything that has to do with women is automatically crazy! I am trying to find a way to speak back to this use of "the woman" in this crazy-making way, as if there is only an Imaginary mother. And there is something about how these clinicians use 'the father' in these discussions that seems off to me as well.

RM: Often, clinicians suffer from two biases. First, that women are outside the Symbolic and they are therefore psychotic. The mother is crazy, and the father needs to make a break between the mother and the child. On the other hand, the father in the family can undermine his own function by being narcissistic, sexist, and chauvinistic. A lot of people do speak about fathers in that way, but it is partially true! We have to own that, and masculinity has to own that. That's why there is feminism.

EW: Are you saying at all that it is simply part of human beings' relation to each other, that there is always going to be an element of narcissism. As if, yes, we can be interested in the other, but there always must be a narcissistic element to that.

RM: Yes, but narcissism is gendered – it's part of sexuation. It's not a neutral narcissism.

EW: [*Agrees*] There is the mother's narcissism and the father's narcissism.

BB: This is the idea of some analysts that I cannot accept: that the mother's narcissism is different and is supposed by those whose ideas I am arguing with, to be way, way worse than a man's.

RM: This is because clinicians are trying to treat a new neurosis with new symptoms. They call this the borderline condition. However, the borderline can also be seen as a new hysteria that also happens in men, and this is why the borderline is considered to have gender identity diffusion. There are, in fact, different levels of narcissism. Freud described two forms, primary narcissism, and secondary narcissism. In my 2008 book, I describe four levels of narcissism, some of which are not pathological: primary narcissism, secondary narcissism, tertiary narcissism, and quaternary narcissism. They are all necessary.[2] They only become pathological when they are not transformed in steps to their next form.

EW: I feel clinically there are different forms of narcissism, like there is a universal maternal narcissism which I completely claim cheerfully, and which I think has to be worked with developmentally, but is part of the whole thing, and is not inherently problematic. Then I think there is the kind of thing that is talked about sometimes in the mentalization literature, which is the mother who, really, in a more pathological way cannot get that the infant has reality outside of her.

RM: Right, so what we say is that what creates that is the problem with the intervention of the paternal function.

BB: So, what's the limit of the father's narcissism? The intervention of the maternal function?

RM: It's symbolic castration. The father is under castration, so if the father does not accept his own castration – symbolic castration – then the father puts himself in the position of "I am the law and you have to do what I say because I came up with this and it's my idea, the end … regardless of whether it makes sense, you have to do this".

BB: I understand.

RM: So, that is the masculine trying to defend against castration by appealing to this myth of the primal father; namely that he has everything, that he can do whatever he wants, there is nothing binding him, he doesn't have commitments to women or his own sons, and so on and so forth.

BB: So, are you saying that the mother moves into the Symbolic place through the mark of the paternal function and the father moves into it by castration?

RM: The mother moves into the Symbolic through the acceptance of her father's name. The father enters symbolic castration through accepting his subordination to his own father. And then they both need to go beyond castration.

EW: Let me ask you about that. Again, I am trying to link it to clinical experience. It's tended to be my experience when a mother is really not able to be very interested in the infant or sees the infant in a kind of utilitarian extension of her own needs, that often there is something going on with the mother, like the mother is depressed or the mother is really overburdened, or in some way doesn't have access to the full range of psychological flexibility. So, I am trying to make a link between that …

RM: … right, she's stuck with Imaginary femininity, with being an Imaginary mother, trying to see her child as something that completes her. That it is about her rather than about the child.

EW: Yes, but how does the paternal function come into that conceptually? I mean we are not necessarily saying you have to have a literal father show up at that point, although it would certainly help her if a literal father showed up. But, as far as the function, how does the paternal function intersect with the mother's depletion?

RM: Right, so the way that Lacan thinks about castration is that castration is not the losing of the anatomical penis, you know, as in Freud, but it is the breaking of that fusion of mother and child based on the mother's object of fantasy. Where the child is functioning as an Imaginary phallus of the mother … that phallus needs to be castrated. That's what the paternal function does.

EW: I see, okay. Maybe the link between what I am trying to get at is that the mother cannot tolerate castration or accept that castration because she's just too depleted or depressed, and she clings to the Imaginary phallus.

RM: Right, she's depressed maybe … I mean, who knows the details of each circumstance. It's not like the environment does not interact with this question either. [*EW agrees*] So, it's complex, right. And we are not disabused of the notion of how complex this is because otherwise, it would not be so hard to treat or to figure out. Let's say the mother was hoping that the pregnancy would give her something that she is not feeling in her life. Sometimes women when they get pregnant, you know, they are a mess, they don't know

> what to do with their life, and so on. And then, all of the sudden, just getting pregnant kind of focuses them completely. So, they get a boost from that. Other times, the mother may think that this is going to solve the problem and it doesn't, so when the child is born and she loses that fusion in her body with the child, then that triggers grief and loss.

Now, there is also the question, what if there is no father that is accompanying her in that process of producing a child and raising a child. That's also another aspect of this question of the paternal function. It's complicated, because the paternal function is not identical to the presence of a father in the family, and it's not unrelated to that either, because when the father steps in to help the mother who needs a break, he is also helping the child separate from the mother, but as a father, not another mother. If you think that the Other is just two parents, then the child does not learn the difference between desire and prohibition that the paternal and maternal differentiation brings. If there are two females or two males raising the child, then the functions have to be distributed. I would argue the rationale for saying that, yes, of course, children can be raised neurotically and heterosexually, being raised by two women or two men. But, in my opinion, when that works, it's because the desire of the mother and the name of the father has been distributed in those two males or those two females as opposed to the two males or the two females being two parents that are the same in the relationship to the child. Barri, do you want to push the question further?

BB: We don't have time, but I think I will push that question for at least the next year or two! [*All, laughter*] Thank you, Raul!

Notes

1 *Agalma* is the term Alcibiades used to grasp the hidden yet fascinating object he believed to be enclosed in the depths of Socrates's hideous body.
A mysterious gem whose preciousness he had savored as a young man during a privileged moment of revelation, the *agalma* had sparked Alcibiades's infatuation with Socrates and served to justify his eulogy of Socrates's attractiveness. *The Encyclopedia of Psychoanalysis*, https://nosubject.com/Agalma.

2 Primary narcissism is needed to create a union between mother and child. Secondary narcissism is necessary to create a body image and sense of self. Tertiary narcissism is needed to create values and ideals. Finally, quaternal narcissism is necessary to create a self beyond imaginary ego identification.

Supplemental References

Aristotle. (2009). *The Nicomachean Ethics*. Oxford World Classics. Cambridge: Oxford University Press.

Dahl, R. (1982). *The BFG*. United Kingdom: Penguin Books.

Freud, Sigmund. (1920). *Beyond the Pleasure Principle*. SE 18, 7–64.

Freud, Sigmund. (1927). *Essais de Psychanalyse*. Paris: Payot.
Kristeva, J. (1941). *Desire in Language*. New York: Columbia University Press, 1980.
Lacan, J. (1972–1973). *Encore. The Seminar of Jacques Lacan, XX*. New York: Norton, 1998.
Moncayo, R. (2008). *Evolving Lacanian Perspectives for Clinical Psychoanalysis. On Narcissism, Sexuation, and the Phases/Faces of Analysis in Contemporary Culture*. London: Karnac.

Chapter 6

Apparatus of Jouissance, a New Ego in the Real, and the Question of a Protolanguage

Moncayo Seminar February 16, 2017, *Encore, Seminar XX*, pg. 39

RM: Okay, do people want to start reading?

TEXT: The Other, in my terminology, can thus only be the Other sex. What is the status of this Other? What is its position with respect to this return on the basis of which the sexual relationship is realized, namely, a jouissance, that analytic discourse has precipitated out as the function of the phallus, whose enigma remains utter and complete, since that function is articulated therein only on the basis of facts of absence?

RM: Any questions? Or should we continue reading?

EW: The part that talks about "the function of the phallus whose enigma remains utter and complete, since that function is articulated therein only on the basis of facts of absence"?

RM: That's the Symbolic phallus, which is missing by its very definition.

EW: Okay.

TEXT: But is that to say that what is at stake here is, as people all too quickly thought they could translate it, the signifier of what is lacking in the signifier? That is what this year ought to put an end to and it should say what the function of the phallus is in analytic discourse. For the time being, I will say that what I put forward last time as the function of the bar is not unrelated to the phallus.

RM: Right, because the Symbolic phallus is related to the phallic function, and the phallic function is the function of castration. So, you have it because you don't have it. And, that functions differentially for men and women, and it also depends on the sexual orientation.

EW: Can you say more about that? It would make sense to me that it would be different for men and women, but hearing about that in more detail and also how that differs with respect to sexual orientation would be helpful, at least, to me.

DOI: 10.4324/9781003424581-6

RM: So, for a heterosexual woman, like just say for the sake of clarification … she accepts that she doesn't have the phallus and that's why she wants it from a man in phallic jouissance or in the sexual act. The fact that she doesn't have it doesn't take anything away from her, because the function of castration also gives her access to feminine jouissance. Then, the neurotic tendency for a woman would be to think that if she wants it from a man, and she doesn't have it herself, that somehow she is less than a man. And, for a man, on the other side, in order to have it in the Symbolic, he also has to not have it first – not have the Imaginary phallus. The access to the phallic function goes through the Other.

For example, when men go to sex therapists for help with erectile dysfunction, the sex therapist forbids it [sex]. Or they go to couple therapy and the therapist says, "I don't want you to have sex" or "you should not have sex for the next two weeks". And then the couple comes back and says, "Gee, we cheated, we had sex", when they were having all these problems having sex to begin with! That's a paradoxical intervention, a different mode of working, but it functions out of the same principle. What the therapist is enacting there is the phallic function of castration so that the guy can function sexually. Then, if there is a different sexual orientation … if a woman assumes that another woman has the phallus or will give her phallic enjoyment … this woman may likely think that she is less than the other woman, because after all she is a woman, and lesbian couples can get into the same kind of conflict. For a gay man, to give you an example of an analysand, he wanted to cheat on the boyfriend but did not want to lose the boyfriend, and the guys that he had fantasies cheating with were presumably heterosexual. So there was a potential break of a prohibition there if the guy succeeded in having sex with them – and these were guys who he was to meet in some kind of sleazy way – so that there would be a judgment of him somehow degrading his sexuality in that way. He was going to fantasize about some co-worker or some boss that he has in the scene of seduction. And that seemed, for him, to have a lot more jouissance and intensity than having sex with his partner who was somebody that he knows already and is predictable and safe. So he doesn't want the partner to say, "no, I don't want you to be with anybody else" – but, in a way, his jouissance requires castration. It requires that he encounters this "NO" in his mind, one, he should not have sex with a co-worker; two, you should not try to seduce a married, heterosexual man; and three, you should not be meeting men in uncertain, sleazy conditions where you don't know if it is safe sex or not. All of those served as a stimulation for jouissance. I am not sure if these examples are exactly the same thing Lacan was talking about, but I hope it gives you a general idea.

MK: Well, do you have models for thinking about how to use this language to talk about the 'healthy' sex lives of couples? Like something that doesn't involve cheating or infidelity.

BB: That's an interesting question!

RM: Well, a man may be anxious in thinking he is not a man in relationship to his girlfriend or his wife, so to be given permission "not to be a man" then helps him to "be a man". In other words, to be given permission to be castrated, and it's okay and he can accept that, then he can function sexually. It will also depend on what the spouse's or the girlfriend's position is with respect to this question of castration and this holding of her own femininity. Obviously, the spouse or girlfriend may want the partner to function sexually, and yet, in other ways, behaves in ways that (even though they are not sexual themes) interfere with his sexual capacity to function because he is struggling with accepting being in a feminine position in relationship to a woman. Does that make sense?

BB: How does a woman accept castration if she doesn't have a penis to begin with?

RM: Precisely that's why there is no material castration in women because they don't have a penis. But culture requires symbolic castration: both sexes must lose something or give something of themselves to the big Other. This renunciation creates a sexual difference that will facilitate the sexual relation and reproduction. The boy loses what he thought he already had (the Imaginary phallus). When the girl realizes that she doesn't have a penis, she clings to the Imaginary phallus. This phallus the girl must renounce in order to be constituted as a woman.

MK: Yes, but I am wondering what's the place for feminine jouissance. If jouissance comes out of castration and prohibition, how does a woman find it?

RM: By giving up the Imaginary phallus and accepting castration, and by not interpreting the man's phallic attribute as meaning she is less somehow or that she is less of a woman, because the question of being a woman is on a different level than this question of who has the Imaginary phallus or who doesn't.

MK: Okay. [*Continues reading*]

TEXT: There is still the second part of the sentence linked to the first part by an "is not" – "is not the sign of love". This year, I shall have to articulate what serves as the linchpin of everything that has been instituted on the basis of analytic experience: love.

People have been talking about nothing else for a long time. Need I emphasize the fact that it is at the very heart of philosophical discourse? That is precisely what should make us suspicious. Last time, I had you catch a glimpse of philosophical discourse in its true light – as a variation on the master discourse. I also said that love aims at being, namely, at what slips away most in language – being that, a moment later, was going to be, or being that, due precisely to having been, gave rise to surprise. And I was also able to add that that being is perhaps very close to the signifier *m'être*, is perhaps being at the helm (*l'être au commandement*), and that therein lies the strangest of illusions (*leurres*).

RM: Okay, so here's a meaty paragraph, right? So, the fact that love has been discussed in philosophy since Plato … we don't have to go there, even though Lacan does teach a seminar on the transference based on the banquet where Socrates is asking everybody to say something about love – which goes to the question of why does Alcibiades love Socrates. And this is the same question of why does the analysand love the analyst. Then he says, "I also said that love aims at being, namely, at what slips away most in language – being that a moment later, was going to be, or being that, due precisely to having been, gave rise to surprise". So, 'Being' is what 'slips away' in language, or Being's language is in language, because Being escapes language or appears as 'nonbeing' within language.[1] Remember that Lacan says that language, when you are speaking or writing, has a certain kind of direction – sort of like in 'goal-directed' speech. But, the last word of the sentence, where the sentence closes, may be a successful sentence in language … but where the sentence was really going, for Lacan, was 'Being'. But, since 'Being' cannot be said in language, then 'Being' is substituted by a word that gives meaning to the sentence, and closes the meaning within the Symbolic, but fails to access 'Being'. So being in that sense is [only] within language but also beyond language. Or, and it is precisely due to 'having' Being, then maybe if you do manage to access 'Being' or contact Being through language, then that will appear as a surprise – as something fresh and original! It's like what Heidegger called 'thinking at the origin of being', where something fresh and surprising will manifest out of language. But then he goes on … "I was also able to add that that being is perhaps very close to the signifier *m'être*"[2] … in reference to when he was discussing the 'master's discourse'. So, … "being at the helm" … is it because of the mastery of language that being is able to reach Being? Is that what the master is? Is it that the master is a master because precisely the master fails the encounter with Being? Those would be two different definitions of 'master' – like 'master' in Spanish is *amo* (which is really 'owner' or 'I love' in Spanish) and the other meaning of master is 'teacher' [*maestro*]. I guess a good teacher is one that can make the contact with 'Being' in speech and have the skill to be awake and excited, as opposed to the teacher that closes speech with speech so that the contact with Being is alluded (and then everybody feels, "Oh, this is boring, what does this have to do with me …and I am listening to the teacher talk about this, but I am thinking about the things that really interest me" … and that kind of thing). So, that would be the good teacher and the bad teacher, and so 'master' has that ambiguity, because in English people sometimes use it positively, like a teacher, and sometimes people use it in a negative way, as an agent of oppression like in the master/servant dialectic. The master here is a tyrant – so, it has that double meaning.

Being at someone's orders – 'therein lies the strangest of illusions'. Because authority seems to rise from the Other rather than the subject. This raises the question of how the sign can be distinguished from the signifier. I am not sure how he is using 'sign' there, because usually in Lacan 'sign' means that which has a direct relationship to the object as opposed to the mediated relationship to the object that constitutes the signifier. The signifier has a mediated relationship to the object, while the sign has a direct relationship to the object. That's what we were discussing earlier, the difference between the sign and the signifier in Peirce and Lacan. The sign for Peirce begins by a direct relationship to the object where the sign is either close to the object as in being an icon or whether it has a part of the object in it as in an index.

For Lacan, the index is like the unary trait – you identify with the part of the object – and the icon is given by the Imaginary, by the totality of the image. For Lacan, the Imaginary rather than being a semblant of the object is coded by the interpretant (using Peirce's language). For Lacan, the interpretant is the code, the battery of signifiers. So I am not sure how Lacan is using 'sign' there, whether he is using it in the way Peirce does or whether he uses it as somehow representing an indirect relationship to the object – which he doesn't believe in anyway.

GF: I get the sense that love is somehow being portrayed like a phenomenon or an agency here, and this idea of a "sign of love" is that which somehow aims at Being. Love, then, could be seen as a phenomenon that is akin to an energy. Is it possible that this notion is at play, especially if we move to the last line in the text, "Hence we have four points – jouissance, the Other, the sign, and love". Love here is kept somehow outside the battery of signifiers or from being conceived of as merely 'a' signifier.

RM: For Lacan, feelings are an interpretant, in that sense of using Peirce's language. Love is determined by signifiers or representations. Now, within love, there are physical properties – there is energy and there's jouissance. What gives the definitions of these energies and jouissance as love is a signifier, like 'the lover' or 'the beloved' relationship, and all the rituals that we have in culture about love. And, with love, there is Imaginary, Symbolic, and Real love. So, the Imaginary love is the love people have for the other based on their own narcissistic fantasy, and that is why they fall in love – that's the romance – and it is a real romance-killer to think about it this way [chuckling]; so, when you live in the Imaginary you just have to live in the Imaginary. [*ALL chuckle*] Even analysts live in the Imaginary when they fall in love, but we are not fooled by the fantasy. We are not fooled by the fact that there is a narcissistic object there when you love the other, and when you are ready to sacrifice yourself for the other, that's a false altruism because the sacrifice for the other is based on a narcissistic fantasy of thinking that the other is going to be our object of love. Their object of love is located elsewhere rather than in the interpersonal Other.

With respect to a sign of love representing a love for Being, Symbolic love is manifest in the commitments that one makes in relationships that may sustain a relationship over time in relationship to Being or where the hope of Being in the relationship is not extinguished. But Real love – what Lacan says ultimately is love is empty – meaning what we are looking for in love is the emptiness of the other, which somehow feels the same as our emptiness. You can also formulate that in terms of lack, that we are seeking to discover the narcissistic object in the other but we only find it missing. And then we fall out of love – that's the Imaginary dimension of love. But ultimately, if what we are seeking is the lack in the other, to discover this lack in the other that is different from the object of fantasy. This shows that what really is behind that fantasy in the Real is emptiness.

So, love includes all that complexity across the three registers, and this gives a kind of bird's-eye view of how to think about love in terms of Lacan, because Lacan says that love is what 'covers over' the difference between the sexes. What happens when you fall in love, these differences are temporarily suspended. Once the romantic phase goes away, then the differences return, and as a consequence, that illusionary function of love, of bringing two people together, is gone. Then other factors have to come into play ... and that is why relationships are so difficult – and why he says, "there is no sexual relation".

GF: That's very helpful, because it seems as if the analogy of 'love' to 'being' would really play out then in all the registers.

RM: Right, so this love for Being – that would be a love for emptiness – that is another way of talking about love for Being, because the essence of Being is emptiness, since it cannot be described within language, and it remains outside of language. So, it's Nonbeing, in the sense that whatever being you think about, Being is always on the side of language, it's not it. I think that is consistent with Heidegger and Eastern [religious] thought in terms of the nature of Being and emptiness.

GF: It's like the empty plenum.

RM: Yes ... should we keep reading?

TEXT: Hence we have four points – jouissance, the Other, the sign, and love. Let us read what was put forward at a time when the discourse of love was admittedly that of being – let us open Richard of Saint Victor's book on the divine Trinity. We begin with being, being insofar as it is conceived – excuse me for slipping writing (*l'écrit*) into my speech – as "be-ternal-ing" (*l'êtrernel*), following Aristotle's elaboration, which is still so moderate, and under the influence, no doubt, of the eruption of the "I am what I am", which is the statement of Judaic truth.

RM: Okay, so he is saying "be-ternal-ing" is sort of "being" as in Christianity. Being is conformed to the [Christian] Trinity. And, of course, for the existentialist Catholics, like Teilhard de Chardin, the French theologian, he had no problem with thinking of G-d as Being. But, in philosophy and science we have a problem of thinking about Being as G-d, because being seems to have different attributes than the stories that we hear in the Old Testament and in the New Testament. Although, when you get to the mystical part of both traditions, then the problem that G-d is emptiness is not a problem at all when you get to the deeper spiritual interpretation – and this goes well with "I am what I am". Do you know this story?

EW: This is when God passes before Moses.

RM: Yes, Moses has escaped Egypt, because he was a prince of Egypt – he thought he was Egyptian, but he finds out that he was a Hebrew slave. There's that story about the Pharaoh's sister finding him in a bassinet in the river because his mother did not want him to be killed since Pharaoh had commanded all the first-born Hebrews to be killed. So, the mother, to protect him, sent him down in the river and Pharaoh's sister found him and never told Pharaoh the story. Everybody grew up thinking Moses was an Egyptian. So, then one day he sees a Hebrew being killed by an Egyptian, and Moses kills the Egyptian. Then, realizing what he has done, he runs away and ends up in the field of Jethro, who is a Midianite priest (the Midianites are the ancestors of the Druids in Israel, who are nomads). And, Jethro had a beautiful daughter, and although they are not Hebrews, Moses takes Sephora as his wife. And, over the next few days, he is walking around among the bushes in this field of Jethro (so the assumption is that the Jewish G-d is also the G-d for non-Jews) and then he sees the 'burning bush' – he sees that the bush is burning but not being consumed.

Then he hears the word of God saying, "Moses, Moses". Then Moses says, "here I am", and God tells him to go back to Egypt and free the Jewish people. Then Moses asks, "who should I say sent me?" and God replies with the famous answer (there are many translations of it), "I am who I am", "I am who I will be", "I am this that I am", and so on. So God gives an enigmatic answer. This is the name basically that is coming from the Real … this enigmatic name. The enigmatic name is YHWH, it is "Yahweh", but Yahweh is just a way of writing the divine name with vowels … otherwise it's just four letters that don't mean anything. And so you have to read it in some way for it to mean something. Yet, the name itself is senseless, and that's supposed to be part of the enigma of the Name. And the "be-ternal-ing" … I guess "Being" requires three, and Lacan is really trinitarian with respect to his three registers. He thinks the Catholic religion is the true religion because it has the Trinity, of course, which confirms his "knot" theory.[3]

EW: In the Jewish tradition, you would never say those four letters because they are supposed to be pure Being. You're not supposed to use a word for it.

RM: Exactly.

GF: I think that it is possible that Lacan may have acquired his understanding of Aristotle through Aquinas, which would transmit more of a Trinitarian Aristotelian position when it comes to speaking of G-d. And, even Aquinas, at the end of the day, talked about the Tetragrammaton as the unspeakable essence of G-d.

RM: Yes, Aquinas taught that, and that is part of the Trinity, right? That's supposed to be the Father. So [perhaps] the Father is the Real, the Spirit is the Symbolic, and Jesus is the Imaginary … that doesn't really work out well for Christianity! [*Chuckling*] Those would be fighting words that Jesus was Imaginary!! [*ALL laughing*] But, that might be what the Jews would say! Anyway, let's keep going!

TEXT: When the idea of being – up until then simply approached or glancingly touched on – culminates in this violent ripping away from the function of time by the statement of the eternal, strange consequences ensue. There is, says Richard of Saint Victor, being that is intrinsically eternal, being that is eternal but not intrinsically so, and being that is not eternal and does not possess its fragile or even inexistent being intrinsically. But there is no such thing as non-eternal being that is intrinsically. Of the four subdivisions that are produced by the alternation of affirmation and negation of "eternal" and "intrinsically", that is the only one that seems to Richard of Saint Victor to have to be ruled out.

RM: That's an interesting arcane 'turn of the phrase' or argument. So, there is no such thing as non-eternal being that is intrinsically – so, intrinsic being has to be eternal. It depends, however, on what he means by eternal. Do we mean 'no time'? Do we mean 'infinite time'? Because, you know, there are two infinites – the 'bad' and the 'good' one [*chuckling*]. The 'bad infinity' is the decimals that go on to infinity, so that you can never define an exact number for a concept, so it always slips away. That's the kind of slipping away of the sliding of the signifier, the infinite sliding. That's one kind of infinity, or just the infinity that you get if you follow the 'x-axis' or the 'y-axis' to the end – it just keeps going and going. God [or Being] would not be that kind of infinity in extension. So, then there is the infinity where the numbers don't apply, because it cannot be sectioned off or turned into some kind of diacritical concept … so, that's the same as no time. That's the paradox of time that Einstein encountered when he was riding on the beam of light – the faster he went, the more he stood still – meaning there is 'no time'. So, that's the place where 'time' and 'no time' meet, and that's a different kind of infinity – the kind of infinity that is 'intrinsic' to Being.

MK: What would you call that?

RM: What did I call it, guys? I just forgot! [*Laughing*]

MK: The place of the intersection of time and no time is …?

GF: Intrinsic?

RM: The place of time and the meeting of Being and being or emptiness and form are the two forms of time that erase each Other which is the, found under erasure, *sous rature*.[4] Why emptiness? Because emptiness is Being's own nonbeing, the denial of Being is already part of the equation that Heidegger represents as 'under erasure'. The intrinsic Being is the being that both is and is not in time or partakes of both forms of time: synchronic (no time) and diachronic (time, as usually understood).

MK: The translation of 'intrinsically' means … [*reads footnote*]

RM: Yes, well I guess "by itself" is the same thing as "in itself" – there is no differentiation within Being, so Being is the thing "in itself" in that sense, or "by itself". It [the footnote] says, "In certain contexts, it can take on the sense of and seems quite clearly to refer back to Aristotle's καθ αθτο".

GF: It means "of itself" or "self-based".

RM: Yes, but, 'self-generated', 'self-caused'. There 'self', I think, has a different connotation. It just means it's the same with itself or self-as-sameness. The same with itself, non-differentiation.

GF: For Aristotle, it would be *sui generis*.

RM: Hmm, okay … but if you read it like a 'small s' or 'self-generated', then you are talking about it as if you were self-creating yourself, right? It's like the illusion of autonomy – only I know what's best for me – only I know more about myself than anybody else and I am the master of my own destiny. That is the illusion that Freud says psychoanalysis marks and Darwin broke for us, because self-generation would be more in the sense of how we evolve over time. That is identified more with a species' being rather than one specific individual. We are self-generated in that sense, but here he is saying that G-d is not created, right?

[*ALL agree*] … We will need to stop now … thank you so much!

Notes

1 Being is capitalized to signify Being as empty in its own nonbeing. Just like in Zen, lower case dharma is phenomena, while uppercase Dharma is Noumena. Derrida, for his part, places a bar on the capitalized 'Being' to indicate that there is no being or jouissance outside the text. Derrida believed that Lacan reduced everything to the phallus as a signified of meaning. However, he misses that throughout Lacan's work, Lacan defines the phallus as a signifier of a lack.

2 The French allows us to read either "the signifier *m'etre*" or "the *m'etre* signifier," *m'etre* being a homonym of *maître*, master (thus, "the master signifier").

3 Lacan first takes up the Borromean knot in the seminar of 1972–1973, but his most detailed discussion of the knot comes in the seminar of 1974–1975. It is in this seminar that Lacan uses the Borromean knot as, among other things, a way of illustrating the interdependence of the three orders of the real, the symbolic, and the imaginary, as a way of exploring what it is that these three orders have in common. Each ring represents one of the three orders, and thus certain elements can be located at intersections of these rings. (In his view, these orders are tied together in the form of a "Borromean knot". The "Borromean knot" is a linkage of three "string rings" in such a way that no two rings intersect. The structure of the knot is such that the cutting of any one ring will liberate all of the others. Lacan used the theory of knots to stress the relations which bind or link the Imaginary, Symbolic, and Real, and the subject to each, in a way which avoids any notion of hierarchy or any priority of any one of the three terms.) *Encyclopedia of Psychoanalysis*, https://nosubject.com/Borromean_knot

4 *Sous rature* is a strategic philosophical device originally developed by Martin Heidegger. Though never used in its contemporary French terminology by Heidegger, it is usually translated as 'under erasure', and involves the crossing out of a word within a

text but allowing it to remain legible and in place. Used extensively by Jacques Derrida, it signifies that a word is "inadequate yet necessary"; that a particular signifier is not wholly suitable for the concept it represents, but must be used as the constraints of our language offer nothing better. https://en.wikipedia.org/wiki/Sous_rature

Supplemental References

Aquinas, T. (1966). *Summa Theologica.* T. Gilby (Ed.). OP. 60 vols. Cambridge: Blackfriars.

Aristotle. (2009). *The Nicomachean Ethics.* Oxford World Classics. Cambridge: Oxford University Press.

Heidegger, M. (1927). *Being and Time: A Translation of Sein und Zeit.* Albany: State University of New York Press, 1996.

Lacan, J. (1972–1973). *Encore. The Seminar of Jacques Lacan, XX.* New York: Norton, 1998.

Lacan, J. (1974–1975). *RSI. The Seminar of Jacques Lacan, XXII* (Gallagher, C., Trans.). Retrieved from: http://hdl.handle.net/10788/179

Peirce, Charles S. (1940). *Philosophical Writings of Peirce.* J. Buchler (Ed.). New York: Dover, 1955.

Chapter 7

S_1–S_0 Relations

You Only Know the Unmarked Zero by First Knowing the One Mark

Moncayo Seminar, February 9, 2017 (no text – open discussion)

RM: I want to make it up to you for the missed encounter last time. I thought it might be helpful, given everything that we discussed and the context you're in there, to talk a little bit about the similarities and differences between Peirce's notion of the sign and Lacan's use of the signifier. Maybe that will help clarify some of the terms, how we are working with these concepts, and how to apply them. Would that be helpful, to take a little time to do that today?
[*ALL agree*]

RM: One of the core ideas behind Peirce's understanding of the relationship between a concept and an object … let's start there, because that's where he begins to describe the nature of the sign. And, he says, that the content of a concept is revealed in the effects that the concept has on the object. He says, "our conception of the effects is the whole of our conception of the object", meaning the effect that the sign has on the object. So, what's at stake here is whether the concept determines the object, or the object determines the concept. And, with regard to this, the least we can say is that the object and concept arise together or mutually determine each other. Concepts are embedded in perception in the same way that language is unconscious and constitutes the background of perception, right? We are perceiving, but we are not necessarily conscious of how language is determining our perception of the reality of the object. Language is unconscious, in that sense, from the point of view of the perceiving subject. When we are perceiving, language is unconscious, we are perceiving objects, but we are not perceiving how the signs and signifiers are determining how we see the object. So far so good?

What the subject instead perceives, in the immediate perception, is the naive reality of the object, as if the object presented itself without being determined or mediated by the use of language or the use of the signifier. So he uses the terms object, representamen, and interpretant – those are the three aspects of the sign for Peirce. The representamen and the interpretant are also in a relationship such that

DOI: 10.4324/9781003424581-7

the interpretant is also a representamen and the representamen is also an interpretant. Are you familiar now with what I am talking about? [*All agree*]

The interpretant of a sign is typically a second sign. Thus, it becomes a good example of the concept rather than the word. More importantly, interpretant refers to the use of code. So the second sign would be the second representamen, which is determined by the primary sign to refer to the same object to which the primary sign refers and which translates the meaning of the primary sign. The signifier or the representamen refers to the object – defines the nature of the object – and then the second signifier or the interpretant defines the meaning of S_1. (The interpretant in the Lacanian system would be S_2, and the representamen would be S_1.) S_1 defines the meaning of the object. That's an easy way to walk across the two models.

For Peirce, the object and the interpretant are the two correlates of the sign, one being antecedent, meaning the object comes first, and the interpretant or the representamen is the consequence of the first or of the sign. So the problem with Peirce, where Peirce and Lacan differ with respect to the theory of the sign, is that Peirce conceives of an original relation between the sign and the object, as if the connection between the sign, or the signifier, or the representamen came in some way representing the object that the sign had derived from a quality of the object, instead of the sign determining the meaning of an object world. Do you see the difference there?

MK: Can you say it again?

RM: For Peirce, in terms of the original relation between the sign and the object, or the representamen and the object, or the signifier and the object is that the signifier has something, a quality shared with the object, so that the representation was somehow included in the object instead of the object being determined by the signifier.

BB: Is that referring to the way that some languages started to use ideograms that looked like the objects they were describing and that these were later replaced by a letter?

RM: Right, exactly. So, for Lacan, the early form of the signifier, in the form of the unary trait, the letter, or the tally – how they used marks to tally or count things – is derived from the object. So, there he [Lacan] seems to coincide with Peirce, but not from a part of an object that is represented by the sign, as Peirce believed, but from the quality of the object that originally represented the death or the killing of an animal.

I will unpack that a little bit. An initial mark or unary trace represented the dead animal, and from these, early marks, letters, and systems of numbers would evolve. So, for example, as it was mentioned before, the letter 'A', aleph, or the first letter of the alphabet is said to represent the icon. So an icon refers to an image of an object or in this case, the head of a cow, bull, steer, or bovine specimen turned upside down. That is, if you take the head of a cow and turn it upside down, then you have some form of the letter 'A'.

This example seems to corroborate with Peirce's idea that the sign takes and represents part of the object. However, with a letter, we have a sign [but] not a system of signs. So, it is of the order of the structure that we forget the iconic origins of letters, for letters to constitute words or phrases or statements. The place of the origin of the sign of the object is replaced by the void left in the absence of the object. So when you get a letter, you have an iconic link to the object, just the image of a head of a cow turned upside down, and that becomes the letter 'A'. For the letter 'A' to evolve into a system of letters and a system of signifiers within language, this place of the origin of the object is replaced by a void left by the absence of the object. So, then we have a kind of separation between the reality of objects and the reality of signs and signifiers because the system of signifiers is a mediation of the world rather than the immediate relationship to the world of objects. Does that make sense? We are discussing the notion of symbol in psychoanalysis because Peirce really does not talk about psychoanalysis, right?

BB: I believe you.

GF: Right, he [Peirce] was a contemporary of Freud.

RM: He was a contemporary, but he did not really mention his work.

GF: No, he probably would not have known much about it.

RM: Yes, he was a contemporary, but he wouldn't have known of his work.

GF: Peirce died in 1914, so he wouldn't have known much about Freud. When did Freud come to Clark University? 1909?

RM: Right, but Freud published *The Interpretation of Dreams* in 1900, and the Metapsychology in 1915, so yes, he [Peirce] would have been a bit early for that, correct, I agree. In psychoanalysis, the symbol represents the absence, the death, or the loss of the object. The symbol is tied to this sort of jouissance, associated with lack and with loss. Death or the unmarked behind the symbolic system is what kills the direct or immediate link between a sign and its object because the object is missing. Right, so if the mark is a mark of the unmarked and the unmarked is the killing of the death of an animal, for example, that becomes lost from the fact that signs become independent from that death or that loss, and then are used for other representational purposes. It's as if that background remained there in the unconscious.

The 'unmarked' – do you understand what I mean by the 'unmarked' when I am using these notions of the 'marked' and the 'unmarked'? The mark is obviously part of the sign, and it is part of semiosis. But the 'mark' is a more general concept than the signifier, and Lacan, of course, builds it into the structure of the signifier by representing the unary trace as an early form of the basic unit of the signifier, because the signifier has different units. The unary system is the first type of sign and functions as an early form of the signifier.

Then you have authors who separate semiotics from the theory of the signifier and where the semiotic or the trace becomes more representative of a pre-symbolic, proto-symbolic system presided by the mother rather than the father. In Lacan, you find a continuity across the unary trait between the early and later forms of the signifier. Early and later periods of the signifier cannot be divided because they are related through a metaphor. The mother and the father, as the focus of psychoanalysis, cannot be split because they are both part of an equation or paternal metaphor. The 'unmarked' refers to the work of G. Spencer-Brown in the 'Calculus of Indications'. Spencer-Brown was a British logician. I do not know if Lacan knew about the work of Spencer-Brown, but a lot of Lacanians do. The 'unmarked' refers to what in the Real doesn't have a sign or a mark – that's the 'unmarked'. The 'marked' is always the sign of the 'unmarked'. And we can say what is 'unmarked' is what is repressed, although the repressed also breaks down into the signifiers that are repressed and then the unconscious of the Real which is outside the 'mark'.

In *Encore, Seminar XX*, we find a differentiation between two types of unconscious. The 'unmarked' occupies the empty place of a placeholder function that will be filled or stuffed by other symbols or signifiers. So the 'unmarked' tends to get replaced by other signifiers. The 'unmarked' is really this empty place of a placeholder function representing the void. Once a symbolic system has emerged, the sign will represent a signifier relation that will define the nature of the object. You see how the signifier and the signified will define the relationship to the object more than the sign representing an iconic part or trace of the object. The connection to the object world is lost, and it will remain in the form of the register of the Real. The sign and the signifier will retain a relation to the Real of the object in the form of jouissance. Even though we lost the original connection between the sign and the object, meaning the sign representing a part of the object, we still relate to that object world in the Real through jouissance.

GF: I find this really helpful, and I just want to add that I think Peirce was onto something in terms of how he laid out the notion of icon, index, and symbol, and when he spoke about symbols being 'thirds'. His system of semiotics, which had a metaphysical [architectonic] schema at its foundation, was developed using the concepts of 'firsts', 'seconds', and 'thirds'. He claimed that we always interpret within the realm of 'thirds'. We are always using our signs and representations to interpret objects that we ultimately cannot fully know in their essence or 'firstness'. It seems that Lacan has a better sense of the loss and the repression [of the object], and he links it with jouissance which Peirce would not do, of course. [*RM agrees*] So, it's helpful to understand that Peirce realized that one can only traffic within the representations given to objects – in a symbolic register or a semiotic register – as he also shows that one cannot fully comprehend the real object in itself, even though a clock is [indexically] connected to time somehow, or a painting somehow represents the object.

RM: Yes, so there, the reference to the terms 'first', 'second', and 'third' – the 'first' would be the 'object' for Peirce.

GF: That's correct, the thing in itself … it's the Real, the undetermined Real.

RM: Right, but for Lacan, the first is the 'S_1' … the signifier.

MK: It's not the 'S_0' [S–zero]?

RM: Right, that's the paradox between the S_0 and the S_1, because in mathematics you derive the 'zero' from the 'one'. So, first the 'one' existed, and mathematics only had the concept of 'one' in Europe until they got the 'zero' from India (through the Muslim invasion of Spain) from the Sanskrit cipher. Then, the 'zero' became more fundamental than the 'one'. So, you only know the zero by first knowing the one. The 'zero' (S_0) then becomes whatever the 'one' (S_1) doesn't really capture in a relationship to S_2. The S_1 is defined by S_2, which is the interpretant, the signified or the second signifier. But, when the S_2 defines the S_1, when the second representamen or the second signifier, or 'the second' functioning as interpretant defines the S_1 (which in Peirce's system would be the 'second'), there's something in the S_1 that is left undefined as a residue – undefined by the S_2. That's then where we find 'zero' as a function of 'one'.

MK: It's just that all you know initially is a 'something', and then you only know a zero and then nothing in relation to the gap between the 'something' and the 'something else' (i.e., between the S_1 and the S_2). So, we need to have 'one' first before you can have a concept of none.

RM: Right, you must have '1' and '–1', and then you get 'zero'. But 'zero' is more than the absence of something, because the absence of something is just a deficit in the Symbolic. However, Lacan says that the Real is a plenum, so the 'zero' is also a plenum, meaning it is not the absence of something. It's more in the place occupying the place of the object that is not represented by the sign or that it is missing from the sign. So, from the point of view of the sign, there is something missing, but from the point of view of the Real, there is nothing missing. This is the same logic he will use to understand femininity – in terms of whether femininity indicates a lack of a signifier, a lack of the phallus, or whether that is just one way of talking about femininity in the Real from the point of view of the Symbolic. If you think of femininity separate from the Symbolic, in relationship to the Real, then there is nothing missing in femininity. From that point of view, the concept of penis envy would not mean anything. It both means something and doesn't mean anything at the same time, so that is his way of reconciling the claims of Freud and feminism. That's Lacan's way of reconciling those antithetical claims.

MK: Can you remind me what the 'minus 1' is?

RM: Yes, so, if you have an orange, you have '1'. If you have the absence of an orange, you have '–1'. But we also speak about 'zero' there, because where there was an orange, now there is no orange. So, that's 'zero', although we count it as –1. In this case, zero is used as a placeholder representing the absence of the orange or the 'null set' of orange. But 'zero', or the Real, is more than the absence of the orange (again, numerically counted as –1). It's the world without a system of signs to represent it. Freud and Peirce engaged the Symbolic (or the representational system) to highlight mind-consciousness and not just behavior. To do so, they needed to represent the mind in a way that represents a void. If we want to represent the void, we have to place a mark or sign on it. So, in this sense, the entire symbolic system is based on nothing (an emptiness that is full). We communicate our hunger, for example, which is a void or absence that seeks to be filled to reestablish the homeostasis of the organism.

This is another pivotal point. The representational system is tied to modifications of mind-consciousness, and for Freud, in his Metapsychology, there are different types and energetic qualities in the representations. Not only are there different types of representation – meaning representamen, interpretant, signifier, signified, and signification – there is also the energetic quality of the representation, there's the jouissance that is not there in Peirce. In the Metapsychology we have three systems – the perception consciousness is the first system. Then the preconscious consciousness is the second system. The third system is the preconscious unconscious system. Should I flesh those out a bit for you?

BB: Yes, they are familiar, but it would be nice to have you flesh it out.

RM: Perception consciousness refers to how we perceive the world. To perceive the world, Freud says there must be a layer or a quality of the mind that doesn't retain any signs or traces, so that you can perceive new things. Otherwise, your mind would be completely saturated, and you could only find what you already know. There must be a layer, he calls it 'like a screen' or 'a shield', or membrane, that is transparent. Since stimuli coming from outside the mind or from inside the mind do not saturate that layer, we can perceive new things in the world and the world can appear 'fresh' in each moment. So, that's the system of 'perception consciousness'.

The system of 'preconscious consciousness' is whatever is in our consciousness that is not the focus of our attention in the moment. This is like all the structure of language, our history, whatever is there when the analyst listens. The analyst has to listen first with the perceptual consciousness system – this is what Bion says, "Listen without memory or desire", without the theory and without your thinking. The mistake is to say: I am going to channel everything the patient is saying into some kind of theoretical frame that I have. Doing that is not going to allow me to perceive anything the patient is saying that is somehow outside my frame, the theoretical frame I have? We have to let go of the theory 'in the room' or in the session. To let go, we do not need to repress a preconscious theory. We don't need to because the preconscious comes and goes from awareness. It's just there! We may use it or not use it. So that's the 'preconscious conscious' system.

In the same way that language is there, oxygen is there, and all we need to do is breathe. With language, all we need to do is speak. Oxygen is to breathe, as language is to thinking. Oxygen does not create an obstacle for breathing and language facilitates rather than obfuscates thinking. Otherwise, it would be terrible if we were perceiving, and language was always intruding upon us. In a way, psychosis is like that – language has lost its empty quality and has this intrusive quality that doesn't allow the psychotic to perceive the world in any other way other than the construct that he has. That is why Freud said that psychotics are attached to their delusions like analysts are attached to their theories. The 'preconscious conscious' has a nice relationship between the perceptual consciousness – the layer that remains free and open – and this other layer that contains a receptacle of memory and knowledge and representation. The layers and systems in Freud are abbreviated as perceptual awareness (*Pcpt. Cs.*), the consciousness that is determined by Others (the *Prec. Cs.*), and the unconscious preconscious (the *Ucs. Pcs.*).

The third system, the unconscious preconscious, is that within all those things that we assume that we know although we can use them intuitively in the moment ... within those things that we assume that we know and that we could recall to consciousness. ... Oh, the patient is talking about this, and that makes me think of when so-and-so was talking about this other concept or that concept, or this other point of view. But, within that, they are repressed. Within that reservoir of representations, there are repressed representations. That is where Lacan says the link between S_1 and S_2, the link between representamen and interpretant, is mediated by repression. So that's why the signifier and the signified, the bar between the two represents the defense of the repression. That's why the system of signs can function in different systems. That is how we can say the representational system or 'the Symbolic' involves modifications of mind-consciousness.

GF: Could you say a bit more about how S_1 and S_2 are mediated by repression?

RM: Alright, so, for example, I was reading something there was the example of ... let's say a patient is talking about a pastoral scene where they were having an interaction, having a little picnic in the countryside. Let's say a mother and a daughter were having a little picnic in the countryside, and they are talking about whatever it is that they are talking about – there's a narrative there – and then there is a comment about the tree they are sitting next to and, some of the branches, you know, the daughter associates the branch of the tree to some extraneous signifier that doesn't seem to belong to the narrative that is being discussed. And, that signifier that seems to be extraneous to the narrative then leads you to other repressed signifiers.

BB: By a metonymic chain? Is that metonymy that you are talking about?

RM: Well, no, that would be metaphor. For example, an extraneous signifier (i.e., 'ranch' for 'branch', or 'two' for 'too') associated with a tree, is a metaphor for some other signifiers that are repressed. For instance, other connotations that the tree could have between the mother and daughter...

GF: I was thinking about the actual use of the word 'mediation', and to me that implies that the S_1 and the S_2 are linked together somehow causally by repression. So, it seems that the repressive moment must put one away and then also bring one forward – how would that work?

RM: Right, let's say the narrative is S_2, and the narrative is having the function of representing something – a story – but, at the same time, this expression has the function of concealing something at the same time. Concealing other signifiers where the scene or the conversation of the narrative could have a different meaning. The S_2 there is replacing the links that the S_1 could have to other signifiers, because there is a link between S_1 and S_2, but the link is also both a connection and a separation at the same time. Something gets linked, and something gets separated, even though there is a link between the narrative and whatever the S_1 could represent with meaning. What we are trying to talk about in this story, the fact that S_1 is connected to S_2 functions to repress other connections that the S_1 could have. And, those connections appear by the associations that the daughter may have to this word, or this signifier, that she used in reference to the branches of a tree. Does that answer your question?

GF: What I am picking up there is that there is a possibility of an S_2 creating new links to other S_2's and somehow the S_2 becomes the S_1, moving away from the earlier S_1. The antecedent S_1 gets lost or becomes now only a potential link if one were able to uncover it again.

BB: It would be like, so there is the mother and the daughter having lunch at the picnic, and they end up talking about this day because the little girl saw a bumblebee in the tree. And so, she says 'bumblebee' to mom, and the mom and the little girl know between them that 'bumblebee' stands for the 'bumblebee in the tree'. But, then later, when they are saying 'bumblebee', 'bumblebee' starts to take on another meaning. This is why I thought it was metonymic because it [the signifier] starts to take on other links to 'bumblebee' that have to do, in a contiguous way, but not in a representative way, 'bumblebee' isn't the tree, but it links to 'a moment' of the tree. Then, 'bumblebee' comes to mean other things. That's why I got confused when you said metaphor.

GF: Well, the metaphor does operate within the metonymic chain always …

BB: It does, but I thought metaphor and metonymy were opposite. Like metaphor represents in a vertical way, and metonymy represents time in a contiguous way …

GF: They work together as well, constantly, because if you start talking about the bumblebee going to the hive and making honey, you then could talk about the biological development of 'birds and the bees'.

BB: Then, to go back and say, here we are, mom and daughter underneath the tree, in our own intergenerational 'something', and it would be linked that way, too.

RM: The 'bumblebee' is, let's say, related to a memory she had as a younger child, where there was a different kind of scene that gets represented by the bumblebee. Metaphor and metonymy are the movement of signification across levels …

BB: Which levels?

RM: The level of the bumblebee as a signifier for another scene, the bumblebee for that signifier in the moment, and what's taking place between the mother and the daughter. There's the original signifying context that is latent underneath the manifest content – which is the narrative that they are talking about – then, the bumblebee is a signifier of that other scene. Then, the bumblebee functions as a signifier in this new scene, and the meaning that it may have within the context of that story that they are talking about (whatever it is that they are talking about). So, whatever they are talking about, there is the signifier of 'bumblebee', and the signifier 'bumblebee' refers both metonymically to the other scene and to this current scene. So, metonymy is the movement of signification, the horizontal movement of signification, and the metaphor is the vertical replacement of one signifier for another.

Okay, let me just say a few more things. Another thing that Peirce brings up is where he brings his connection to psychology, because he was considered to have also contributed something to psychology in the concept of 'habit'. The concept of habit is something that relates more to behaviorism in psychology. Psychoanalysis doesn't usually use the concept of habit, although habit is a part of character formation.

BB: And learning, and identification, isn't it? It should be part of psychoanalysis!

RM: Okay, maybe! [*All laugh*]

BB: Well, there's the patient who picks up the gesture of their analyst, whatever it is. [*RM agrees*]

RM: Okay, so how does he [Peirce] think of habit? They are the effects that concepts have on the object in terms of how we were talking about the definition of the object by the concept or whether the concept is shaped after the object. The relationship between the concept and the object is also expressed in 'habits of action' or involved in beliefs in relationship to an object. So, there's a connection between beliefs and habits – they are also connected. For instance, we think that being clean and hygienic is an important habit to develop for health and character, whatever, versus you're an artist and you love chaos, and you hate sterility, and you just like to live in a messy, kind of dirty environment, and you think that is more expressive of your beliefs about nature rather than the other one. So, that's how habits can either represent the Id (the instinct) or the Superego or the ego.

BB: That's cool!

RM: [*Laughing, agreeing*] So, he says that a habit is an interpretant. So, a habit is a 'signified', we could say, 'in action'. Or, in other words, the effect that the relation between S_1 and S_2 has on actions and the interaction with objects of social reality and utility. Habit is both an interpretant and another signifier. So, instead of the way we think in psychoanalysis, an unconscious signifier or representation has an impact on the body, or the discipline of the body. For Peirce, where the rubber hits the road for the signifier, is on habit as a basic unit of action and behavior. So, that's the connection with behaviorism, where habit is the unit of action or activity. The notion of habit that's not so behavioral, it's more psychoanalytic in Peirce, is when he considers habit as a form of disposition, whether inborn, innate, or acquired. So, that opens the whole question of the drive in the instinct. So, that's the link to psychoanalysis. Peirce says:

> "...habit or disposition, that is some general principle working in a man's nature to determine how he will act ... then, an instinct, in the proper sense of the word, is an inherent habit ... or, in more accurate language, an inherited disposition".[1]

Habit introduces the question of acquired characteristics and the whole debate between what's innate or inborn and what's acquired through learning and in relationship to the environment – whether it be the natural environment or the social environment. Then you have the differentiation between things that are maybe inborn or innate and what's genetic (meaning, what's associated with the genes). Right, because for Freud, the Superego could be inherited, even though we think of it as a cultural acquisition – but it's not genetic in the sense of the study of genes in the study of biology. The new field is epigenetics. Epigenetics refers to hormonal changes that are not part of the gene, but over time they become part of the genetic code.

Note

1 Charles S. Peirce. Collected Papers of Charles Sanders Peirce, Vol. 2, ed. C. Hartshorne and P. Weiss. Cambridge, MA: Harvard University Press, 1931–1935. p. 170.

Supplemental References

Bion, W. (1961). *Experiences in Groups*. London: Routledge.

Freud, Sigmund. (1895). A Project for a Scientific Psychology. *SE* 1, 283–397.

Freud, Sigmund. (1900). Interpretation of Dreams, *SE* 4.

Freud, Sigmund. (1915a). Instincts and their Vicissitudes. *SE* 14, 111–140.

Freud, Sigmund. (1915b). Repression. *SE* 14, 143–158.

Freud, Sigmund. (1915c). The Unconscious. *SE* 14, 161–215.

Lacan, J. (1972–1973), *Encore. The Seminar of Jacques Lacan, XX*. New York: Norton, 1998.

Peirce, Charles S. (1867, 2009). *The Essential Peirce: Selected Philosophical Writings. Volumes 1 and 2*. Peirce Edition Project (Ed.). Bloomington & Indianapolis: Indiana University.

Peirce, Charles S. (1940). *Philosophical Writings of Peirce*. J. Buchler (Ed.). New York: Dover, 1955.

Spencer-Brown, G. (1969/1979). *Laws of Form*. New York: Dutton.

Chapter 8

Being, Language, Love, and 'Be–ternal–ing'

Moncayo Seminar April 04, 2017, *Encore, Seminar XX*, pg. 51

RM: [*Seminar in progress*] … and then at CFAR, and you all know the Freud Museum. It's my second year there, and it was really a huge crowd … a lot of young people. In England, we seem to have the youth. And, then CFAR … I don't know if you know CFAR … it's the Center for Freudian Analysis and Research. It's kind of like a sister school in London, which is also as old as the LSP [Lacanian School of Psychoanalysis]. It has been there for 30 years, it's the oldest Lacanian group … of course, they chose to call it the Freudian Center for Analysis and Research. It seems that the Freud Museum is interested in Lacan because we seem to be the ones that still study Freud – the British Society being more Object Relations. CFAR uses the College of London … it also had huge crowds … crowds like we do not see in the US. From there I went to Edinburgh, and it was really very interesting. I had never been there. I do not know if you have ever been there? It's a beautiful, 300-year-old city still standing up pretty well. They were shooting an Avengers movie – I don't know if it was Avengers 2 or 3 [*chuckling*] and they were closing off the streets. You know, there is a 'royal mile' that goes from the Castle to the Queen's palace there, when she visits, and you couldn't pass through after 6 PM. There were huge crowds … everyone wanting to get a view of the action, but I wasn't that interested. There were blowing [up] cars and they were allowing action to happen inside the cathedral, because for them, they hired a lot of local people for the film. And, apparently, they had just made a deal, because there are so many Hollywood movies being made in Edinburgh that now they are going to have a Lucas film institute or something. A major site for film right outside Edinburgh, and they are all very happy about it. Of course, The Avengers was not that interesting to me [*again, chuckling*] but … and, what else … yeah, I was invited by Calum Neill from Napier University (he's an editor of a Lacanian series with Palgrave McMillan publications) – a really wonderful, amazing guy – and they have a program there at the University – they grant the PhD there in Psychology, but without rigid disciplinary boundaries, so you can potentially get a

DOI: 10.4324/9781003424581-8

PhD in Psychology and study, you know, not just clinical stuff. You could study all the stuff that Lacanians study! You know, all the stuff that nobody else studies! So, they have a lot of flexibility as to what might go into the PhD, so I love that! And their students were great. Of course, I am not going to move to Edinburgh. It's way too cold, and I have my life here ... but I will be a visiting professor once a year and we are going to establish some links with the school.

MK: Cool!

GF: Congratulations!

RM: Thank you. I found there was a huge statue of David Hume outside where I was staying and it reminded me of the Hume Center at UC Berkeley where they are always trying to convert students to empiricism! Although David Hume died in abject poverty and they paid no attention to him at the time, he now is recognized as the Father of Empiricism. They are still very interested in him in the US, but in Edinburgh they are now interested in Lacan!

In London and Edinburgh, I got a lot of praise for my new book, you know, and it's something special when you feel that people want to appropriate you. [*ALL chuckling*] You know, they feel proud of you even though I am Chilean, and I have a Spanish name or whatever ... you know, I am one of them ... and that felt very good. I often don't feel that in the US. I feel more on the margins ... but I still want to live here.

MK: Yeah, I often feel like I was made to live in the 1950s.

BB: Really!? I don't think I ever feel like that!

MK: Just at a time, you know, when psychoanalysis and group relations and all that ...

RM: What did you say about living in the 50s?

MK: It's just that I often feel like I was made to be living in the 50s, not now. All of the things that I am interested in were cool back then, but they are not cool anymore.

RM: Well, but it was so different. You know, psychoanalysis in the 1950s was very different from psychoanalysis today, both in the Lacanian field and in the Object Relations field. It was really a different culture. It's back to the future in any case! British society has all the old people, and the Lacanians have all the young people. So, that's kind of interesting.

EW: I think there are some advantages at times to being in the minority. I don't know, maybe it gives you a little more freedom to explore. I certainly have the feeling that in the 50s, when psychoanalysis was the 'thing', you really had to adhere to what everyone thought it was ... [*Chuckling*]

RM: Right, so it was a more dogmatic position. [*EW agrees*] I am sure that if that ever happens to us, we are going to be at risk for that ... for becoming institutionalized.

MK: Raul, are you on *das unbehagen.listserv*?

RM: No, but Jamieson Webster and Patricia Gherovici came to the School the day before I left for London, so I was with them all day on Saturday. We spent a whole day online. Were you there?

MK: No, I wasn't there.

RM: Okay, so, we had a whole day of a workshop, and it was really nice. But, anyway, so I know about her and the group …

MK: Yes, it's a fantastic group to be a part of and the listserv is extremely active. It's primarily Lacanian discourse. I highly recommend it.

RM: Yes, it looks like she invited me to come at some point, and I have to think when I can do that … she doesn't define herself as Lacanian because she was trained in the mainstream institute… [*MK agrees*] … but, of course, she is very Lacanian. Anyway …

GF: Who was it that you just cited? Was it Gherovici?

MK: Yes, Patricia Gherovici.

GF: Thank you. I was recently reading an essay, I don't recall the name of the author, but he was European, and he was talking about the split in psychoanalysis, involving a constant battle between those who utilize the methods of hermeneutic interpretation in psychoanalysis versus those who look to establish the biological drive and lean toward making psychoanalysis a science. It's really interesting to think about the period when Lacan was working to establish psychoanalysis as a scientific modality but yet, it was still strongly based in a hermeneutic and philosophic tradition.

RM: Right, well, Paul Ricoeur, do you know who he is? [*GF acknowledges*] Ricoeur wrote several books on psychoanalysis and hermeneutics, and he attended Lacan's seminars early on, and then he continued on his own. Of course, the Relational School in the United States uses hermeneutics quite a bit, but Lacan thought that hermeneutics was too limited as a framework, because usually the way people interpret hermeneutics, aside from the question of interpretation … and, of course, the distinction comes from Wilhelm Dilthey, the German philosopher, between the natural sciences and the social sciences (and also Derrida) … is with the idea that there is 'nothing outside the text'. Then, everything is a social construction, part of social constructivism. While for Lacanians, there is a Real outside – the social construction is through the Imaginary and the Symbolic. The Real provides something that is outside the text. In fact, it interacts with the text, but you cannot reduce it to the text. So, that is why the unconscious will never be just a social construction. That doesn't mean that it is biological either. [*EW and BB acknowledge*] And, therefore the appeal to topology and mathematics, and all of that, is used to construct the notion of a structure outside language. Well, should we go through some text?

MK: Yes, we are still on the first page of chapter Five, pg. 51 [*Encore, Seminar XX*].

TEXT: In dealing, a long time ago, a very long time ago indeed, with the ethics of psychoanalysis, I began with nothing less than Aristotle's Nicomachean Ethics. "All art and all research, like all action and all reflected deliberation" – what relation could there possibly be among those four things? – they tend, it seems, toward some good. Thus people have sometimes had good reason to define the good as that toward which one tends in all circumstances. "Nevertheless, it seems that there is a difference between ends".

RM: Okay, so that's the telos idea, right? This idea of purpose or purposiveness. Which is also tied to the idea of causality in Aristotle, in terms of the different aims and purposes of the various forms of causality.

MK: It seems weird that Lacan is talking about 'the Good'.

RM: Is there a discussion of the distinction between the pleasure of the good and the good of pleasure?

GF: Well, I believe so, but more in Plato's philosophy. I am sure Aristotle picks up on it, too, but he splits the concepts, talking about pleasure as being something distinct from discourse on 'the good'. 'The Good', as we know, is the metaethical measure – the ultimate standard by which all other forms are built. And everything is conceived to have the aim of the Good. It is that which was thought of as a first cause, and that which is the final cause … the alpha and the omega.

EW: That's a focus that is common among Greek philosophers – that is, what is 'the Good', and how do you know 'the Good' and what it really means.

GF: That's right. Plato was all about that, and Aristotle categorizes it according to the different casualties. But Aristotle still maintains the Good as the telos you mentioned.

RM: Okay, so, a couple of points. So, you can have a contrast between 'pleasure' and 'the Good' – sort of like the 'id' and the 'superego'. Lacan is breaking down that distinction by talking about 'the good of pleasure' and the 'pleasure of the Good'. Well, of course, I am sure that Aristotle would differentiate between the good and something that may not feel so good … the relationship between the good and frustration, for example, or privation. That has to do with the formation of character. And, of course, pleasure feels good, but it is not necessarily good … but it's not necessarily bad either. So, where Lacan deals with this is in the seminar on *The Ethics of Psychoanalysis* (VII), and out of that comes a distinction between morality and ethics. So, the Lacanian sense of ethics includes the ethics of desire, where he says, the only thing that you should feel guilty of is having given up on your desire (as opposed to feeling guilty about having desires, which is the traditional view associated with conceptions of "the Good").

And yet, at the same time, he says, it's not a form of hedonism in the bad sense of the word, because with hedonism usually nowadays people think of 'I just can't get no satisfaction, but I try, and try, and try', you know! And you have Mick Jagger and so on! That would be more jouissance than desire in Lacanian theory because desire is always in relationship to the Law. Lacan did not think like Freud – Freud thinks in kind of a traditional, ethical way – like you have the biology, and the id, and the instinct of nature – which is a poor way of understanding Freud, but many people read it that way. And then you have the law of culture on the other hand – Lacan says these two are intrinsically related so that you cannot have desire without the Law. But in the same token, then, if you choose desire – which is the example of Antigone – if you choose desire, then it means you are willing to pay the consequences. You don't just act out without knowing what you are doing, right? If you make a choice to follow your desire, you have to be willing and you know that there are going to be consequences and that you are willing to pay the consequences. So, that's what's ethical about it – that it is not just an impulsive act.

With the whole emphasis that we have now in our profession in this country, the profession is highly regulated because of all the scandals and all the problems there have been – but that's more of secular morality and not really ethics. The only reason to call it ethics is that it seems to be rational in terms of consequences – meaning that professional behavior is tied to the Law, and that generates a series of consequences. It's really a question of practical reason. The very way of being able to talk about it is that it is rational, meaning that there is the boundary of 'the good' on one side and 'the bad' and the legal consequences on the other. But there is no way of creating space where that can be talked about other than simply having a gut reaction that 'this is good' and 'that is bad'. The complexities of what takes place, which seem to be more the spirit of Freud, when the field was newly growing, and there were some boundary violations – not that they were promoted or advanced as part of the profession! – but when they did happen, Freud had more interest in understanding what was going on. We see that with respect to Jung as well, who had more boundary violations than Freud as far as we know. But he (Freud) was more interested in treating it analytically rather than legally or morally. So, what we call ethics in the United States seems to be more of a secular form of morality rather than ethics in the strict sense of the term, as distinguished from morality. In England, CFAR sued the government to prevent the regulation of the profession, and they won in court. But Darian Leader, one of the founding members of CFAR, says it is just going to happen again because somebody's going to do something stupid, and that's going to trigger a legal case and the desire to regulate the profession is going to come back.

TEXT: They [the *Internationale de Psychanalyse*] would have liked to see preserved, all the same, my reflections on what psychoanalysis brings with it by way of ethics. It would have been sheer profit [for them] – I would have sunk to the bottom while *The Ethics of Psychoanalysis* would have stayed afloat. That's an example of the fact that calculation is not enough – I stopped my *Ethics* from being published. I refused to allow it to come out because I'm not going to try to convince people who want nothing to do with me. One must not convince (*convaincre*). What is proper to psychoanalysis is not to vanquish (*vaincre*), regardless of whether people are assholes (*con*) or not. [*ALL laugh*]

RM: Do you want to read the footnote …?

TEXT: In the present context, *un con* means an idiot, an asshole, a jerk, and so on; as an adjective, *con* means stupid, idiotic, and so on. In playing on the words *vaincre* and *convaincre*, Lacan is saying that in psychoanalysis, there is no point trying to win over or convince jerks.

RM: Well, you know, the ethical problems that Lacan had with the International [Psychoanalytic Association]. It was a time when Ego Psychology was the dominant force, and he was critical of that. Then we had the conflict between the French and the Americans, and, of course, the American Psychoanalytic was the dominant force in international psychoanalysis at the time. So, there were theoretical differences – the reason they gave was primarily the variable length session. But, when you talk to them more closely, they also say that they objected to the fact that his [Lacan's] analysands came to his seminars and they considered that unethical. Several leaders of APA and IPA psychoanalysis had ethical problems, but they were not banned from the institution. And Jungians do not reject Jung, and he was known to have had at least one affair with a patient.

EW: I don't know if this is the right way to think of it, but I tend to think that there is a huge tension between Ego Psychology and the Lacanian view of what's desirable in clinical work. And, that Ego Psychology is all about adaptation while I tend to think Lacan is about freedom from adaptation … or, not necessarily adapting. [*Chuckling*]

RM: Well, the thing is, you adapt to what? Even nowadays, adaptation is a term borrowed from Darwin. And, when you talk to Darwinians these days, they say adaptation is a two-way street. The genes adapt to the environment, but the environment also adapts to the genes, so it kind of goes both ways. It's not just that we have a static society that people adapt to – it's a moving target. Not that there isn't adaptation, but it goes both ways, and if you put the society in a static place, then people feel how minorities feel, since that kind of adaptation goes with the 'melting pot'. That is still going on now between those who think, 'well, if you want to have immigrants then they should adapt to our way of life and our beliefs and love the way we are instead of criticizing us'. But, you know, it always goes both ways. I think that's why this notion of adaptation was rejected, because it was made similar to the 'melting pot' idea. And, you know, Ego Psychology is practically gone anyway. So, what we have now … the American version of psychoanalysis … [there is] either the 'relational' school or the 'object relations', which is the middle, British Object

Relations school. Ego Psychology cannot be blamed on America either because this came from Freud – the second theory [Id, Ego, Superego], right? So, the whole thing is more complex and political than it appears, in any case.

TEXT: There's no reason not to put oneself to the test, not to see how others before Freud saw the terrain in which he constituted his field. It is another way of experiencing what is involved, namely that this terrain is unthinkable except with the help of the instruments with which we operate, and that the only instruments by which accounts are conveyed are writings. A very simple test makes this clear – reading the *Nicomachean Ethics* in the French translation, you understand nothing in it, of course, but no less than in what I tell you, and thus it suffices all the same.

RM: Okay, and also, not to say it's the only incomprehensible text of Aristotle ... I don't know if you have tried to read Aristotle, but it's quite difficult to follow!

EW: I think I blamed myself for that! It's good to know it's a more general problem!

[*ALL laugh*]

MK: Just to note, the title of this section is called 'Aristotle's headache'!

RM: I think that's an ethical position that you took ... to take it on you rather than blame the author. You should feel in good company! [*Laughing*]

TEXT: Aristotle is no more comprehensible than what I talk to you about. It is even less comprehensible because he stirs up more things and things that are further from us. But it is clear that the other satisfaction I was talking about earlier is exactly the satisfaction that can be seen to emerge from what? Well, my good friends, there's no escaping it if you force yourself to look at it closely (*au pied du truc*) from the universals: The Good, Truth, and Beauty.

FOOTNOTE 8: Lacan has modified here the usual French expression *être au pied du mur*, to be up against it or with one's back to the wall by saying *si vous vous mettez au pied du truc*. That implies, it seems to me, putting yourself up against it, but also evokes the expression, *prendre quelque chose au pied de la lettre*, to take something literally.

RM: Ah, so he's translating 'looking at it closely' with 'taking it literally'. Do you know the double entendre of 'taking it literally'? Because, usually, we say, 'the spirit of the Law' and the 'letter of the Law', right ... that's the traditional distinction. That's a distinction that comes from a contrast between Judaism and Christianity. Christianity is supposed to be the 'spirit of the Law' and Judaism is the 'letter of the Law', and in the West, the Christian view has prevailed in general because it is considered to be the less dogmatic position – that you don't read the Bible literally. Therefore, people say that the Enlightenment comes out of Christianity for that very reason. Lacan sort of reads it the other way because the literal refers to the letter – literal[1]– and linking it to the letter, you have to take the letter literally. So, he takes a more Jewish position in terms of reading the text, and in order to understand the secrets of the text, you have to take the letter literally – which, of course, doesn't mean that it is a dogmatic position. It takes away this notion of being literal as equivalent to being dogmatic and to say that you cannot change anything and everything has to remain just the way it is. It's just a way of listening or interpreting, going back to hermeneutics.

[*ALL agree*]

TEXT: Culture, insofar as it is distinct from society, doesn't exist. Culture is the fact that it has a hold on us (*ça nous tient*). We no longer have it on our backs, except in the form of vermin, because we don't know what to do with it, except to get ourselves deloused. I recommend that you keep it because it tickles and wakes you up. That will awaken your feelings that tend rather to become a bit deadened under the influence of ambient conditions, in other words, due to what others who come afterward will call your culture.

RM: So, he is distinguishing culture from socialization, right, which would refer more to society.

EW: He was saying that we need something to wake us up. What are 'the louses' that irritate us and wake us up? Or 'the lice', I guess, that irritate us and wake us up?

RM: The way I read that, if I am correct, is that there is a difference between culture and socialization – that culture breaks up the monotony of social habit.

EW: I see, so it's annoying!

TEXT: It will have become culture for them because you will have already been six feet under for a long time and, with you, everything that you sustain qua social link. In the final analysis, there's nothing but that, the social link. I designate it with the term discourse because there's no other way to designate it once we realize that the social link is instated only by anchoring itself in the way in which language is situated over and etched into what the place is crawling with, namely speaking beings.

[*ALL laugh*]

MK: So, we are all vermin?!

RM: Yeah, so there are several terms here that are running around. There is the 'social link' and there's 'discourse'. So that's the definition that he gives us of discourse: a discourse is a social link. Now how to break down discourse as a social link in terms of 'culture vs. society' is something that somebody could write a nice paper on.

MK: We will need to tackle that next week!

Note

1 There is a tradition of biblical exegesis that comes from the Middle Ages. This tradition was literal and exact in its meaning. Along with the Enlightenment, this literalism is rejected in postmodernism and post-structuralism and metaphor becomes more important for the reading of the text. Lacan is not a postmodernist, because he sought to avoid the disorders of postmodernism (borderline personality) while not returning to the Freudian conventional Oedipal structure that Deleuze rejected. Lacan creates a nonconventional Borromean knot of four that goes beyond convention and post-conventionality without structure. The letter is more important than the word or the later forms of the signifier. Thus the letter is Real, while the word becomes Imaginary.

Supplemental References

Aristotle. (2009). *The Nicomachean Ethics*. Oxford World Classics. Cambridge: Oxford University Press.

Jagger, M. and Richards, K. (1965). *('I Can't Get No') Satisfaction*, from the Rolling Stones' album, Out of Our Heads.

Lacan, J. (1959-1960). *The Ethics of Psychoanalysis. The Seminar of Jacques Lacan, VII.* New York: Norton.

Lacan, J. (1972–1973), *Encore. The Seminar of Jacques Lacan, XX.* New York: Norton, 1998.

Chapter 9

A Logic and a Grammar That Cannot Be "Arithmetized"

Moncayo Seminar, May 4, 2017, *Encore, Seminar XX*, pg. 56

RM: So, were we on pgs. 55 or 56? I remember talking about the primary and secondary processes.

MK: Yes, we are toward the bottom of page 56.

TEXT: That is what I am saying when I say that the unconscious is structured like a language. But I must dot the i's and cross the t's. The universe – you might realize it by now, all the same, given the way in which I have accentuated the use of certain words, the "whole" and the "not whole," and their differential application to the two sexes – the universe is the place where, due to the fact of speaking, everything succeeds (*de dire, tout réussit*).

RM: He's asking for trouble there! I don't know what that means. Let's keep reading a little bit. Well, there's a note there, no?

NOTE: Rater means to "fail," "botch," "screw up," "mess up," and so on. I have translated it in a number of different ways in this chapter.

TEXT: Normally I would expect to hear some snickering now – alas, I don't hear any. Snickering would mean "So, you've admitted it, there are two ways to make the sexual relationship fail". That is how the music of the epithalamion is modulated. The epithalamion, the duet (*duo*) – one must distinguish the two of them – the alternation, the love letter, they're not the sexual relationship. They revolve around the fact that there's no such thing as a sexual relationship.

RM: There, that last point is related to this question about romance covering over the sexual difference. And, before, what he says about the universe … he's talking about the universe in terms of the whole and the not whole, and the different applications to the two sexes … "the universe is the place where, due to the fact of speaking, everything succeeds". I guess, both the whole and the not whole reference … Okay, so the universe he's referring to is the universal, the category of the universal, and the particular in the Aristotelian

DOI: 10.4324/9781003424581-9

logic, so the universal is the 'all women' or 'all men' under castration. And then, there is the alternative logic, which is 'not all of a woman' is under the phallic function. And, then there's the question of the interaction between the two sexes – what a man is looking for in a woman, and what a woman is looking for in a man. This refers to the graph of sexuation, which I don't know if you have it ... whether you know it in your mind or not. Are you familiar with that graph?

BB: I think I might have it, but not in a way that I can reproduce it. Can you describe it to us if I don't?

RM: I have it in my files ...

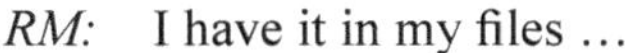

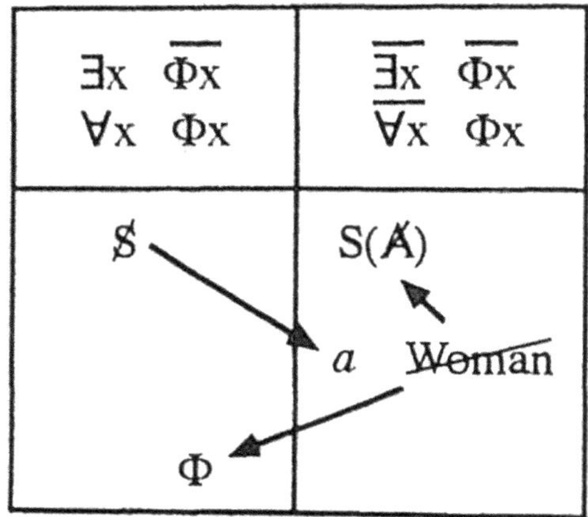

RM: Okay, so you can see there is a vertical line and a horizontal line. Then you have two formulas on the right and two formulas on the left. And so, the left is for masculinity, the right is for femininity. Do you see it?

BB: Yes.

RM: So, on the left you have the particular categories for masculinities – there does exist one man not subject to the bar of negation on top of the phallic function. There does exist one man, 'x' is 'one man', not subject to the law of castration, and that would be the primal father.

MK: Can you just tell us what these symbols mean Raul? The 'backward E' [∃] and the 'x'?

RM: In symbolic logic, the '∃' is there exists ... that's the way you read it, and the 'x' is the particular variable, or the particular individual. In this case, it would be 'one man'. There does exist one man.

EW: And the 'backward ∃x' with the line over it?

RM: Right, so the backward '∃' represents 'there exists' and the opposite of that is 'it does not exist'. And the ∀x, that's the primal father of *Totem and Taboo* that castrates all his sons and has all the women. And, that fantasy, that myth of Freud, is modeled after Darwin, who said that in animal species there is one dominant alpha position, usually occupied by a male, a biological male, who is larger. In some species, like the hyena, it is the female who occupies the alpha position, who is larger. So, in a way, it's like the alpha is the master discourse. Sometimes it can fall on the side of the female, sometimes on the side of male. In most species, it falls on the side of the male.

So, the alpha ape … of course, with Darwin, we came from the apes – we evolved from apes – so then the first social family would have had a similar alpha male who is larger and bigger. And usually in those species, the bigger alpha male is a threat to the smaller males and keeps the smaller males under submission. That gives the alpha male access to all the females to reproduce with. And the females also want to reproduce with the big male. Now, the alpha male is not always nasty, you know, but that's part of the function. So Freud naturally says, there must have been a first family, a first horde of human beings that was modeled in the same social organization as the apes. Then he says, this primal father exists in the unconscious, and just like the species went through that development phylogenetically, ontogenetically, the primal father also appears in psychical structure … and that what creates the fantasy of patriarchy – of having one master who has this kind of power and authority and who dominates the other men and has all the women. So that's that position. Now, for Lacan, that's an impossible position that doesn't exist, only in fantasy, because the formula underneath tells us that all the "x's", all the men, are subject to castration. They are all subject to castration and experience castration in this kind of imaginary way, and so they all fantasize to be the "number one" guy. But that dream needs to be given up. And the ones who don't give up that dream or fantasy suffer great consequences, eventually. That's why patriarchy can never be an ideal if it is understood in that kind of way, and it was never the ideal in psychoanalysis … although many people thought it was. Fair enough?

BB: Isn't there more here? There's an 'S' with a slash and an 'A' …

RM: Right, let's do the feminine side. It's important that it's not biological femaleness, but psychical femininity. These are logical, not biological categories. Then the right side says, there does not exist a single woman not subject to the phallic function of symbolic castration. And then, underneath that one …. so, you see how they are reversed … the particular now comes in the form of the singular. So, on the feminine side, you have … the top formula is the particular – there's 'one guy' – and then there's the universal below. So that is why he is using the category of the 'universe'. That's why he's mixing up the 'universe' with the category of the 'universal' in the formulas of sexuation. And that's why he blends things like this and it makes it very hard to follow … so you have to break it up to be able to follow it.

BB: I got lost on 'the woman' … so there does not exist a single woman not under castration … and that's the particular?

RM: Right, and underneath that is 'not all of a single woman is under the phallic function'. So, that means that it is not that there is the 'one woman', because there is the fantasy – you know, women wanting to be 'the one' … the one who walks down the street and all; the heads are turned of both women and men saying, *wow! what a woman!*, right? That would be 'the' 'one woman'. So, there is no 'one woman' because that would be the equivalent of the 'one man'. So, what he is saying [rather] is 'not all of a single woman' is under the phallic function, meaning there is a floor or a level within feminine subjectivity that is not under the phallic function – not 'all' under the phallic function.

BB: Isn't the lower place on the feminine side the particular? I wasn't sure you said that right.

RM: On the feminine side, the lower is the equivalent of the higher on the left side for masculinity, but instead of being the particular, he is using the singular.

BB: Oh, that's right, the 'single woman'?

RM: Which doesn't mean a single … because a single woman would just mean a particular woman. Like if we said, Megan and Barri … those are two particular women, right? But, within Barri and Megan, there is a level or dimension, or an aspect or a floor, however you want to say it, that is not all under the phallic function – so, it escapes the logic of the phallus and castration.

EW: I am not clear on the 'A'.

BB: We have not done that yet, or the 'x'.

MK: That's the phallic function.

BB: That's the phallic function, and it's the same for the man and the woman.

RM: And the inverted '∀' is 'all' and 'not all'. I don't know why, in symbolic logic, they like to invert letters vertically or horizontally [*chuckles*] … that exceeds me! But that's what it means. It's the inverted '∀', it's 'all', and if it has a bar or a negation on top, it means 'not all'. And the same with the 'x'. So, the bar of negation is the horizontal line above them, so you have to know that it means the bar of negation. And then, underneath the feminine side, you have the signifier of the lack of the Other. Now, why is that on the feminine side? Do you want me to explain that?

MK: Which symbol is this?

RM: The S of the pure signifier is not barred. Next to it is the barred Other (*Autre* A→ Ø).

EW: What does that mean again?

RM: That's the signifier for the lack of the Other.

BB: Is that a small 'a' other or a 'big A' Other?

RM: That's the big Other. It's just that in French, the formula with the 'A' in French comes from *Autre*. In English, we place the 'O' there instead of the 'A'. English has the advantage in using the 'O' instead of the 'A', since the barred 'O' is also the symbol for the null set, which Lacan will eventually use for this same matheme. So, eventually Lacan will write it with an 'O' in certain places, but because he is using it, he's invoking the null set there – the symbol of which in logic is a big 'O' with a bar across. [*Tacit agreement*]

Okay, so what does that mean then? This refers to, that for both sexes, the empirical reference for castration is a woman who doesn't have an imaginary phallus. In Freud's system, it would be a woman who doesn't have a penis. And so for both sexes that means that there is such a thing as a human being that doesn't have a penis, and then, you know, Freud speculates that children, in their sexual theories of childhood, they theorize that she had one and then she lost it. So that's the castration fantasy. Both sexes reject castration, and for the same reason, they reject femininity, irregardless of what the society says about gender in this respect.

So, there are three levels of reality that can be confused – psychical, sociological, and biological. Is the rejection of femininity due to patriarchal society placing less importance on women ($-\varphi$), as the culturalists would say? For example, Frieda Fromm-Reichman, Erich Fromm, and Clara Thompson precisely argued that. Freud's theory argues that psychical sex is independent from social gender, although it interacts with it. What is independent of whatever the society places on one sex or the other? The question of a structural, not environmental lack.

The lack is first placed or discovered in the mother. The mother at first appears as omnipotent, because the mother has the power of the gift – to give love or to not give love. To love the child or not love the child. And the child is helpless in the universe in the face of that question vis-à-vis the mother. And, so, the mother is omnipotent … and at some point, the mother has to fall from her omnipotence. When she falls from her omnipotence, because she also has other desires or needs that she needs satisfied by her partner or by the Other, then she's perceived as lacking. And then the omnipotence is transferred to the father.

The father then appears as omnipotent, but eventually, the father also has to fall off from that position of omnipotence, and then the lack in the Other has to also be realized in the father. So the realization of the lack in the mother and the realization of the lack in the father mean that neither of them is omnipotent anymore. So, this idea of completeness or omnipotence only comes with an unbarred Other. This is the later Lacan (beginning with *Seminar IX*). So that's why a signifier of a lack in the Other is placed on the feminine side, because it's something that is first … the lack is first discovered in relationship to the mother … and the rejection of the lack is what is at stake in the rejection of symbolic castration – the attempt to resist the separation [of the infant] from the mother, and leading to also a devaluation of femininity for misunderstanding the lack as a defect. But, in reality, women don't lack anything.

MK: What's the barred 'LA'?

RM: There's the barred 'the', right, at the bottom …

BB: It says barred LA, is that French?

EW & RM: that is 'La', as in '*La familie'*.

RM: I have the formula in English, so in English it is the crossing of 'the' … there is no 'the' woman and there is no 'the' man either, as when people say, "you are my main man!" That's a colloquial kind of English, right? So, there is no 'the' woman because that would be … 'the' woman would be sort of the equivalent of the primal father … that she has it all. She is all. So, the fact that the woman is not all under the phallic function is misconstrued as 'she has it all' or that the desire of the woman or femininity is to have it all. So, but in reality, as a structure, the All doesn't exist, so that woman has to be represented by the 'the' or the 'la' barred. There is no 'the' woman. There is only 'a' woman. Not 'the' woman. And, so, there you see the 'a' up here. So 'a' woman is a singularity. And 'a' woman refers to the aspect of the *objet a* that escapes the logic of the phallus. Right, the *objet a* in the Real escapes the logic of the phallus – so that's the other side of 'a' woman who has that 'je ne se pas', you know. It's interesting, the women, I have to say in this case, have disappeared from the screen! [*Laughs*] [*ALL laughing*]

RM: Where did they go?!

MK: There are no women!

RM: No women! [*Laughing*] Right, so that's the offensive statement of Lacan, 'the woman does not exist' ... when he said that it caused a huge furor. Doesn't that tell us what patriarchy has been telling us all along, that women are just, you know, doormats, nonexistent ... and, precisely, he doesn't mean that ... precisely, it means 'the' woman does not exist ... meaning the unbarred woman who is the phallus and who 'has it all' only exists in fantasy.

The same way that the primal father, 'the guy', 'the man' – he's 'the man', he's 'the number one', you know – that master doesn't exist either. So, in the Imaginary they exist, but in the structure, they don't. So, the *objet a* in that sense also, the *objet a* in the Real doesn't exist in the same way. It's that kind of aspect of femininity, the *je ne se pas*, the 'something' (like the George Harrison song – *Something* [in the way she moves...]). That well could be that she is 'it', she's the 'all', or it could mean there is something about the object of desire that's in the Real and escapes logic and the signifier. So, you can only write poems about it!

Then, on the side of masculinity is the divided subject, which is the one, the subject divided under the law, having lost the object, having lost the union with the mother, and trying to get it back. And below that, masculinity represents the phallic function. And so the barred woman is looking for the symbolic phallus. And that is the ambiguity of looking for the object that the masculine could have that maybe is attractive to a woman. That's the ambiguity ... when a woman wants to be desired by a man and she succeeds in that, that's a success. But, on the other hand, the success also means that now she has become the object of his lack. And by that same token, when you succeed, you fail – because now, the man is not 'the man', the man is lacking. And 'the women' has become the object of his lack and that's where his desire is centered ... which is both a blessing and a curse for a woman.

EW: So, with the arrow pointing from the barred '*LA*' to the phallic function, that's saying, it's the fact that the woman cannot be 'the' woman that makes her pursue the phallic function?

RM: Right, because she is not 'the' woman, meaning she is not the phallus, she doesn't 'have it', so she has to look for an object of desire in a man. Symbolic castration gives a woman access to the phi (φ) or Imaginary phallus that a man is supposed to have in the sexual relation and the NoF, and the Symbolic phallus (missing) gives her access to the culture and to power.

TEXT: There is thus the male way of revolving around it, and then the other one that I will not designate otherwise because it's what I'm in the process of elaborating this year – how that is elaborated in the female way. It is elaborated on the basis of the not whole. But as, up until now, the not whole has not been amply explored, it's obviously giving me a hard time.

RM: Okay, so you see how he is using the 'all' and 'whole' the 'not all' and 'not whole' as equivalent terms? Because, in the formulas, the 'whole' appears as the 'all' …

TEXT: I picked an absolutely ridiculous title for my lecture to the Milanese, who had never heard anyone talk about such things before, "Psychoanalysis in Reference to the Sexual Relationship". They are very intelligent. They understood it so well that immediately, that very evening, the following was printed in the newspaper, "According to Dr. Lacan, Ladies – le donne – Do Not Exist!"

There is one thing that provides dazzling evidence of this not whole. Consider how, with one of these nuances or oscillations of signification that are produced in language (*langue*), the not whole changes meaning when I say to you, "Regarding feminine sexuality, our colleagues, the lady analysts, do not tell us… the whole story!" (*pas tout*!). It's quite striking. They haven't contributed one iota to the question of feminine sexuality. There must be an internal reason for that, related to the structure of the apparatus of jouissance.

RM: That's a somewhat extreme statement … not to make any friends among the women analysts! To say they haven't contributed one iota to the question of feminine sexuality … that's a little extreme to say! It makes me a little embarrassed, you know, as a Lacanian, when I hear statements like that said without much explanation. Because, of course, there are a lot of women analysts who have made contributions to the literature. But I think what he is trying to say is that they only interpret the whole castration complex in a purely imaginary way – as something bad being done to children and women by men. That's the problem that the feminine analysts interpreted that way, or Marie Bonaparte, who was really into identifying with women as the phallus … and I think she even had a statue of a woman in the shape of the phallus.

MK: I guess I really don't take him that literally. It's surprising that he means it as literally as maybe he does …

RM: He doesn't take it literally, but it could be read that way. That's why he said there was one feminist in the audience who was totally outraged, and the newspaper wrote it in a very provocative way.

EW: I guess part of the way I take it, and I don't know if I have this wrong ... and I do think it is possible to flatten and make a caricature out of what Lacan is saying ... but there is a way that for him the point of view on the sexuality of women is something that belongs to the Other – that it is not something that the subject is male and the other is female, and that is something that is hard to get away from. So, it is kind of like he's saying, what's wrong with the women analysts that they haven't explained the issue of female sexuality. As though, it's a little bit like saying, what's up with men that they haven't helped us understand male sexuality better.

RM: [*Agrees*] Well, I'm not sure about why Freud places libido and sex on the side of masculinity. In this instance, the subject, the divided subject, he places on the side of masculinity, and the Other, and the lack, is on the side of femininity. Yeah, it would apply to that Oedipal formulation that I gave you, in terms of the 'Other' being encountered first as omnipotent, and then, as lacking. And that first 'other' is the mother. Then, out of that loss of the first 'Other', out of the loss 'in' the mother and the loss of 'a' mother – so loss 'in' and 'of' – loss 'in' the mother because she desires something else other than the child, and therefore she has desire, she has lack, she wants something else ... or, 'of' the mother, because that also implies the separation ... and, both of these is what constitutes the subject. That would be true for both a girl and a boy, and then there is a feminine subject and a masculine subject depending on how they position themselves in relationship to the father and the Other – the second 'Other' rather than the first one being the mother. So, I am not sure about placing the subject entirely on the side of masculinity.

EW: Yes, I am not suggesting that Lacan's theory of the subject is always male. I don't have the feeling that he is saying that. I just more have the sense that he cannot get away from his predisposition to think the subject as male.

RM: Yes, and I would say masculine, not male [*EW agrees*], since that creates confusion. If we stick to the nomenclature using 'man' and 'woman' as psychical masculinity and psychical femininity and 'male', 'female' is the biological gender, then with the formulas of sexuation according to Lacan, you can enter sex or gender as either a male or female. You can enter on one side or the other as a male or a female.

BB: Did you want to say anything about the jouissance that he refers to at the end? I was wondering about the internal reason for him saying that. He's assuming women have not contributed one iota to the question of feminine sexuality. Is he assuming that it is related to the apparatus of jouissance?

RM: I would say, because of the confusion between femininity and the 'jouissance of the Other', and the difference between 'phallic jouissance' and the 'jouissance of the Other', and phallic jouissance and the 'Other' jouissance. Because, usually, when women want to access an alternative theory for femininity outside psychoanalysis, then they seek refuge in the early bond of the mother and the child and that kind of fusion without separation or difference. And that's often a predicament of many women-to-women relationships ... for women ... for female homosexuality it's called, what is it? The 'deathbed'? Where the sexuality dies because they enter into this kind of fusion [trying] to articulate this kind of femininity purely in terms of the dyadic relationship to the mother, versus the femininity that Lacan is trying to carve out; namely, a femininity based on the Third jouissance, not the first jouissance, that does require the prior intervention of the father or the Other in order to give access to something that lies beyond that. And, in femininity, it [the Third jouissance] can be accessed either through the body, through feminine sexuality, or it can be also accessed through the same way that men can access the Third jouissance, through something more mental like the 'jouissance of meaning' or the 'jouissance of the mystic'. Although mystics have been traditionally understood as being more feminine than the typical [man], the male mystics have been typically understood as being more feminine than the typical male.

EW: Would you mind saying what the Third jouissance is again?

RM: Yes, so the Third jouissance is what's beyond the phallus, and it has three forms: feminine jouissance, the jouissance of the mystic, and the jouissance of meaning. And that is where you find a meaning that is not necessarily phallocentric or organized around the phallus. But it does require the prior intervention of the phallic function of castration. Castration ultimately is also turned against phallic jouissance ... meaning, okay, is this all there is to it? ... having sex, is that the ultimate thing for human beings? And it's always a question of who's more, who's less, who's more desirable, who's less desirable ... *I want this one, no I want the other one* ... and that process goes on ad nauseum, ad infinitum. So, there has to be something that leads the psyche and subjectivity beyond that. And, what helps in the transition beyond phallic jouissance to the Third jouissance is the phallic function itself, because the phallus is missing. So, therefore, that becomes a kind of placeholder for substituting the phallus for other things or other forms of jouissance that are not phallic. Did that cast some light and some further shadows, as usual ...?

ALL: *[Laughter] ... goodbyes*

Supplemental References

Freud, Sigmund. (1913, 1919). *Totem and Taboo: Resemblances Between the Mental Lives of Savages and Neurotics*. New York: Moffat, Yard and Company.

Freud, Sigmund. (1920). *Beyond the Pleasure Principle*. SE 18.

Harrison, G. (1969). '*Something*', from the Beatles' album Abbey Road.

Lacan, J. (1961–1962). *Identification. The Seminar of Jacques Lacan, IX.* New York: Norton.

Lacan, J. (1972–1973). *Encore. The Seminar of Jacques Lacan, XX.* New York: Norton, 1998.

Chapter 10

The Ethics of the Second Death in Psychoanalysis

Moncayo Seminar, May 29, 2018 (no text – open discussion)

RM: So, what would you like to do?

GF: Well, I would like to talk a little bit generally about Lacan and *Encore, Seminar XX* if you're game! In particular, I've been mulling over this question in my mind about the way Lacan differs from Freud in understanding the operation of drives. More specifically, with respect to the death drive as it relates to the pleasure principle, and how that *Eros* and *Thanatos* distinction may or may not be different in Lacan versus the Freudian perspective. That is not exactly what is discussed in Chapter 3, but I was trying to figure out a way of relating the text to these considerations by zooming out a little bit and generally discussing these two thinkers in relation to one another.

RM: And the whole thing is very confusing, paradoxical, and perplexing, right, because in Freud you have the 'pleasure principle', you have the 'reality principle', then you have the 'Nirvana principle' – and then you have the 'constancy principle'. And these principles are given quite different names throughout the length of his work. So, just keeping all those straight is kind of a task unto itself. And then Lacan just has a very particular definition of the pleasure principle.

GF: How does he address that?

RM: Well, basically Lacan talks about the pleasure principle in the seminar in terms of the signifier. But the pleasure principle is a principle of defense, so Lacan collapses the pleasure principle with the reality principle. But, in Freud, the pleasure principle has two sides, seeking pleasure and avoiding displeasure. So, one side is 'seek pleasure', which seems to be tied to the drive and to hallucinatory wish fulfillment. For example, when the child is trying to go back to the first experience of satisfaction, they're trying to go back to that experience of pleasure they had at the breast with a mother. So that's seeking pleasure and the drive for satisfaction. Now the other side of the pleasure principle, which is to avoid displeasure, has to do with repression. So, you see, it works for both, because in Freud, you have the duality

DOI: 10.4324/9781003424581-10

between the drives and defenses – that's basic in Freud. But the pleasure principle seems to be a concept that works for both sides.

GF: That is profound.

RM: Lacan, on the other hand, is using the pleasure principle mostly as working for defenses to avoid anxiety and avoid unpleasant feelings. The paradox then, also, is that when seeking pleasure, people may also be seeking to release tensions. So, pleasure in itself could be defensive in that sense. And when avoiding unpleasant feelings, people may also be seeking to feel better rather than the unpleasant feelings. So, you see how there's a duality, but then constantly the duality is overturned, because it's dialectical rather than dual.

GF: Is that the way the death drive and the pleasure principle are also dialectically intertwined?

RM: So, what Freud will say in *Beyond the Pleasure Principle*, which is the paper where he introduces the death drive and where he redefines the theory of the drives, is that the ego drives are also narcissistic and libidinal so that the old dichotomy between sexuality and life preservation doesn't hold anymore. He originally had this principle of 'neuronic inertia' in the project for scientific psychology – that's what he first called it [death drive]. That's how we first called it – the principle of neurotic inertia. *Beyond the Pleasure Principle* is now considered a very paradoxical text which some people reject because it doesn't seem like he [Freud] is able to arrive at a clear distinction and formulation of the two drives. So, he asks, well, is the pleasure principle the expression of a more fundamental principle? The more fundamental principle would be this principle of neurotic inertia, which he relabels the 'Nirvana principle'. The Nirvana principle would be the more radical expression of the pleasure principle, but, at that point, the Nirvana principle is working for the death drive to bring all the organic tensions to the lowest level of tension available in inorganic life. He borrows the tendency, the concept of the Nirvana principle, from Barbara Low, who was an English analyst, who suggested to him the principle coming from Buddhism. So, he defines the Nirvana principle as a tendency to reduce all excitation to level zero.

GF: Yes, I've seen diagrams describing this.

RM: But again, the paradox is whether that's the principle that regulates defenses – that defenses want to bring tension down – or is that what pleasure is looking for? So, in other words, is the Nirvana principle an ascetic principle, or is it a hedonistic principle? That's another paradox. You know the rock group Nirvana? [*GF acknowledges*] The fans think Nirvana is like heroin, so they misinterpret nirvana for heroin, thinking 'nirvana' is a kind of high, or blissful state, or something. But, in Buddhism, that's a kind of misunderstanding of the concept of Nirvana when you're looking for some high, or some pleasure, or some rapturous feeling. Instead, Nirvana in Buddhism is more like equanimity – equality in pain and pleasure, rather than finding an exceedingly intense form of pleasure or not having any kind of tension at all. But then Freud introduces a third principle, which he calls the 'constancy principle' in *Beyond the Pleasure Principle*. This is how Freud reconciles it – the constancy principle is to bring the tensions as low as possible. It emerges from Nirvana but tries to achieve it by reducing tensions as much as possible. So, in other words, that there has to be some balance with tension and relaxation. You know, to be alive you have to have some tension – otherwise you are inorganic or basically dead. So, there has to be some stimulation and excitation arriving to the nervous system or to the psyche. That lets you know that you're alive. And it creates certain conditions for motivation or for making work happen. So, constancy is to try to bring tension to the lowest possible level and keep it constant instead of reducing tension to level zero. And then, it's unclear whether reducing to zero is sort of a principle of the defenses or whether that's jouissance which is always asking for more.

GF: And that would move into hedonism?

RM: Right. So, jouissance in that sense is always asking for more – asking for excess. But then, the further complication is that Lacan comes with different types of jouissance. And the one that's inconvenient, the one that has to do with addiction and fixation to libidinal objects or narcissistic objects – this inconvenient jouissance is always asking for more in an attempt of returning to this fusion with a mother that we read as inconvenient. But there are entire schools of thought that regarded that as the basis for utopia and people who considered the refusal of abandoning that kind of fusion with a mother as something positive to oppose, not something to overcome. That's also another aspect of this duality. Some people in the Frankfurt School, even Marcuse,[1] argued that we are to refuse to abandon this primal connection with the mother, because that's the root of all the emancipatory feelings and root of compassion and whatnot. But the way Lacan reads it is that fusion is something to be lost because that kind of jouissance is 'inconvenient'.[2] And so, to the extent that it still operates, this kind of oral fixation, this fixation to withdraw, this fixation to an object of pleasure, this fixation to a bad relationship – that's an inconvenient form of jouissance that needs to be stopped. But, when it stops, it gives rise to a new form of jouissance, which then itself needs to be stopped. So, there's a mechanism within jouissance that also brings jouissance to a stop. In order to find some satisfaction, it also has to be inhibited to some degree – that tendency to always be asking for more – and that's the phallic function. You know, the negative is what stops one particular form of jouissance and attains a new one. So, in the case of fusional feelings, where often in relationships individuals fuse as a couple, the sexual relationship around phallic jouissance dies. So that's the basic outline of the complexity of the problem.

GF: I wonder if we could discuss some text in *Encore, Seminar XX*? [*See pgs. 32–33*]. In thinking about how jouissance emerges and moves from one type to the next, and tends to peak out or is brought back down or reduced somehow, I'm assuming you are talking about the relations of Imaginary jouissance and phallic jouissance …?

RM: Well, actually, I wasn't directly, but it kind of works that way. To clarify, the first one is the jouissance of the Other. That's the imaginary relation of the mother and the child to the *objet a*.

GF: And then the second is phallic jouissance?

RM: That's where it's a question of having or not having or being or not being the phallus.

GF: And there is a Third jouissance?

RM: The last one, the Third jouissance, is the 'Other jouissance'. So, it's important to distinguish the first, 'jouissance of the Other' and the third, 'Other jouissance', which comes in three forms – jouissance of meaning, jouissance of the mystic, and feminine jouissance.

GF: Okay. I feel clearer about that now. So, in *Encore, Seminar XX* on the top of page 33, Lacan asserts the idea that "*men, women and children are all but are but signifiers. Man is nothing but a signifier. Woman seeks out a man qua signifier*". That seems to define the movement from 'jouissance of the Other' to 'phallic jouissance'.

RM: Well, here he's focusing on highlighting the determination by the signifier or by the Symbolic, meaning that there's no prediscursive reality or there's no being outside language because language indicates the limit where Being becomes the 'beyond language'. So, he says, "There isn't the slightest prediscursive reality, for the very fine reason that what constitutes a collectivity – what I called men, women, and children – means nothing qua prediscursive reality. Men, women, and children are but signifiers". Except that he'll also say there's no signifier for femininity and a woman is outside the signifier, right? So those are the two sides – how the signifier also indicates what is outside the signifier. Both are simultaneously created in the [Borromean] knot, as opposed to thinking that the Real preexists the Symbolic in some way.

GF: This seems to me to really sit right at the heart of Lacan's work … I mean if you've got a psychological issue that already presupposes a divided subject because of the language in which one operates to discuss any of the relational components whatsoever, you're already split! You're not able to get full meaning from the signifier, but you're also reading the signifier while the signifier is reading you, and it's sort of a wild and wooly battle of interpretation.

RM: You can think about it like the infinite line, like the line on the X axis, for example, on the Cartesian plane. So that's an infinite line, but the infinite line doesn't come into existence until you put marks on it. And the marks are units – the numbers … you know, 0–1–2–3–4–5. And so they all depend on the infinite line to be marked. But the infinite line doesn't preexist the marks. So, the marks and the infinite line both arise together. So that's sort of like the relationship between the Real and Symbolic ... you don't have the Real until you have the mark, and then when you have the mark, you have also the unmarked – that which has no marks and that which has marks both arise together. That's the structural predicament and what he's saying here in terms of the signifier and men, women, and children. A woman seeks out a man qua signifier. A man seeks out a woman qua emptiness. This will strike you as odd that a woman's emptiness can only be situated in discourse since, if what I claim is true, namely that a woman is not whole, there's always something in her that escapes discourse. So, women look in men for a phallic signifier and men look in women for the *objet a* – and here, the *objet a* is being defined as something that escapes discourse. So that's how this knot between the Real and Symbolic is also intertwined in the relationships between men and women. That is knotty! Very knotty! Lacan is a very naughty boy! [*Both laughing*]

GF: No doubt! So, going back to our previous discussion, is the death drive for Lacan located in castration?

RM: No, the death drive is the opposite of the pleasure principle. So, the death drive is seen as a characteristic of all drives because it's the jouissance of 'encore'; always asking for more. So, there's a kind of infinity there with jouissance ... a bad infinity which is represented by the jouissance of the Other and it's also the jouissance of perversion, because perversion is always looking for some other forbidden pleasure that's supposed to be better than bourgeois, normal pleasure. So, the pervert is always trying to entice the subject with a forbidden jouissance that would be much better than phallic jouissance or that would be much better than heterosexual jouissance. You don't know what you're missing ... you know, there's this other jouissance and you know you like it and blah, blah, blah, right? So that's also associated with perversion, and it leads to a destructiveness that's associated with that – for one, in that case, it is outside the law ... whether it's incest, fusion with a mother, or some other perverse pleasure ... it is outside the law in that sense. So, it's deadly [the drive] and has deadly consequences in that sense. The most extreme example of this would be the serial killers, who are mostly men, and they're trying to extract the *objet a* from the body of the woman – so they cut her into little pieces. So, that would be 'I love you, I mutilate you'. That's what's deadly about sexuality or how sexuality with serial killers is all an enticement through sexual seduction. That's how they draw in their victims, kill them, and then there's a ritual act by which they try to extract the *objet a* in them that hasn't been symbolized ... it's taken as a 'concrete' of what a man is looking for in a woman. That is an example of how it takes the form of death or something deadly.

GF: So that's kind of the pleasure side, acting with unbridled pleasure. Is there another form, like unbridled or extreme defensiveness or something like that?

RM: Yes, you would see that in the example of the obsessional, where the obsessional is obsessed with the law and with the defenses, and with regulation, and ordering everything. And so, that's an example where Freud, in the *Beyond the Pleasure Principle*, gives the example of the death drive and of Nirvana as also what the defenses operate under. It's like the example that he gives of the cheese that is exposed to the environment – when the outer layer of the cheese hardens, that's the ego. And the soft cheese inside is the id. And, so the hardcover, which becomes hard through exposure to the elements, as a kind of defense against the elements, is seen as deadening the living tissue. It desensitizes – it's how the defenses make you desensitized, which is related to the whole thing about systematic desensitization in behaviorism which intends to serve as a way of strengthening the defenses. And the obsessional is all obsessed with death. So, Freud connects that with the death drive located in the defenses. The death drive also operates within the defenses in order to deaden the aliveness of the drive. But apparently, it has an adaptive function there as well. And you find that in Lacan with his theory of the two deaths, which he doesn't explicitly connect with this theory of the death drive, but the word death is used in both cases. The theory of the two deaths, which he develops in *Seminar VII*, uses the example of Sophocles's *Antigone*, because Antigone would rather be killed than betray her brother. So, Antigone, by burying her brother, is upholding the law of the gods as greater than Creon's law, and so is sentenced to death. That death is under the Symbolic and is an example of living and dying through symbolic ideals. Here, the physical death is one death, but the other one is the death under the signifier where the Symbolic regulates that function which has to do with what the Law regulates. And, in its regulating, it deadens.

GF: Yes. How does that fit in with the notion of foreclosure? Or does it?

RM: No, it doesn't, because what we're just talking about depends on primary repression, because repression is part of the Symbolic order, meaning the division of what you should do and what you shouldn't do – the question of morality and the Superego. The superego also has a deadly aspect, right? The Law has a deadly punishment since the state, in principle, is the one that's entitled to have the power over life and death. Otherwise, its nature. But, with the state, the state assumes the power over life and death. So that's another aspect of the second death in the Symbolic.

GF: Right. But, why doesn't foreclosure fit in?

RM: Because foreclosure is the foreclosure of primary repression – the foreclosure of the Name of the Father. And primary repression is action associated with the Name of the Father, the phallic function, and of castration. Primary repression is also that separation from the mother and the child, which also creates a separation within the psyche or creates a structure with different levels within the psyche. Interpersonally, it is the father intervening and separating the mother and the infant that generates not just family structure, but also intrapsychic structure. So that's what establishes primary repression. Foreclosure, on the other hand, is the defense against that action of primary repression, against the action of castration or the Name of the Father and so on. In this instance, psychosis is the use of foreclosure instead of primary repression. Primary repression leads to an erotic structure, while the defense for neurosis is primary repression. The defense for psychosis is foreclosure.

GF: And, of course, neurosis is the healthier of the two?

RM: Yes, psychosis is where you have foreclosed the intervention of the Name of the Father and the Symbolic, and then you're caught in this kind of fusion with the mother and her desire.

GF: I see. So, it's kind of like an imprisonment of the mind in the Imaginary.

RM: You're escaping the repression or the Symbolic only to fall prey to the tyranny of the Imaginary.

GF: That's very helpful. This idea of being caught in the signifying chain has its limits but also opens up the potentiality to have a relationship of love. I guess it's just a matter of how lack is given expression in the symbolic chain in relation to the Other.

RM: Right, and then there's a question of whether there's demand in that love or not.

GF: Yes, the impulse of love demanding love.

RM: To love is to want to be loved. So that's one definition of love. It's not the Christian definition of love, but rather it's the mundane definition of love. So, you may be loving, but you're loving because you want to be loved back. That's more love in the Imaginary. So, the question is, are there forms of love when there is no kind of demand. Parental love is kind of a combination, because some parents have those demands – they want to be loved, they want to be admired, they want their kids to identify with their ideals. They want the kid to become a great football player or something because they never were a football player, or just to make the parents proud or whatever. So, that's closer to Imaginary love in parental love. But the parental love where there isn't so much a demand is just a kind of joy where the parents relinquish their own personal satisfactions in order for the child to be fulfilled or satisfied as who they are.

GF: It's a very difficult balance to allow your kids to do their own thing while relinquishing the expectations. I've struggled with that quite a bit, actually.

RM: Or even to try to help them without them noticing that you're trying to help them!

GF: Right, so true!

RM: Or, supervising them without them knowing that you're supervising them, you know, so their autonomy is preserved ... it gets complicated! But parental love has Symbolic love, too. And, it has Real love – you're committed ... you have to take care of your kids and you have to show up. You have to put up with the tantrums, you have to help with the homework. There are all these agreements that you have to fulfill as a parent and they're the first ones to tell you when you fail at your symbolic commitments. Like if you don't show up for an event or something that was special to them, they'll have to go to a therapist to talk about that! So, there's this Symbolic obligation, but then there's something else there, too, that one experiences with one's children and I would say that's more of the empty love. But most of the love that we're talking about in psychoanalysis is more of the Imaginary love, except when talking about agape or the love of ideals. For instance, Freud couldn't believe in the maxim 'love your neighbor as yourself'.[3] Why would I want to love my neighbor as myself? Maybe I don't like my neighbor, so why do I have to feel like I have to love my neighbor … you know, maybe I hate my neighbor! So, Freud had a lot of trouble thinking about the different kinds of love. And I think with Lacan, it's a little bit easier to be able to sort out the different types of love because of the multidimensional framework of the three registers.

GF: Well, I guess that's a discussion for another day. It reminds me of Lacan's *Seminar VIII* on transference in relation to that question and how there's all these different relational interplays that make loving such a slippery slope.

RM: Right, so when in the transference, Lacan highlights where Socrates speaks to Alcibiades … there where you think I am, something like an Imaginary phallus, a knowledgeable guy, a sexy guy, a powerful guy … those are all the things you think are in me and that you love me for. But ultimately, there, where you see something, I am not – 'I am nothing'. So, the ultimate power that's behind all those semblances[4] is this nothingness, or this emptiness, which drives people to think that there are all kinds of objects in Socrates – the knowledge object and the phallic object, since the Greeks were tolerant of homosexuality. There's a clear implication of a kind of homosexual love between Alcibiades and Socrates, or at least Alcibiades is thinking of Socrates in a sexual way, thinking that he has the Imaginary phallus because of his knowledge. And then he [Socrates] says, it's not only because of my knowledge but because of my emptiness.

GF: Well, we'll have to pick that up some other time. And thank you as usual!

RM: You're welcome! … [*End of recording*]

Notes

1 This is the Marcuse linked to the young Marx, who believed that all social repression is the same as oppression. However, Marcuse also was critical of this point of view with his concept of 'surplus repression'. The latter claims that the drives can be repressively desublimated, so that when people act out the drives, this is a form of oppression rather than freedom from oppression. Foucault made the same point when he said the history of sexuality is the history of the construction and repression of sexuality (see Michel Foucault, *The History of Sexuality, Volume 1: An Introduction*, New York: Pantheon Books, 1978).

2 Lacan says that jouissance must be forbidden to those who speak (*Écrits*, p. 93). This is what Lacan means by an inconvenient jouissance because his definition of the Real with respect to jouissance is that it was inconvenient and destructive.

3 See Freud, *Civilization and Its Discontents*, p. 56.

4 See Moncayo, *The Emptiness of Oedipus*, p. 180. The concept of semblance first appears in Lacan in *Seminar IX* where semblance appears as distinct from the notion of

reality that appears in classical art. Reality, as opposed to the Real, is determined by the Symbolic and the Imaginary. Even though the Middle Ages is full of talk about God and belief in God, the Real escapes them except for the mystics. So, we spell God 'G-d' to indicate the mystery of the experience.

Supplemental References

Freud, Sigmund. (1920). *Beyond the Pleasure Principle*. SE 18.

Freud, Sigmund. (1930). *Civilization and Its Discontents*. SE 21.

Lacan, J. (2007). *Écrits* (B. Fink, Trans.). New York: WW Norton.

Lacan, J. (1959–1960). *The Ethics of Psychoanalysis. The Seminar of Jacques Lacan, VII.* New York: Norton.

Lacan, J. (1960–1961). *Transference. The Seminar of Jacques Lacan, VIII.* New York: Norton, 2001.

Lacan, J. (1961–1962). *Identification. The Seminar of Jacques Lacan, IX.* New York: Norton.

Lacan, J. (1972–1973), *Encore. The Seminar of Jacques Lacan, XX.* New York: Norton, 1998.

Marcuse, Herbert. (1955). *Eros and Civilization. A Philosophical Inquiry Into Freud.* Boston, MA: Beacon Press

Marx, K. (1818). *The German Ideology*. New York: Prometheus Books, 1998.

Moncayo, R. (2012). *The Emptiness of Oedipus: Identification and Non-identification in Lacanian Psychoanalysis*. Routledge/Taylor & Francis Group.

Plato. (1999). *The Symposium*. New York: Penguin Books.

Sophocles. (1993). *Antigone*. New York: Dover Publications.

Chapter 11

The Language of the One and the Language of the Other

Moncayo Seminar, April 20, 2017, *Encore, Seminar XX*, pg. 56

RM: Well, I think we were on Section 2, right?

GF: Yes.

RM: So, I made a note and I just wanted to share it with you … basically, with the first sentence … could you read that?

TEXT: Reality is approached with apparatuses of jouissance.

RM: So, the 'apparatus of jouissance', it's interesting, because I don't know if there is such a thing as an 'apparatus' of jouissance, and it is a term Freud used to describe the psychical apparatus. This was not one of his happiest expressions, because it makes it sound very apparatchik … you know how they talked about government workers in Russia in the past, they were the apparatchik. So in Freud it refers to the structure of the psyche which has to do with the functioning of repression and desire in mental formations that is kind of described as an apparatus – but that does seem to reify it in some way. So, how could it apply to jouissance? In language, in the apparatus of language … because then he says …

TEXT: That is another formulation I am proposing to you, as long as we focus, of course, on the fact that there's no other apparatus than language. That is how jouissance is fitted out (*appareillée*) in speaking beings. On that basis, language is clarified, no doubt, by being posited as the apparatus of jouissance.

RM: So, language then is the apparatus of jouissance, but language is tied to the existence of repression. And repression is necessary for psychical structure. That's an ambiguity that we have in Freud's theory, because repression is both good and bad for Freud. Without repression, you have no apparatus, you have no structure. And yet, repression, at least in the first theory, was considered the main reason for suffering, and therefore repression had to be undone. So, in the first instance, it is necessary, and in the second, it

DOI: 10.4324/9781003424581-11

> needs to be undone. But, when you undo repression in analysis, you don't undo primary repression, which is what creates a structure. So, the primary repression is associated with the Name of the Father (NoF) and the function of metaphor in language. And, also, language is about having to represent things that are absent. They can be absent because they are not present, but they may also not be present because they are repressed. So, the fact that you learn to speak about things that are absent … it's like with the beginning unary mark, when the first traces were used to mark the killing of an animal … the fact of the killing of the animal was totally repressed.

What remains is just the mark and then the usage of the marks, and then the marks turn into numbers and letters and so on. But the fact that originally arose as a marking of the deed of the killing of an animal gets repressed and gets lost. So, in the same way, the fact that repression arose out of the equation between the Name of the Father and the Desire of the Mother – which is how primary repression, and psychical structure is established – and also forgotten or lost. So, there is the question of representing the mother's desire … that's one of the early preoccupations. And the mother's desire, with the resources of language, is signified or it becomes substituted for the metaphor of the NoF.

So, when you are trying to say something about the mother's desire, you end up with language that inevitably involves the NoF, which then becomes a signifier – and the signified of that signifier is the mother's desire. The mother's desire is captured through language, mediated by the structure of the paternal metaphor. And that separation between language and the mother subsumes the Desire of the Mother under the NoF. This is both a blessing and a curse, because something about the mother's desire is not symbolized other than being a signifier of what the mother wants from the father. But the question of the mother's desire in relation to the child doesn't get symbolized either, and so that's where it can proliferate into fantasy. That is part of the psychical apparatus which has to do with desire, not jouissance.

Proliferation here is linked to metonymy and to the displacement of the objects of desire. A monkey, for example, jumps from vine to vine, trying to find the fruit in a tree. They have so much energy, and searching for fruit is how they spend their day when they are not fighting or reproducing.

The alpha male is always seeking to reproduce with a female. But human beings are reproduced by genetic design, meaning we want one or two children, or many or none. The culture dictates this and fashions certain possibilities, while animals have no free will. They are determined by a mathematical structure mediating reproduction. Here, we see how language is a more evolved form of signification than mathematics. On the other hand, we also say that numbers are purer and more exact than the signifier. Why? Because for beings that have no free will, it is better to have a pure structure determine them. For animals, oversight is not random or by chance.

Further, we cannot say for sure what the Real is, and the mystery is trinitarian. But while the Real cannot be discriminated (discrimination is egotistical), it nevertheless can be discerned. The positive form of discrimination is to be happy discerning differences and semblances. Despite nondiscrimination as a necessary approach to the Real, it is discerned by three forms: jouissance, mathematics, and the exterior real as unknowable. Then there are still three forms of jouissance to be discerned (jouissance and the Real are interchangeable here): the Real beyond number, the Real beyond the signifier, and the highest Real, which is the exterior Real (e.g., the discourse of birds which is simply a song that has numbers but evokes something beyond numbers). Once we are clear that there are three forms of jouissance and three forms of the Third jouissance, we can see what Lacan may mean by an 'apparatus of jouissance' – or multiple forms of enjoyment. Here, lalangue is the jouissance of meaning which is the third form of the Third jouissance. Lalangue is thus a special form or usage of language.

GF: Could you say something more about the distinction between desire and jouissance?

RM: Yes, for Lacan, jouissance, the way he initially conceived it, was inconvenient. So, it's kind of an excess, for example, being overly agitated or having anxiety. So, that is an inconvenient (unpleasant) jouissance that's derived from how the relationship with the mother becomes problematic, or the relationship with the mother as fantasy object becomes problematic and needs to be stopped or transformed in some way. So, Lacan says the jouissance needs to be stopped in order to be reached through the "inverted ladder of the Law in relation to desire". So, jouissance needs to be transformed into this more neurotic way of handling desire through the Law. So that is one definition of how he differentiates jouissance from desire. The other one is that desire itself is a limit on jouissance. And there, jouissance, I would say, is also not only tied to some excitement that could be pleasant or unpleasant, but is more generalized and not personalized, while desire is personal, in the sense that you desire and have romantic feelings and sexual feelings toward somebody in particular – an object of desire – someone that you desire. Someone that you desire is also a substitute, but it's still one particular person as opposed to the jouissance that seems to be more generalized as a form of jouissance or sexual pleasure with anybody (or anything for that matter).

MK: What's confusing to me is that the apparatus of jouissance is tied to repression because I thought jouissance was unstructured and unbound?

RM: What's tied to repression is the psychical apparatus, and Lacan is using the word 'apparatus', which, again, he took from Freud. He doesn't tell us that he is doing that, but that is where Freud talked about the 'psychical apparatus', and the psychical apparatus has more to do more with Desire and the Law than with jouissance. But Lacan is using a word that was tied to that model to now refer to jouissance – but jouissance is something different

> than that, right? So, why is he using the word 'apparatus' for jouissance? I guess the answer to that would be that jouissance is functioning within language as well. But, how does desire and jouissance function differently within language? That would be the question. Reframing your question slightly: How do desire and jouissance function differently within the structure of language? The easy way to resolve that, but in a way, it is too easy, is to say desire refers to the language of the Other, or language as the battery of signifiers of the Other, and jouissance instead refers to lalangue, which is the language of the 'One' rather than the language of the Other. If the language of One here refers to lalangue, then the question becomes, well what's the difference between language and lalangue?

So, lalangue ... and here is the equivocal point: Is lalangue the language of the unconscious? That is, as distinct from how the 'regular' language is unconscious? Is there a difference between the regular language being unconscious and the repressed unconscious, meaning things that are repressed and that potentially are absorbed by the primary process? And then the way the primary process manifests is through lalangue rather than through the use of social, grammatical language that nowadays people also think is unconscious. And the question of lalangue is more linked to the Desire of the Mother, while language is more related to the Name of the Father. And so here we could say that in lalangue, it's just more a question of expressing desire for a child or expressing joy to a child as opposed to using language as an attempt to socialize the child – which is something that happens later.

So we can also say that lalangue is related to this early kind of proto-language that is used by the mother ... and the father, too ... but more by the mother to interact with the child. And you could say that's an 'apparatus of jouissance,' in the sense that lalangue is being used to express the jouissance of the Other – the jouissance that the mother has with the child and later in development the 'language of the One' (Real) will have to be replaced by the' language of the Other' (Symbolic). Just like in development, the mother presides over the relationship with the child in the first year or two, and then, as a child grows, the impact of increasing socialization moves the child more in the direction of the Other and the father and so on. Therefore, the language of the Other replaces the language of the One. But these two always remain linked in ways that we don't fully understand yet.

GF: Would you say that lalangue is socially accessible in the Imaginary, so that it sets up a different kind of social connection? Regular language is conventional, and it functions in the Symbolic register, while lalangue does not necessarily, or its manifestation can run aberrant to the Symbolic. But it also seems to have an almost wider social accessibility because lalangue allows for the Imaginary register to operate as a platform for social connection.

RM: Well, you could say that. I would say that lalangue is between the Real and the Imaginary, and the language of the Other is between the Real and the Symbolic. But it is not so clear. Let me give you an example. With one

> of my first analysands, we were having a conversation about him coming either once a week or twice a week to sessions. And, in my kind of inexperience, I got into a polarity with the patient whether it was my agenda that he come twice a week or whether this was something he wanted ... and if he wanted it, was it really that he had a desire for it or whether he thought that it would be better for him, for where he wanted to go professionally...that it would be better for him to have analysis twice a week rather than thinking of the treatment as a once a week psychotherapy. And then, the next session he came in and told me that the waiting room in my office was "too weak". That's an example of the 'two a week' versus the 'too weak'. The way I understood that ... I mean, he was really struggling, and it was hard for him to come to analysis and to be in the session.

He would experience a lot of humiliation and he was kind of narcissistic ... he was always posturing and trying to present himself in a favorable way. And if I made any inroads to issues that he needed to work on instead of talking about his successes, he would experience that as a kind of humiliation – a kind of Imaginary castration[1] – if he had to acknowledge certain symptoms that he didn't think he had or that contradicted the image he had of himself. So the question was, did he feel "too weak"? Was it "too weakening" for him to come twice a week? Or was it that I was "too weak" – that I wasn't enough of a good analyst for him to make that kind of time and money investment, because I was just getting started. But you 'hear here' the homophones – the similarity of the sound of 'week' and 'weak' – seems to be within the language of the Other. So that's what's confusing, because sometimes the lalangue seems to function within the language of the Other – just the similarity of sound for the associations – and sometimes it seems to be pointing at something different than that. Because, in his case, lalangue didn't represent desire, nor was it a reference. Lalangue represented more his struggle with his father rather than representing an early desire for his father or an early feeling of feeling like the object of the mother's desire ... anyway, I'll stop here because I think I am talking too much. Sorry, I get into this jouissance where I just keep talking!

[*ALL laughing and appreciating*]

TEXT: When we say "primary" and "secondary" for the processes, that may well be a manner of speaking that fosters an illusion. Let's say, in any case, that it is not because a process is said to be primary – we can call them whatever we want, after all – that it is the first to appear. Personally, I have never looked at a baby and had the sense that there was no outside world for him. It is plain to see that a baby looks at nothing but that, that it excites him, and that that is the case precisely to the extent that he does not yet speak. From the moment he begins to speak, from that exact moment onward and not before, I can understand that there is [such a thing as] repression. The process of the Lust–Ich may be primary – why not? It's obviously primary once we begin to think – but it's certainly not the first.

RM: I think this is of importance for psychoanalysis because there is this confusion about what's primary and what's secondary – the 'primary process' and the 'secondary process', which were Freud's terms. And, Bion says that sometimes the primary is secondary and sometimes the secondary is primary, so there seems to be a form of primary processes that, in analysis, when we are doing free association, that's a primary form of thinking that is not 'secondary process', and yet it is not the primary process that we associate with psychosis and 'loose associations'.

So, free association is a kind of primary process, because if it were a secondary process, then you would have a patient doing their narrative, and telling you stories, and you know, telling you their theories about themselves and about the world and whatnot, as people often do. But that kind of secondary process is not good for analysis. While the way that people talk about the secondary process is like what you need in order to not be crazy, in order to not be psychotic ... in order to have an integrated ego and be able to think rationally, and so on. And what seems to be a necessary achievement, a developmental milestone, precisely becomes an obstacle to analysis. So the secondary process can be productive or unproductive and the primary process can be productive and unproductive. And it seems that both Bion and Lacan have this kind of understanding of 'primary' and 'secondary', which is different from the way Freud and [modern] psychology talks about it. So, it's the difference between the archaic and the ancient! You know, it's like when people talk about antiquity, they think of these cultural things that are passé and that are 'long gone' and no longer relevant for scientific modernity. It's the 'old way' of thinking. So that's archaic, primitive – whereas the 'ancient' is old, but it is not primitive. Then, we talk about the 'knowledge of the ancients' ... that Freud is passing on to us ... continuing that lineage of ancient knowledge that is very advanced – it's not primitive, but it's old.

BB: Can you define what you mean by 'primitive'?

RM: Yeah, it's sort of the way that Levi-Strauss criticized the notion of primitive mentality that was ingrained within psychiatry, of thinking that children and psychotics are like primitive people – they behave like primitive people. Because he thought that was a kind of Western bias that doesn't recognize the wisdom in old cultures, and that, in some ways, they may have some forms of wisdom more advanced than the ones we have, and yet we call it 'primitive'. So, that's the difference between the ancient and archaic. The 'archaic' would be to think that they are just stuck in a lower stage of development and an earlier form of culture, and so on and so forth, and we are the enlightened and advanced West, when in fact this idea we have of being the enlightened and advanced West is just this secondary ego process that is not that profound. So, in a similar way, the 'primal' is not necessarily 'primitive'. So, these are different ways of thinking about the primary process.

TEXT: Development is confused with the development of mastery. It is here that one must have a good ear, like in music – I am the master (*m'être*), I progress along the path of mastery (*m'êtrise*), I am the master (*m'être*) of myself (*moi*) as I am of the universe. That is what I was talking about earlier, the vanquished idiot (*con-vaincu*). The universe is a flower of rhetoric. This literary echo may perhaps help us understand that the ego (*moi*) can also be a flower of rhetoric, which grows in the pot of the pleasure principle that Freud calls "Lust-prinzip," and that I define as that which is satisfied by blah-blah.

[*ALL laughter*]

RM: So, he is equivocal in how he is using blah-blah. On the one hand, the blah-blah could be lalangue. On the other hand, the blah-blah could mean that people are just mouthing off but saying nothing, right? *Blah-blah, blah-blah* ... people often use that expression. But what he is handling here, what I talked about last time, is about Freud saying that there is an original, 'real ego' prior to the 'lust-ego', or 'pleasure ego', and then there is the 'reality ego'. So, those are three different things – there is a 'real ego' before the 'pleasure ego' before the 'reality ego'. And, that real ego refers to just the drives for self-preservation – let's say, the suction reflex, the grasping reflex, that are inborn the way Ego Psychology talks about them as 'inborn apparatus' – that would be the real ego. And, then the pleasure ego is the one that is involved in the development of the hallucinatory wish fulfillment once the breast becomes more than just an object of need and becomes an object of pleasure and fantasy – which then requires the reality ego to intervene. So, those are three different elements.

The Master – because we have this triple notion – when we talk about the Master in social and political contexts, the Master has a negative connotation – he's a despot or an autocrat. But even when Freud talked about the impulse that the Ego wants to master the trauma of the repetition compulsion, that mastery refers to something necessary ... a necessary acquisition to have some degree of autonomy and control, and so on. And that's the way they talk about mastery in Ego Psychology – but, of course, Lacan collapsed that notion of master with the political notion of mastery which is negative.

And this dilemma between these two types of 'master' is replicated in how nowadays people talk about 'spiritual masters' and whether to think about a spiritual teacher as master where the teaching gets reabsorbed into some kind of social, egotistical discourse where they idolized the guru or the master, and then the master uses the power they have to take advantage of their position with regards to sex, violent behavior, or the inappropriate use of monies and so on. So people are always not knowing which master they are dealing with, the good or the bad one! [*Chuckling*]

GF: So, this idea of the 'vanquished idiot' is the master I think I am as an ego in reality and a "being of the universe"?

RM: The 'vanquished idiot' … of course that refers to the 'victor' and the 'vanquished' that is part of the master's struggle. So, that's a master that oppresses you or that you are struggling with.

GF: Right, so when being 'of the universe', the universe is my master. Yet I think I am the master of the self. So, in that respect, the idea of the vanquished idiot is …?

RM: Okay, but it is unclear what he means because first he says, "I am the master of myself, I am the master of the universe", and we know he is saying that facetiously. He is saying that ironically, because Freud says we are not the master of ourselves – we are not the "masters in our own house". And then, Galileo and Darwin dethroned us because we are not 'masters' because we descended from apes, and we are not 'special people'. Galileo dethroned us because the earth is not the center of the solar system … the sun is, right? This 'being master of the universe' is part of the hubris of the human condition and masculinity in particular, whether in males or females. I remember when I came to the US and the whole computer-thing was starting to take off, and there was a *Time Magazine* cover (June 1995) with the CEO from Microsoft with the title, "Master of the Universe". But rather, I think that Bill Gates is kind of a geeky, humble guy, so, this kind of doesn't fit him exactly. But then Lacan gives this funny sentence … "The universe is a flower of rhetoric". What do you think he means by that? And, then he says the Ego can be a 'flower of rhetoric'.

BB: That it is created in a game of speech … in a 'speech game'. And, it has a life cycle. There would be no universe or no universe as we know it without the 'language game'[2] or without the 'speech game'.

RM: Yes! Well, it is sort of like, do we describe the universe in our 'human-centered' way, thinking that language is the same as the order of plants, the order of bacteria, the order of photosynthesis, the order of light or [other] physical phenomena, and language is just equivalent to that. So, if language is just one more expression of this universal rhetoric, then the rhetoric of the universe would include not just language but all the codes that nature uses. Or does it mean the other way around, which is that we are presenting the universe in a human-centered way. But I think that sentence is beautiful, and if the universe is a flower of rhetoric, then it probably includes both meanings. I am not certain about what he means by 'rhetoric' either – is it a good thing or not a good thing? I guess he means well spoken? Although rhetoric is also what is used in politics to manipulate public opinion, so that would not be so good. But, if it is just a poetic expression, then whatever universal principle is at work in a beautiful, poetic expression, or a beautiful way of using words, is the same power that is at work in the beauty of the universe. Looking at the night sky, or the beauty of the galaxy, the beauty of light or whatever.

BB: So, can I define 'rhetoric' for us? I am reading from the internet: "Rhetoric is the art of discourse, wherein a writer or speaker strives to inform, persuade, or motivate particular audiences in specific situations. Also, as a subject and formal practice, rhetoric has played an essential role in European tradition. Its best-known definition comes from Aristotle who considers it a counterpart in both logic and politics and calls it 'the faculty of observing in any given case the available means of persuasion'. Rhetoric typically provides heuristics for understanding, discovering, and developing arguments for particular situations, such as Aristotle's three persuasive audience appeals – logos, pathos, and ethos. The five canons of rhetoric which trace the traditional tasks of designing persuasive speech were first codified in classical Rome, and they are – invention, arrangement, style, memory, and delivery (along with grammar and logic). Rhetoric is one of the three ancient arts of discourse" … and it goes on.[3]

RM: I don't know … it's more the political rhetoric, right?

BB: Why do you say that?

RM: Because he is saying it's the 'art of persuasion' and the faculty observing the means of persuasion. And the Romans all used rhetoric to convince everybody to submit to them.

BB: But isn't that what we do when we form identifications and find someone to mirror us?

RM: Well, it is hard to dissociate rhetoric from the 'master's discourse', because rhetoric is the art of governing and how to govern and use words in order to govern well or to be able to persuade the masses or the citizens. And, how citizens engage in public discourse around politics and policy. So, I don't know, in that sense, if the universe is a "flower of rhetoric" as Lacan states. I guess the universe is a flower of poetry, or the universe is a literary invention … that would be different. He is using 'the master' and also, he differentiates between discourse and speech. Then he differentiates between 'the saying' and 'the said' or 'the saying' and 'the statement'. And what we are aiming at in analysis is 'the saying' rather than 'the statement' and speech rather than discourse, because 'discourse' is discursive. It's like when patients come in and want to talk theory and we don't see that as so productive for analysis, because what we are looking for is speech or 'the saying' rather than discourse.

BB: Why?

RM: Because speech articulates the subject of the enunciation, and that is where desire appears. And usually speech and discourse in the narrative contradict each other because speech includes unconscious formations. Discourse can be written or not spoken. The statement (*le dit*) refers to what you are trying to say but enunciation (*énonciation*) is what you actually say – you may have a slip of the tongue.

MK: This would be a good place to pause … [*Thanks and farewells*]

Notes

1 One example of imaginary castration might be when a child is asked by a parent to go to bed. The child refuses to go to bed because he is playing with his object. The object for the child is a video game, but the video game represents the Imaginary, and losing it, represents loss, frustration, and anger. So we call this protest against separating from the video game an equivalent loss to that of the mother and breast.
2 A language game (German: *Sprachspiel)* is a philosophical concept developed by Ludwig Wittgenstein, referring to simple examples of language use and the actions into which the language is woven. Wittgenstein argued that a word or even a sentence has meaning only as a result of the "rule" of the "game" being played.
3 https://en.wikipedia.org/wiki/Rhetoric.

Supplemental References

Bion, W. (1961). *Experiences in Groups*. London: Routledge.
Freud, Sigmund. (1920). *Beyond the Pleasure Principle*. SE 18.
Lacan, J. (1972–1973). *Encore. The Seminar of Jacques Lacan, XX*. New York: Norton, 1998.
Levi-Strauss, C. (1967). *The Elementary Structures of Kinship*. Boston, MA: Beacon Press.
Levi-Strauss, C. (1978). *Myth and Meaning*. London: Routledge.
Wittgenstein, Ludwig (1953). *Philosophical Investigations*. New York, NY, USA: Wiley-Blackwell.

Chapter 12

Sexuation and Three Forms of Jouissance Beyond the Phallus

Moncayo Seminar, June 15, 2017, *Encore, Seminar XX*, pg. 61

TEXT: In the end, if this jouissance comes to someone (*celui*) who speaks, and not by accident, it is because it is a bit premature. It has something to do with the renowned (*fameux*) sexual relationship, concerning which he will have only too many occasions to realize that it doesn't exist. It is thus second rather than first. There are traces of it in Freud's work. If Freud spoke of *Urverdrängung*, primal repression, it was precisely because the true, good, everyday repression is not first – it is second.

RM: Okay, is that transparent, or do we need to deconstruct the paragraph?

BB: I would like it if you could say something about primal repression and its difference from 'everyday' repression.

RM: So, in Freud, there is primary repression, secondary repression, and tertiary repression. So, if we use the first model of mind, the topographical model, when we speak, we have to decide about what to say and what to leave out – and what's left out, what's selected out, may be for a variety of criteria. There's also the assumption about what could be said that is being pulled back into unconscious repression. So that censorship, between consciousness and the preconscious, Freud calls suppression – and it's one of the three operative types of repression.

BB: You said 'suppression', correct?

RM: Right, he calls it technically, suppression, even though generically we could just say it is one type of repression. Then, there is another line between the preconscious and the unconscious. So, the preconscious, as we have said before, is anything that could be in your mind that is part of your history, your biography, [something] part of the culture, [something] part of rational thought, et cetera, that could be in your mind from which one selects – you're not going to talk about everything at the same time! But what is not available in that preconscious is an effect or the barrier between the preconscious and the unconscious … so, that barrier is unconscious. You do not make a conscious choice here to select something out or not select something out, because that is already being done for you. And that means that you have

DOI: 10.4324/9781003424581-12

> a structured mind ... you have a structure within your psyche as part of your constitution as a human being ... and, that structure is established in culture – you are not born with the structure.

And then, within the unconscious itself, there is another barrier that was never conscious. Maybe it was conscious at a particular moment, but you didn't have the cognitive structure to process that representation and that then will never become conscious experientially. But it creates a dynamism because it pulls everything in the direction of repression. It has a certain kind of gravity or centripetal force, a certain kind of mass, even though it doesn't have any mass. So that is why Lacan likens it to a black hole that doesn't have any mass, but yet it has an enormous amount of gravity.

Now, this is me speaking and my thinking here – that there are two types of primary repression. In *Seminar XXIII, The Sinthome*, Lacan speaks of a 'true hole' and a 'false hole' [Moncayo 1998], which applies to the question of primary repression in Freud. So, the true hole would be ... it is sort of how people say, well, you know, children have this kind of naiveté and ingenuity in their discovery of the world, but they don't have the conceptual categories established to be able to differentiate the perceptions or have some kind of understanding of what it is that they are perceiving. They don't have a code, so they are perceiving the world in this kind of 'mythical moment' prior to the establishment of psychic structure and cultural structure, and so on, in a way that they don't have words for it.

And this is similar to the experience of the 'mystic', where the Real manifests in experience. For the mystic, the categories are there but they are just in abeyance. For the child, they [the categories] are not there yet, so it's forgotten because there is no reference to create a memory about it. So that would be one type of primary repression, meaning our forgetting of that originary experience of the world. And this is not so psychoanalytic. It's not typically Freudian, although Freud did include the unconscious in the sense of the unknown or even the unknowable. But it does have to do with Lacan's understanding of the (Real) unconscious. What is it about our perception of the world that still to this day, despite all our structure, despite all our fantasies, there is still something about our experience of the world that is left unmarked ... something that contains that Real dimension within the Borromean knot, which, for the child, in originary experience, was all they knew. So the Freudian repressed unconscious specifically refers to the 'false hole' because there is something there. And what is there refers to "what (object of fantasy) am I for the Other?". What fantasy do I occupy for the Other? How is the Other seeing me? What do you want from me? So that's the child asking the first Other – the mother – what do you want from me? What object in your fantasy am I for you? So you could call it *objet a* or you could call it Imaginary phallus, depending on your preference or depending on the situation – one might be more relevant than the other. One is more loaded with phallocentrism, the other is not. So we have options in Lacanian theory. But that's the object that is kind of intolerable to actually know – what fantasy object was the infant for the mother. This is what gets repressed under primary repression. That's what is there behind primary repression – that's what the theory predicts.

BB: So, when they say 'ordinary', is that 'everyday' repression?

RM: Yeah, he's talking about it in a generic sense. 'Everyday repression' could be, yeah, you know, I thought something about somebody, but I am not going to say it because it would be a matter of poor judgment to say it. If you were to say something that just occurs to you in a fantasy while in a conversation with the other, you wouldn't know what your place is at that moment and it would be inappropriate to say something like that – so, that's 'everyday repression'. But that everyday repression is tied to all these other series of repressions.

So, there is always an excess of jouissance, and we all experience that to some degree or another depending on how emotional we are. In our speech, there is an excess, meaning that we do not say completely what our jouissance or our desire is – but it can be read in the voice, it can be read in the emotional tone, and it can be read when somebody says, "oh, this person is so bubbly because this person is just effervescent!" And that is a nice expression, a nice aspect of jouissance – this kind of bubbling excess – like when you open a bottle of something that has gas in it and there's a kind of 'bubbling up'. And, at times it is wonderful ... somebody is so energetic, vital, and full of life where there is an excess of jouissance. But at other times, somebody may say, "oh, that person is too much ... can you modulate your affect a little bit"! That's also an excess of jouissance. So Lacan is saying that this excess of jouissance goes back to this unmetabolized signifier under primary repression. So it appears in our everyday conversation, this whole mythic structure is right there in the moment even though it may have taken eons to develop. The unmetabolized signifier might take eons to develop and has multiple rather than restricted relations with other signifiers. Therefore, it represents a form of disorderly chaos, while form represents the realm of form and repression. The realm of form and repression can be positive or negative, thus there are two forms of primary repression. For example, the right hand is symmetrical to the left hand, so it is the same hand. However, inside the fingers and the palm of the hand (and wrist) there is a multiplicity of nerve endings and fat. So what is an easier form to perceive becomes an entangled web of nerve endings or cables. Just speak to a car mechanic or a computer engineer to determine the impossibility of sorting out the cables completely. Yet the cables are connected at both nerve endings.

GF: So, is the primary repression repeated, or is it something that happens once and for all?

RM: It's Freud's 'Big Bang' theory. So, it's 'once and for all', but it's always active, because there is always this gravity, this pull of gravity that structures.

That's why the 'black hole' is a good metaphor for it, because it is this intense gravity from something that doesn't seem to have any mass, and yet it affects the whole positioning of the galaxy. It's affecting what is going on in the entire galaxy even if you are not near it.

MK: Raul, I have some note from many years ago about the ideal of analysis being the transformation of a 'false hole' into a 'true hole' …

RM: Yes, I probably said that somewhere, sometime! [*ALL laugh*]

MK: Yes, the action of replacing the Name of the Father from the Real as opposed to from the Imaginary …

RM: So, in a way it's like the Imaginary phallus doesn't exist and the *objet a* dissolves in the face of the Real.

MK: Then, what are you left with?

RM: When you get close to the *objet a*, it vanishes. So, that is the process of transforming a 'false hole' into a 'true hole'. Something that is there that you are seeking in analysis, which eventually when you get to it, it kind of 'empties out'.

MK: Is this the traversal of a fantasy?

RM: You could look at it that way, but it's not exactly the same. The way I am thinking of the traversal of the fantasy these days is like when you localize the fantasy, you can see how it works in you, but you are not fooled by it. Because, you know, we are never going to get rid of fantasy, so it's not like the fantasy of getting rid of the fantasy. But the fantasy may acquire a different quality, so it might become less of a hindrance. It becomes more of a creative force so long as you are not fooled by it. It no longer leads you to do things that become disastrous or where you end up with just one more repetition.

BB: Is it disastrous because of the *méconnaissance*? Is the disaster of the fantasy related to misrecognition – where the fantasy misrecognizes the situation?

RM: Lacan puts the *méconnaissance* more in terms of when we recognize our image in the mirror, we think it is just us [me]. We do not see the Other in the image. We don't see how our image has substituted the Other or how the Other has structured our image. And we also don't recognize the nature of the mirror. Neither do we see our own image in it – that's *méconnaissance*. We misrecognize the place of the Other. But it's a necessary moment of alienation which is a misrecognition that cannot be undone, because otherwise there is a risk of psychosis. Thus, we have to appropriate the Other to have a sense of 'self', and that involves a misrecognition. So, we have to have a conventional sense of self that we can use in society that we identify as 'us' [me or I], because if you start deconstructing everything that you are, then you may not be able to function.

BB: Would it possibly be, too, that there is an echo of this in how fantasy works in terms of understanding others as social phenomena or a social tie as Žižek (1989) has indicated. I mean, if you know it is a fantasy, and are not fooled, it's similar to a kind of mirroring. I think this is what is going on. If I just assume that what I think is taking place in front of the mirror in the specular image phase of development, is the only way of seeing things and that there is no other way of seeing the world than my own, that leads to a certain disaster. How would you say this relates to the experience of "alienation" that supposedly happens when the child looks in the mirror and understands that he is looking in a mirror, and that what he sees reflected in the mirror is being determined by many things – intrapsychic things and contextual things?

RM: This is an example of how the distortion of vision in front of the specular image is a normal distortion that needs to take place for the constitution of the subject. But then, although normally constituted, the subject misperceives his or her self as the Other. The ideal ego sees the Other beyond their own completeness in front of the mirror. Where the Other is lacking in the mirror is where the ideal ego, or the body schema, comes to be established. From then on, the subject goes around the world thinking that their images of the world are real images instead of numbers and symbols. If you took the number and symbols out of the image, the world would vanish. It's in this sense that Buddhism says that the reality of the world is an illusion (exactly as Freud also said regarding religion).

BB: I really feel like it is important to know where the misrecognitions are and to allow misrecognition to be one of things central to discovery in terms of fantasy.

RM: Right, and that's where Lacan says that misunderstanding is the norm.

BB: Is misunderstanding the same as misrecognition?

RM: It's sort of the same thing as it seems to follow from the different ways of using the concept of misrecognition. It's a Hegelian notion – we all want to be recognized. Without recognition, it would be hard to live in the world. And, if you break it down further and say, re-cognition, there is so much there – memory, representation, presentation, cognition, recognition, et cetera – that there exists a whole series of mediations of the world. We always need recognition, but we are often never recognized in the place where we would like to be recognized. There is always something just a little off and dissatisfying in our need for recognition. So, if you think it is a valid thing and you insist – I want to be seen, I don't feel seen! – it may just be that the other does not see you. But it also may be that the other does see you, but they don't see you from the place you want to be seen from.

In actuality, this is kind of the norm. So, in that sense, we have to give up the struggle for recognition because there is a failure built into recognition. So if you take it to the extreme, you will always end up frustrated because they will never recognize you exactly, because you want to be recognized from the fantasy, right? So the fantasy is what is in movement in the desire for recognition, but the fantasy is yours, it is not the other's. The other has their own fantasy, and they also may not feel recognized by you since they want you to recognize their fantasy. And we never recognize each other's fantasies, and that is why there is no sexual relationship. That's why Lacan refers to the "renowned" sexual relationship in which we will have only too many occasions to realize that it doesn't exist.

GF: It's interesting to consider misunderstanding as being something more contextual, as if an understanding only exists within a certain context "x". This makes me think of Heidegger who talks about 'Understanding' as always being a 'case of' ... being something of a particular species under a broader genus understanding. And, if you find yourself 'out of context', you could be even further estranged from your own fantasy as well.

RM: Right, and that's why it is important to define the terms because we may be using the same words, but we think of the words within different contexts. So, for this subject, this word refers to this concept and for this other subject, this word refers to another different concept. And so there is always disagreement about the meaning of the word because the concept of the word within their own [perceived] context is completely different! And, they may be actually agreeing or talking about the same thing, but it is just that they haven't reconciled their contexts or their terminology. And, if they did that, then they may recognize that they do agree! So, that's a misunderstanding that happens all the time.

TEXT: People repress the said jouissance because it is not fitting for it to be spoken, and that is true precisely because the speaking (*dire*) thereof can be no other than the following: qua jouissance, it is inappropriate (*elle ne convient pas*). I already sustained as much earlier by saying that it is not the one that should be (*faut*), but the one that shouldn't be/ never fails.

RM: So, that's where Lacan early on discusses jouissance as being 'inconvenient'.

BB: What is the "it" in that sentence? Is it jouissance all the way through?

RM: [*Citing text*] "I already sustained as much earlier by saying that it is not the one that should be (*faut*)" ... I don't know how he is using that, there is no note about it ... yes, it's the one that should be missing. So, it's the one that you shouldn't say because it would be inappropriate to say ... it would be inconvenient to say ... so, that's what should be censored by suppression. But, nevertheless, it never fails to be there. So, you can expect that it will be there, but you will have to handle the jouissance, because it could become inconvenient.

BB: So, the "it" is the 'speaking of the jouissance'... that is inappropriate?

RM: It is not the one that should be, yes.

BB: That's the 'speaking of the jouissance', not just the jouissance [itself], right?

RM: Yes! So, both "it" and "one" refer to jouissance.

BB: Jouissance or just 'speaking the jouissance'?

RM: It is not the one that should be ... it is not the one that would be appropriate to speak. It is not the one that would be convenient to speak.

BB: Is there a jouissance that is convenient to speak? Or is it by [the] nature of jouissance being jouissance, inconvenient to speak?

RM: Well, Lacan changed his theory over time. Initially, jouissance was always inconvenient. And then, when he [further] developed the theory of jouissance in *Encore, Seminar XX* he introduced feminine jouissance. In *Encore, Seminar XX*, he also introduces the Other jouissance which, in *The Sinthome, Seminar XXIII*, he renames the Third Jouissance.[1] The Third jouissance is not inconvenient. For example, in the case of Dora, Freud said that she was seeking to have the phallus. Lacan goes back and reinterprets the case as an example of the inexistence of femininity. What Dora is seeking is to have the phallus as a lack, whereby lack provides an opening for the emptiness and inexistence of femininity. 'feminine jouissance' and the 'jouissance of the mystic' end the question of the hysterical woman, because the woman is empty and thus can take many identities, including being and having the phallus.

BB: How does it settle the question of the hysterical woman?! I am always interested in this question! You can never say too much about this, okay! I am always going to want more help with that one! [*ALL laughing*]

RM: Meaning that, you are not going to be able to get rid of this excess in femininity, because this excess is driven by the Real. So, the Real of femininity needs to be realized and you will never get rid of that because it's foundational. The Real of femininity and the Other jouissance are convenient but are both confused with the first jouissance which is inconvenient. The first jouissance is called the jouissance of the Other referring back to the fusion with the mother. But the Other jouissance, the Third jouissance, is convenient. So, the One and the Third are always confused, and that's the quandary of femininity: Do women stay attached to their mothers, and do they become phallic women who are or have the phallus? Being close to your mother is not the same as being fused with your mother for a woman. And, if the Third jouissance is not feminine, or if it is not gendered, then it would be the jouissance of meaning, or the jouissance of the mystic (which, again, are all convenient). But with the jouissance of the mystic, Lacan is trying to rescue mysticism from the pathological way of describing it. Psychiatry described the jouissance of the mystic pathologically, which is part of the scientific model – like saying all the Biblical prophets were all psychotic and other kinds of that reduction that a lot of psychiatrists do because they can't think of different types of perceptual experiences as not being psychotic. So, Lacan is trying to rescue mysticism from that by saying, 'no, there is a kernel there that is outside meaning, but where the Name of the Father is not foreclosed'. So, it's not a psychotic structure, although it has an outside meaning. And, if you are too narrow in your rational, scientific perspective, then you miss it entirely. So, in that sense, Lacan is doing classical psychiatry a very big favor. This is nothing new anymore in our culture, but there are some psychiatrists who still think that way.

BB: Yes, there are a lot. And, psychoanalysts, too.

TEXT: Repression is produced only to attest, in all statements (*dires*) and in the slightest statement, to what is implied by the statement that I just enunciated, that jouissance is inappropriate – *non decet* – to the sexual relationship. It is precisely because the said jouissance speaks that the sexual relationship is not.

BB: So, when the 'said jouissance speaks', what kind of 'speaking' are we talking about here?

RM: Well, it's like if you picture a couple and they are arguing and they are at an impasse in their relationship, and they are yelling past each other. And, Lacan says, 'oh, the two versions never add up'! So, there the jouissance between the sexes is being spoken, but there's no relationship because they are just speaking past each other through their own fantasies.

TEXT: Which is why that jouissance would do better to hush up, but when it does, that makes the very absence of the sexual relationship a bit harder yet to bear. Which is why, in the final analysis, it doesn't hush up, and why the first effect of repression is that it speaks of something else. That is what constitutes the mainspring of metaphor.

There you have it. You see the relationship between all that and utility. It's utilitarian. It makes you capable of serving some purpose, since you don't know (*faute de savoir*) how to enjoy otherwise than to be enjoyed (*être joui*) or duped (*joué*), because it is precisely the jouissance that shouldn't be/could never fail.

RM: Yeah, he [Lacan] tries to bring in utilitarianism as a philosophy ... Greg, do you want to give a definition of it?

GF: Well, it basically states that when a community of believers all feel happy or that there is mutual agreement that enough of a resource is distributed to everybody equally within the community, then it is this final goal which determines the direction of an ethical decision practically speaking.

RM: Right, except it doesn't quite fit, because he is saying that that kind of happy common good is something very difficult to attain because the happiness that would be required for each subject is not easily reconciled with the idea of happiness that the 'other' has. So, I'm not sure. But he is going to expand that, because he is going to go onto ethics from here, so maybe we will get a better sense of that.

TEXT: It's on the basis of this step-by-step approach, which made me "scand" something essential today, that we must consider the light Aristotle and Freud can be seen to shed on each other. We must investigate how what they say (*dires*) can intersect and cross over into each other's work.

FOOTNOTE: Scantier is the verb form of "scansion", and is usually translated as "to scan" or "scanning" (as in scanning verse). I have opted in all of my translations of Lacan's work to date to introduce a neologism – to scand, scanding – so as to distinguish the far more common contemporary uses of scanning (looking over rapidly, quickly running through a list, taking ultrathin pictures of the body with a scanner or "feeding" text and images in digital form into a computer) from Lacan's idea here of cutting, interrupting, punctuating, or highlighting something.

In book seven of the *Nicomachean Ethics*, Aristotle raises the question of pleasure. What seems most certain to him, in referring to jouissance, is no more or less than the idea that pleasure can but be distinguished from needs, from those needs with which I began in my first sentence, and with which he frames what is at stake in generation. Needs are related to movement. Indeed, Aristotle places at the center of his world – a world that has now definitively disappeared with the tide – the unmoved mover, immediately after which comes the movement it causes, and a bit further away, what is born and dies, what is engendered and corrupted. That is where needs are situated. Needs are satisfied by movement.

Oddly enough, we find the same thing in Freud's work, but there it concerns the articulation of the pleasure principle. What equivocation makes it such that, according to Freud, the pleasure principle is brought on only by excitation, this excitation provoking movement in order to get away from it? It is strange that that is what Freud enunciates as the pleasure principle, whereas in Aristotle's work that can only be considered as an attenuation of pain, surely not as a pleasure. When Aristotle connects the status of pleasure with something, it can only be with what he calls *energia*, an activity.

RM: That's important because in the idea of energy, which is something mentioned in my last book where Lacan talks about energetics in *The Sinthome, Seminar XXIII,* is only known through an activity and that there also is the connection between energy and mass in physics. They are not the same thing, yet you do not know about energy until it activates into something. But the fact that it is activity doesn't mean that the activity itself can be reduced to energy. So, it's like the difference between kinetic energy and potential energy. All the activity in the brain and the transmission of impulses depends upon activity, but activity depends upon a base level of potential energy in the cell according to its mass.

I am not sure that it is correct to only think about it as activity – maybe that's the way that you measure it or the way you quantify it – that's the way you work with it. It's also like the relationship between steam and the engine of a locomotive train. There's the steam, and the steam is the potential energy that gets the train moving, and so we know it as the activity of the movement of the train. And this is similar to how Freud spoke about drive. We only know about drives, he says, through representations. So, we only know the energy of a drive through the work that it produces in the mind – the mind thinks, the mind sensates, the mind feels, the mind fantasizes – all that is activity, and that's all the activity of the drive. But thinking, sensing, and feeling are not the same as the energy that is the source of the drive.

TEXT: To orient yourselves on the path along which we are proceeding, recall the step we made earlier by formulating that jouissance is centrally related to the one (*celle-là*) that shouldn't be/never fails, that shouldn't be/could never fail in order for there to be a sexual relationship, and remains wholly attached to it. Hence, what emerges with the term by which

Aristotle designates it is quite precisely what analytic experience allows us to situate as being the object – from at least one pole of sexual identification, the male pole – the object that puts itself in the place of what cannot be glimpsed of the Other. It is inasmuch as *objet a* plays the role somewhere – from a point of departure, a single one, the male one – of that which takes the place of the missing partner, that what we are also used to seeing emerge in the place of the real, namely fantasy, is constituted.

I almost regret having in this way said enough, which always means too much. For one must see the radical difference of what is produced at the other pole on the basis of woman. Next time, I will try to enunciate in a way that stands up – that, for woman – but write woman with the slanted line with which I designate what must be barred – for Woman, something other than *objet a* is at stake in what comes to make up for the sexual relationship that does not exist.

RM: So, would you like to articulate that in your own words?

GF: It sounds like he is developing an analogy between the Name of the Father and Aristotle's 'Unmoved Mover'.

RM: Yes! And I was thinking more about what's under primary repression – it's what moves everything. But, what's under primary repression is a 'signified'. So, if we think about it in terms of the signifier and the signified, the signifier would be the Name of the Father and the signified is the fantasy object of the mother. So, both the Name of the Father and the object of the mother's desire are in the place of the Unmoved Mover from the point of view of psychic development.

The Name of the Father cannot be dissociated from the Desire of the Mother – they are a pair. It's a signifier/signified pair. And so the Name of the Father is the primary repression – it's the repressive force – and the object that is the cause of the mother's desire is the repressed in the primal repression. Now, what Lacan is saying here is that, on the one hand, 'yes, Freud was right' ... it's always about who has it and who doesn't have it (who's 1, who's –1 ... who gets the 'short end of the stick') ... and it's all that way in the Imaginary. It's all about this Imaginary phallus that is at play and circulating between the sexes. But where is femininity there, if it's just this $+\varphi$ and this $-\varphi$, which seems phallocentric? So he is saying, although that is going on, there is something more that I have to tell you about 'woman' that is in a different register than what Freud was talking about in terms of the relationship between the sexes as being mediated by this imaginary object. Who has it? Who doesn't have it? Who is it? Who is not it? Who's in? Who's out? Who's the new guy for the woman? Who is the new woman for the guy? So now he is going to begin unfolding his new view of femininity in the Real. And that woman is 'barred' because it doesn't exist – but 'it doesn't exist' means she 'ex-sists'.[2] So when you say "she doesn't exist", you could also say she 'ex-sists'. And I think that is a better way to explain it, because when he said that in Milan, it triggered all the headlines and newspapers in Italy – DR. LACAN SAYS THE WOMAN DOESN'T EXIST! – and everyone went crazy, because doesn't that sound like patriarchy all over again! We are back to square one with a woman not being able to have a self,

just being reduced to this place of nonexistence?! So that's the risk! You could (perhaps) just as well say woman 'ex-sists' or 'the woman' does not exist.
[*ALL thanks ... end of recording*]

Notes

1 Instead of this designation being the Third of the Symbolic, it becomes the Third of the Real.
2 Heidegger defined this as outside of existence when he coined the term *ek-sists*. But Lacan writes with the 'x' rather than 'k' ... it means, for him, what we could experience of the Real before we enter into symbolic sisterhood or that which represents the interconnectedness of the symbolic in the feminine. Why? Because the first other is the mother and it is the mother that introduces the child to the Symbolic order. Lacan also said that the mother represents the structural layers of Mother Earth. So, 'ex-istence' is what stands before the interconnectedness of the system of symbols.

Supplemental References

Freud, Sigmund. (1915). Repression. *SE* 14.
Freud, Sigmund. (1915). The Unconscious. *SE* 14.
Heidegger, M. (1927). *Being and Time: A Translation of Sein und Zeit*. Albany: State University of New York Press, 1996.
Heidegger, M. (1943). "On the Essence of Truth". *Basic Writings* (Revised and Expanded Edition), D. F. Krell (trans.), London: Routledge, 1993.
Lacan, J. (1972–1973). *Encore. The Seminar of Jacques Lacan, XX*. New York: Norton, 1998.
Lacan, J. (1975–1976). *The Sinthome. The Seminar of Jacques Lacan. Encore, Seminar XXIII*, London: Polity Press, 2016.
Žižek, S. (1989). *The Sublime Object of Ideology*. London: Verso.

Chapter 13

Differences among Femininity, Mystical Jouissance, and Psychosis

Moncayo Seminar, December 14, 2017 *Encore, Seminar XX*, pg. 122

TEXT: What cuts a line is a point. Since a point has zero dimensions, a line is defined as having one dimension. Since what a line cuts is a surface, a surface is defined as having two dimensions. Since what a surface cuts is space, space has three dimensions.

The little sign I wrote on the blackboard (Figure 1) derives its value therefrom. It has all the characteristics of writing – it could be a letter. However, since you write cursively, you never think of stopping a line before it crosses another in order to make it pass underneath, or rather in order to assume that it passes underneath, because in writing something completely different from three-dimensional space is involved.

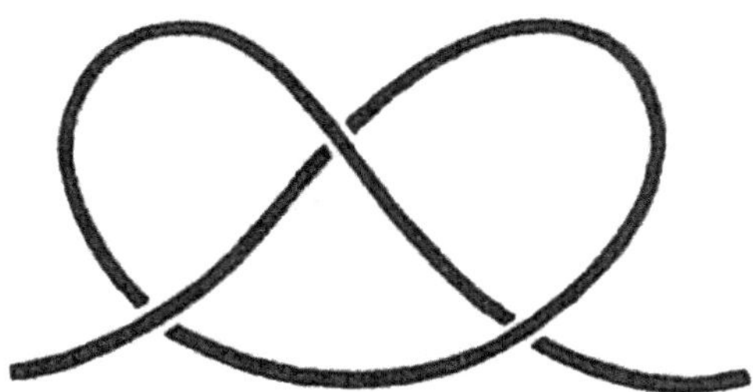

In this figure, when a line is cut by another, it means that the former passes under the latter. That is what happens here, except that there is only one line. But although there is only one, it is distinguished from a simple ring, for this writing represents for you the flattening out (*mise*-à-*plat*) of a knot. Thus, this line or string is something other than the line I defined earlier with respect to space as a cut and that constitutes a hole, that is, separates an inside from an outside.

RM: Okay, shall we unpack this? [*Agreement*] So, there is the possibility of two dimensions versus having more dimensions, right? So, in writing, you just have two dimensions – but, in topology, you have three dimensions. So, with three dimensions, you can see what goes over and what goes underneath.

DOI: 10.4324/9781003424581-13

That's one of the points he is making, because, to make a knot, you have to put the string underneath or over the top.

GF: And, so topology can be something that signifies as well … it could be like the letter?

RM: Yes, but with topology you have significance, because you have a topological structure rather than a linguistic structure. In a linguistic structure, you have signification, but in a topological structure, since the meaning is in the Real, you have significance (*signifiance*). But then he says, you can flatten out a knot, even though it has three dimensions, you can flatten it out to where it just looks like two dimensions. And then, this line or string is something other than the line I defined earlier with respect to space as a cut and that constitutes a hole. I am guessing that he is referring to when you convert a straight line into a circle, then you have a hole inside the circle. So, the surface of the circle, which was the concern of the early Greek mathematicians, is understood to become a hole.

GF: So, is the significance of that the lack that always occurs?

RM: Well, he separates an inside from an outside. That's with the body, right, but I am not sure this is the same thing. In the holes of the body, or the organism, there is a differentiation between 'an inside' and 'an outside'. The inside of the ear, the outside of an ear; the inside of a mouth, the outside of a mouth. Let's say if you think of the circle as a mark, it marks space – it separates the 'unmarked' from the 'marked'. The 'unmarked' has been 'marked' inside the circle. But then if you convert the inside of the circle into a hole, rather than mere space … let me pose this as a question: What is the difference between the surface that is outside the circle and the surface that's inside the circle? What's the difference between that and what's inside the circle as 'hole', which then marks the difference between the inside of the hole and the outside of the circle?

BB: Well, the hole is circumscribed outside by the circle, and the circle is not – it does not have a line around it, so we don't know the limits of the space.

RM: Yes, the space inside the circle is circumscribed, but you could say that of a surface.

BB: But the surface is not the space.

RM: Let's say you have a canvas, and you draw a circle on the canvas. That creates a difference between the inside and the outside of the circle. Now, if you cut out the inside of the circle with a pair of scissors, then you have a hole that is discontinuous with the space outside the circle. So, that's a different notion of inside and outside, isn't it?

BB: Yes, then when the space is the same on both sides, so we are just changing the content.

GF: And one is empty and the other is not. The hole is the null set. So, if it is a circle that defines a surface, it's different from a circle with a hole in it.

RM: Right, that's the question. And I am not clear about the difference between the unmarked outside of the circle, the uncircumscribed space, and the unmarked in terms of what's inside the hole. I suspect that this is something to do with the curvature of space-time, but, again, I am not clear exactly how. But, in any case, the point that Lacan is making is to posit the idea that the 'inside the circle' is not a circumscribed surface or space, but that it's a hole. It's sort of the difference between if you make a hole in the ground, you create a cavity of space, but the space is circumscribed by matter. As opposed to the space that is out there in the universe that's not circumscribed by matter, and it is not subject to the gravity of the matter. So, presumably, there is space out there that is not subject to or not near any body of matter … what's the difference between that space and the space circumscribed within a hole in the earth or a hole within our bodies? I'm happy with just formulating the question at this point.

GF: I think it raises a question that I am assuming was also prevalent in Lacan's time, which was the notion of whether space was relative or absolute. The idea of 'absolute' space implies that all matter exists, or is contained within space (i.e., space is defined as a container), as opposed to 'relative' space, where space is always defined by points, a line, or the distance between some kind of matter.

RM: Right, and with the Big Bang theory there's energy, and then there is matter, and space is a function of the expansion – so, that seems to be relative space.

GF: Yes, I think the problem leaned historically to the relative side, despite a few physicists that have presented strong arguments for the absolute position …

RM: I guess the argument is that the universe has grown so big, so now you have big stretches of space without any matter in it … but it still has small particles that were part of the Big Bang – so in that sense, it would still be relative space. Accordingly, even that space that is outside the circle is still circumscribed space.

GF: Right, so it's always relative to the circumscription.

RM: Yes, it's just that the circumscription doesn't come from the circle.

GF: But isn't there the circumscription the circle represents that then defines the 'outside' as well?

RM: The circle is like a planet, a formation, or a consolidation of matter. But perhaps this is more of a question for physics, and it may not be productive for us at this point, other than raising the question of the nature of space in relation to the hole.

GF: Yes, but it is interesting to think of the circumscription as being a way of defining the inside and the outside, and there also is 'front' and 'back'.

RM: 'Front' and 'back' would be the third dimension and would be a sphere instead of a circle.

GF: Yes, and every circumscription that is geometric, and not just linear, has three dimensions.

RM: That's why it is topological rather than geometrical.

TEXT: This new line is not so easily incarnated in space. The proof is that the ideal string, the simplest string, would be a torus. And it took a long time for people to realize, thanks to topology, that what is enclosed in a torus has absolutely nothing to do with what is enclosed in a bubble. Regardless of what you do with the surface of a torus, you cannot make a knot. But on the contrary, with the locus of a torus, as this shows you, you can make a knot. It is in this respect, allow me to tell you, that the torus is reason, since it is what allows for knots.

RM: Okay, so what he is saying is that in the double torus – the torus is like a donut – you make a knot by putting the string through a hole or putting a line through a hole (and then you create another circle). But, for a torus, it has the distinction of having two holes – the hole that is circumscribed by the tube and the hole that is inside the tube. So, there are two voids there, two holes. Whereas in a bubble, you only have only one hole, only one space inside the bubble.

GF: [*Agrees*] So, why does he say the torus is reason?

RM: I understand it as the articulation between the positive and negative propositions, or the affirmations and negations, and reasoning functioning according to this 'knotting' between universals and particulars, positives/negatives, affirmation/negation, et cetera.

GF: So, reason represents the demarcation or the circumscription – and he uses the term circumspection.

RM: And the relations between the negative and the affirmative or the particular and the universal. We have that in both formal logic and dialectical logic … in the square of oppositions in Aristotle and the dialectical logic in Hegel. So, it seems to pervade different types of reason, not just formal reason – this dialectic between form and emptiness.

GF: I love the analogy of that example! The torus of reason!

BB: Can you say more about that?

GF: My understanding is that the idea of having a demarcation is not only 'making the cut' somewhere between particularity and universality, but the relation of the two is also maintained. So, any time a demarcation is made, a knot is formed, or some kind of stitch. And that is analogous to reason: that is what reason does.

BB: It creates a link between universal and particulars?

GF: Yes, it both circumscribes and divides – it is the ordering structure. Is that reasonable? [*Chuckling*]

TEXT: It is in that respect that what I am showing you now, a twisted torus, is as neat (sec) an image as I can give you of the trinity, as I qualified it the other day – one and three in a single stroke (Figure 2).

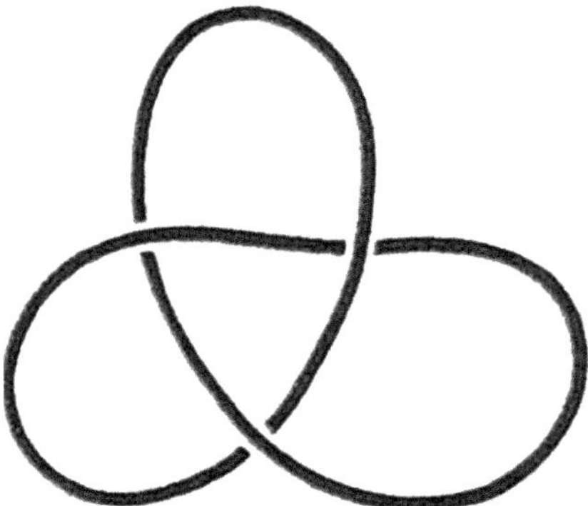

RM: There's another concept that may be helpful in this regard, and that is the distinction between a unary and a binary negation. With the unary negation, what's negated is unmarked, in the sense of the negative pointing to some emptiness, rather than simply to the negation of a positive term. So, unary negation doesn't have a value that is negated. What is negated is simply the 'unmarked', not the 'marked'. So, when Lacan says, "what in the woman is in the Real" or "she does not exist", it means that what she is in the Real is unmarked (other than she is a form of jouissance). Or, if you said, a woman is not a man, then you would be saying that a woman is a negation of man – that's a binary negation. When a woman is something that cannot be described with the affirmative signifier, she is functioning under a unary negation. So, when Lacan says, a woman does not exist, it is not a binary negation, but a unary negation. And you can use the difference between 'not' and 'non', wherein 'non' is a unary negation and 'not' is a binary negation. There you are defining what a woman is by denying her the quality of a man – that's a binary definition of woman versus the definition of a woman on the basis of what is unmarked within femininity … that is, what's outside the Symbolic or what's in the Real.

BB: What this means to me is that there is a way of acknowledging something that exists that is unmarked. So, there is something defined about the way a woman exists that is not like a dictionary definition that requires reference to something else, but rather can be supposed, so that the Real that is a woman is unmarked.

RM: Yes, but it is experienced.

BB: So, people saying, "this is what it is", which leads to a constricting feeling that it is only this one thing that is defined, is different from saying a woman is defined as this something that has two relations – one, to our systems of pluses and minuses (blacks and whites, not this, but that), and two, to its own relationship to something larger that can be experienced, but we don't have a way to mark it or relate to it. I suppose it can be marked by someone else's language, or the Other's …

RM: Right, but the Real always escapes the signifier or signification because there is no signifier for it.

BB: So, it changes the sense for me of the notion 'in itself', which impacts on the quality that feeling the responsibility for a life will take. It feels different. If such a space exists, as the unary negation suggests, one doesn't find one's place in the world by having one's ideal form just come out of one so that one becomes what God made you. There's a passivity to that…

GF: So, is it somehow circumscribed by the phallic signifier?

RM: That defines the position of femininity in relation to the phallus on the one side, and something beyond the phallus on the other side.

GF: Because the phallic signifier cannot be known?

RM: Well, the phallic signifier is always a signifier of a lack. So, an absence of what? But then, in the lack is also an access to the Real. That's an emptiness of presence rather than an emptiness of absence. So, the signifier of a lack is the emptiness of an absence, like the woman doesn't have the phallus – that's a kind of Freudian definition of a woman within the phallocentric signifying system. But, if you interpret the lack as an access to the Real within the Symbolic, that gives you the other definition of emptiness of presence … something that is unmarked, outside the system of marks.

GF: So, the unary trace always comes, not as a mark, but as a mark of the unmarked?

RM: Exactly. That's the first form, the unary numeral system, which is just a system of tallies of marks … and that's a positive … but it was used to mark a death that stays outside the system of marks. Unless you say, it's just all these marks that represent a dead animal (which they did), but, pretty soon, when the marks are turned into diacritical marks, and there is a measurable distance between the units, and you also have a system of numbers and signifiers, then the reference to the unmarked is lost – unless you have a concept of zero.

GF: I see that! So, the originary or unary mark would be marking something that's not there. But, once that mark is made, it's almost as if it creates pressure toward a system to give the mark its understanding. It then shifts to a diacritical position, whereby the unary trace endures but the mark itself is subject to change …

RM: Well, when you have integers, and you have zero and a unit that creates a 'one', and a 'one two', a 'two three', a 'three four' … it's the same unit repeated, instantiated each time. Then you have the system of marks that evolved from the unary system, but it is all discrete. Within the Symbolic, meaning cannot be defined in isolation and is a function of the relative relations between signifiers.

GF: So, the significance of it slips into the system.

RM: Right, they play off each other. But here's the difference ... when the 'one' becomes a diacritical distance, that's a unary trait. When it functions just as a trace, without the issue of distance between the two, then it's just a trace because it contains the reference to the unmarked. It's the mark of the unmarked, whereas the unary trait is just a mark within a system of marks. So, in a sense, masculinity is on one side and femininity is on the other. And, in terms of the feminine, the marks were also used. The oldest marks in the Ishango bones, where you have groups of traces that are grouped together in terms of prime numbers. Those were used to mark the reproductive cycle of a woman, which has to do with life and death. So, the unary system was a product of hunters, where the mark represents a killed animal. And, in using the numeral system to mark the reproductive cycles of the woman is for the purpose of life.

GF: But that is still not a unary trait, is it?

RM: Right, it is not a unary trait because they are still using a tally system.

GF: So, it could either be a negative unmarked or a positive unmarked.

RM: Yes, but at the level of the unmarked, the positive and the negative are the same. So, if you say that it documents the absence of an animal ... I had five cows, and I killed one – now I have four. But the unmarked acquires a larger meaning than simply the absence of a particular animal that was killed. So, there are different types of 'unmarked'. I think that either refers to the absence of something or the presence of something that doesn't have a mark.

GF: I would like to revisit this now that I am beginning to see the differences more clearly.

BB: Yes, me too!

GF: And it is fascinating that we arrived here starting with only a piece of string!

[*End of recording*]

Supplemental References

Lacan, J. (1972–1973). *Encore. The Seminar of Jacques Lacan, XX*. New York: Norton, 1998.

Chapter 14

Agape and Eros, the G-d of the Law and the G-d of Jouissance

Moncayo Seminar, June 29, 2017, *Encore, Seminar XX*, pg. 74

MK: Okay, so we are on page 74 …

TEXT: There is a jouissance, since I am confining myself here to jouissance, a jouissance of the body that is, if I may express myself thus – why not make a book title out of it? It'll be the next book in the Galilee collection – "beyond the phallus". That would be cute, huh? And it would give another consistency to the women's liberation movement. A jouissance beyond the phallus ….

You may have noticed – I am naturally speaking here to the few semblances of men I see here and there, fortunately I don't know them for the most part, and that way I don't presume anything about the others – that now and then, there is something that, for a brief moment, shakes (*secoue*) women up or rescues them (*secourt*).

RM: Interesting how he uses the 'few semblances of men', because he is talking about persons as 'semblances' or 'men' as 'semblances' … okay.

TEXT: There is a jouissance that is hers (*à elle*), that belongs to that "she" (*elle*) that doesn't exist and doesn't signify anything.

FOOTNOTE: "The so-called third person [he, she, or it] doesn't exist".

RM: Yeah, that's a little bit of a different meaning of doesn't exist, because he is talking about psychosis and the way the psychotic talks about the Other as an 'other' that doesn't exist – meaning the other only exists as a fantasy in the subject because the relationship to the [big] Other is damaged. The Other doesn't exist means something different than the woman 'doesn't exist', but he is linking them in some way.

TEXT: There is a jouissance that is hers about which she herself perhaps knows nothing if not that she experiences it – that much she knows.

DOI: 10.4324/9781003424581-14

RM: The outside meaning is different in femininity and psychosis. In psychosis the outside meaning is foreclosed; in femininity it is not, for there is no foreclosure of the Father in femininity. People think that the 'outside meaning' in femininity is the same as the 'outside meaning' for psychosis, but they are not the same because one is a neurotic structure and the other one is a psychotic structure. And, by neurotic structure, I mean normal human subjectivity. That there's a dimension of experience or of femininity that is outside meaning doesn't mean that meaning is foreclosed like in psychosis. But those two often get confused.

TEXT: She knows it, of course, when it comes (*arrive*). It doesn't happen (*arrive*) to all of them.

RM: There's another important statement. Are you familiar with that reference to femininity by Lacan – that femininity in the Real is something that women experience, but know nothing of?[1]
[*ALL agreeing*]

RM: ... because it is not in language. But it is, however, in experience.

MK: What does it mean, 'it doesn't happen to all of them'?

RM: So, for example, and I mentioned this in my last book [Moncayo 2018], Lacan in *Seminar III* [*The Psychoses*] makes a reference to Dora suggesting that Dora was trying to find something out about femininity, but she misses it and instead construes femininity as something related to masculinity (which is something a hysteric may do often) – but what they are really seeking is the Real in femininity. But, since women can't access it, then they construe femininity in a masculine mode. So, this process doesn't happen to all women in that sense. Not all women recognize their nonexistence and emptiness. There are more Freudian women than Lacanian women. Most women identify with masculinity or identify femininity as a form of masculinity.

MK: Yes, I like using the word 'arrive' better.

RM: Yes, it doesn't 'arrive' to all of them.

MK: She knows when it arrives, but it doesn't arrive to all of them.

TEXT: The plausibility of what I am claiming here – namely that woman knows nothing of this jouissance – is underscored by the fact that in all the time people have been begging them, begging them on their hands and knees – I spoke last time of women psychoanalysts – to try to tell us, not a word! We've never been able to get anything out of them. So, we call this jouissance by whatever name we can come up with, "vaginal," and speak of the posterior pole of the uterine orifice and other such "cunt torsions" (*conneries*) – that's the word for it! If she simply experienced it and knew nothing about it, that would allow us to cast myriad doubts on this notorious (*fameuse*) frigidity.

RM: So that whole controversy about whether it's vaginal or not? Whether there are two types of orgasms or not for femininity? Are you familiar with that controversy?

MK: Yes.

BB: She is, I'm not.

MK: Of whether or not women can have vaginal orgasms?

BB: Oh, I thought you were saying there are two kinds of orgasms … I thought this was some kind of deep psychoanalytic something or other …

MK: I think it is just biology!

BB: Yes, biology I get! [*ALL laughing*]

RM: It's a controversy within feminism and it's a controversy within psychoanalysis and for women psychoanalysts.

BB: How can there be a controversy? I don't understand! And we are blushing here – you had to talk about this! [*All laughing*]

RM: This is the uncomfortable part of psychoanalysis, and we have to talk about all these things that are uncomfortable and talk about it in medical terms, and scientifically, but there are things that are difficult to talk about personally. I think there are women who don't experience vaginal orgasm and only know clitoral orgasm, so they think there is only clitoral orgasm, and that the idea of a vaginal orgasm is a fiction – or even a fiction constructed by men. But then we know, through many narratives in psychoanalysis, that some women experience one type, but most women experience both types of orgasms. And, whether a woman experiences one orgasm type or another type, it is psychical, not just biological. I guess you say, biologically, that there is a capacity of the body, the women's body, to experience both types of orgasm.

Whether a woman experiences one or another, these two types are related to phallic and feminine jouissance. What is at stake is whether a woman or a man will gravitate more to one or the other type of jouissance. I do not think that Lacan is going to make the case that vaginal orgasm is related to feminine jouissance more than clitoral orgasm, because vaginal orgasm is also related to phallic jouissance. But that's part of the territory that he is covering now. And, of course, we know Freud's theory that he thought that the clitoris was a residue of an atrophied penis that was part of a vestigial biological development and the acquisition of secondary sexual characteristics, and so on and so forth. We know he said that, and I am not sure we need that particular theory or whether it matters or is the case or not. But, for Freud, vaginal orgasm was more associated with femininity, whereas the clitoral orgasm was more associated with masculinity within females.

TEXT: That too is a theme, a literary theme. And it's worth dwelling on for a moment. I've been doing nothing but that since I was twenty, exploring the philosophers on the subject of love. Naturally, I didn't immediately focus on the question of love, but that did dawn on me at one point, with the abbot Rousselot actually, whom I mentioned earlier, and the whole quarrel about physical love and ecstatic love, as they are called.

RM: Well you know the difference between agape and love or Eros, right?
MK: Isn't agape 'friendship love' or something?
RM: Yes, agape is the non-erotic form of love, as well as the devotional form of love of G-d. However, agape in its proper place does not obstruct eros. What is the proper place of eros under creation? Well, sexual love and reproduction. The same ambiguity between eros and agape is found in the concept of sublimation. The sublime can be the product of socialization or a direct manifestation of the drive which, otherwise, Freud considers sexual. But, for Freud, love was complicated because he considered all these aspects of love, including philia or 'brotherly love', as related as opposed to being able to clearly delineate a difference.

TEXT: Mysticism isn't everything that isn't politics. It is something serious, about which several people inform us – most often women or bright people like Saint John of the Cross, because one is not obliged when one is male, to situate oneself on the side of ∀xØx (see earlier formula).

MK: Wait, don't tell me [referring to formula] ... all men are subject to castration?
RM: No, that's to situate oneself on the side of "not all of an X is in the phallic function". But what that means is that the way that men, or masculinity, gains access to the Real is through the 'experience of the mystic' or the jouissance of the mystic and the jouissance of meaning. So, women can access the Third jouissance through feminine sexuality and not just through the jouissance of the mystic. But, for masculinity, unless a male takes a feminine position, which is also possible ... short of a male taking a feminine position in sex ... the man experiences the Third jouissance in the form of the jouissance of the mystic, rather than through sexual jouissance – whereas femininity has both.

TEXT: One can also situate oneself on the side of the not whole. There are men who are just as good as women. It happens. And who also feel just fine about it. Despite – I won't say their phallus – despite what encumbers them that goes by that name, they get the idea or sense that there must be a jouissance that is beyond. Those are the ones we call mystics.

I have already spoken about other people who were not too bad in terms of mysticism, but who were situated instead on the side of the phallic function, Angelus Silesius, for example, confusing his contemplative eye with the eye with which God looks at him, must, if kept up, partake of perverse jouissance. For the Hadewijch in question, it's like for Saint Teresa – you need but go to Rome and see the statue by Bernini to immediately understand that she's coming. There's no doubt about it. What is she getting off on? It is clear that the essential testimony of the mystics consists in saying that they experience it but know nothing about it.

RM: Okay, so Lacan wants to say that "she's coming",[2] having an orgasm – do you know the statue of Bernini that he is referring to? Which would be, you know, not what the Catholic Church would say of it, but they would say she is in a mystic trance. But he's playing on the ambiguity of both in saying that, for femininity, it's both things. Meaning that there is something mystical about a woman's orgasm that is not the same for what an orgasm is for a man. Although there are traditions like in Tibetan Buddhism you have the union of the Buddha with the consort, which represents enlightenment as the sexual union of men and women, so, in that sense, sexuality could be seen as having a mystical dimension for both sexes. But I think for psychoanalysis, Lacan differentiates that in such a way … and this is interesting … when one of the years when Dany [Nobus] came to give his lectures in the school, I forget the title of his talk, but he had images of orgasms, of men and women that he found online, and he says, for men, it's all about their phallic jouissance, and you rarely see much expression – it's not about the expression at all. Whereas, all the photos of women having an orgasm, it's all about their expression as if the jouissance is all over the body or something like that … as opposed to the masculine orgasm which seems to be more instrumental. I don't know if that makes sense to you … [*ALL agreement*]

RM: But, of course, men want to possess that experience of a women's jouissance as if it were something related to them. Like women often complain that men are worried about, 'oh, how was it for you?', and they want to talk about that? Women are not inclined to talk about it in that kind of way – in that kind of instrumental way. Because men want to think that it is all about them, that they had that experience. Where you could say for a woman, it's more about her relationship to jouissance, or to God, or to the Other that is more involved, rather than being directly a result of phallic jouissance in relationship to a man. And for a man, it is a kind of narcissistic injury that they cannot possess a woman's jouissance because a woman's jouissance is in the Real.

BB: I get it.

MK: What do you get?

BB: I've never clearly understood that before. What is interesting to me is the dialectic created by the questions that focus on where I am looking to find pleasure's source: am I looking to see my pleasure in your pleasure, am I making my pleasure a function of your pleasure, or am I looking for my pleasure somewhere else? The man's pleasure, it sounds like, is that a woman can have an orgasm and he can say that this is about me, this is what I did, this is what I gave her… this is how I am understanding this – I made her do this – so, his potency is somehow demonstrated by how many orgasms she has or how good an orgasm she has. And her orgasm then is a product of his potency. But, for her, it's more an experience of oneness or something, or maybe not oneness, but her experience of a relation to something that is not just the man ... maybe the man is the vehicle there?? But it's already there ... he didn't create it for her. He may have connected her to it. But, for him, he created it. So, if a woman doesn't have an orgasm, then it means he is not a man – which is more existentially threatening for a man. For a woman, if she doesn't have an orgasm, she is not connected to it, to the possibility of orgasms ... I'm not sure she feels less of a woman, but maybe.

RM: Right! She is not connected to her own femininity, or she is not connected to phallic jouissance (either one).

BB: Is 'phallic jouissance' an orgasm? Is phallic jouissance another name for orgasm? Or do orgasms have more jouissance than just phallic?

RM: Aside from the enjoy-meant of the letter, as a preliminary form of pleasure, phallic jouissance is the act of fornication or penetration. And, so a woman, according to Lacan, has both an experience of phallic jouissance with a man, so she partakes of the phallic function in that way, but her orgasm is also in relationship to the Real of femininity. It is hard to say what this is, but this is also what produces this lack of sexual rapport, because there is this kind of built-in misunderstanding that gets translated into that preoccupation with masculinity or femininity as to whether a woman enjoyed it or not based on a narcissistic reference to his phallic narcissism. So, there is a misunderstanding that develops around that.

MK: I don't know if he means this word coming up next ... these 'mystical jaculations'?

RM: What does he mean by jaculations?

MK: I don't know! It's a neologism.

RM: Let me Google it! 'Jaculation' is the act of pitching, throwing, or hurling.[3]

TEXT: I believe in the jouissance of woman insofar as it is extra (*en plus*), as long as you put a screen in front of this "extra" until I have been able to properly explain it. What was attempted at the end of the last century, in Freud's time, what all sorts of decent souls around Charcot and others were trying to do, was to reduce mysticism to questions of cum (*affaires de foutre*). If you look closely, that's not it at all. Doesn't this jouissance one experiences and yet knows nothing about put us on the path of ex-sistence? And why not interpret one face of the Other, the God face, as based on feminine jouissance?

RM: Here he is going against Freud and psychiatry because he doesn't want to reduce the jouissance of the mystic to psychopathology or sexuality in the usual acceptance of the word. The jouissance of the mystic is asexual in reference to the *objet a* in the Real.

TEXT: As all of that is produced thanks to the being of signifierness, and as that being has no other locus than the locus of the Other (Autre) that I designate with capital A, one sees the "cross-sightedness" that results.

RM: Yes, so you are seeing double, and people are perplexed, right?

TEXT: And as that is also where the father function is inscribed, insofar as castration is related to the father function, we see that that doesn't make two gods (*deux Dieu*), but that it doesn't make just one either.

MK: I just ordered a book, *The Not Two: Logic and God in Lacan* by Lorenzo Chiesa …

RM: I have not read it … I know that he is Lacanian. Bernard Burgoyne, one of the founders of CFAR in London, recommended it. I haven't read it. Let me know if you like it and I will buy it.

MK: Yeah, I'll let you know in three years!

RM: If you read it![*ALL laughter*]

RM: So, you understand what he is saying there … isn't there G-d the Father? Or what about G-d the Father versus the G-d of the Third jouissance … are those two gods? If you say that those are two gods in the lower case, then that is idolatry and polytheism. You see, when religious people have an adversarial view of the relationship between the two gods, they are, in fact, committing idolatry. An example is when religious people criticize the mystics, and the mystics criticize orthodox religions.

Because he is saying that also, where the Father function is inscribed, insofar as castration is related to the 'father function', then that is also where we find desire. We see that it doesn't add up to two gods because Desire and Law are not two gods/ things. We need the Law in order to have Desire. We need Desire in order to have Law. We need mystical experience to have the Law: and we need the Law to go beyond it. That is the equivalence between desire and jouissance – they both evoke and escape.

BB: What's the relationship he is construing between the 'father function' and God? I don't want to read too much into it.

RM: Right … the Name of the Father is in the Name of the Father, Son, and Holy Spirit … but the Name of the Father is what Christianity took from Judaism.

BB: So, is the Name of the Father God, but also the Word? Because God says, "I am the Word". Is Lacan speaking about all three when he uses the name God: The Name of the Father, the Word, and ? …

RM: No, I believe he is just speaking here of the Name of the Father. You can relate him, in Lacanian theory, to the question of 'the Word', but God the Father in Judaism is the source of the commandments, and the prohibitions: this or that prohibition. So that's how he [Lacan] relates it to castration – sort of taking away what you are not supposed to enjoy or do, et cetera, but he's contrasting that with the dark G-d of the mystics and the G-d of jouissance which is also a classical kind of distinction within religion. There is the G-d of the mystics and then there is the G-d of the religious traditionalists, and then there is the G-d of the philosophers. You see that clearly in Judaism, where you have the G-d of the Law, and then you have the G-d of the Kabbalah (which is the G-d of the mystics). And the G-d of the mystics refers to the presence of the divine and the G-d of the Law is a remote and absent G-d.

[*Seminar interrupted by visit of Dr. Françoise Davoine, with introductions, etc.*]

RM: So, we were talking about here how Lacan is discussing the difference between G-d as 'Father' and the G-d of jouissance, and the relation between the phallic function of castration and the experience of feminine jouissance and how this relates to the jouissance of the mystics. So, I was explaining a bit about the contexts within the different religious traditions about that. What I was saying is the 'God the Father' or the 'God of the Law' is a G-d that is transcendent and is separate from its creation, whereas the G-d of the mystics is based on presence, the experience of the divine, and usually that is associated with more feminine characteristics. In Judaism, the G-d of the mystics is associated with the feminine side of G-d which is called the Shekinah. So, everything Lacan is saying here is consistent with that ancient tradition when thinking about these kinds of things.

TEXT: In other words, it's no accident that Kierkegaard discovered existence in a seducer's little love affair. It's by castrating himself, by giving up love, that he thinks he will accede to it. But perhaps, after all – why not? – Regine too existed. This desire for a good at one remove (*au second degré*), a good that is not caused by a little a – perhaps it was through Regine that he attained that dimension.

RM: I think this goes back to this distinction between agape and eros – the love that requires a loss or a renunciation versus the love that is based on our satisfaction.

BB: What does Regine mean?

MK: Regine or Regina was the woman Kierkegaard wrote about … it's a reference …

BB: Oh, yes, Kierkegaard …

RM: Right, so Regine would be the Christian or the Roman name for the *Shekinah*. The *Shekinah* is the feminine presence of G-d in Judaism.

BB: So, it seems significant, and just to deepen it … so, Lacan says, "the desire for the good at one remove, a good that is not caused by a little a – perhaps it was through Regine that he attained that dimension" … what's at stake in the desire for the Good at one remove?

RM: 'One remove', that's 'second degree' in French, right? At 'one remove' – are you familiar with the English expression, 'at one remove'?

BB: Yeah, I was just trying to connect it to a conversation we recently had about the man, who, through his jouissance and ability, may be able to give the woman an orgasm through more instrumental means, and the woman's ability to represent, or to link to that something in the Real that isn't instrumental. Is that what we are talking about? – it's not necessarily a fulfillment of her desire, but an enjoyment that isn't necessarily related to the fulfillment of a narcissistic desire.

RM: It's a jouissance that is based on the Real that's different from phallic jouissance. And, so, it's a supplemental jouissance for femininity according to Lacan. So, the good 'at one remove' would be that giving up of love – that it's removed – as opposed to the love that is caused by the experience of the *objet a.*

BB: I always thought it was going to be love through displacement … such as in utilitarian love.

RM: In Kierkegaard, it's not utilitarian. He says it's by castrating himself by giving up love that he thinks he will accede to.

MK: I just read this quote by Žižek where he says something like, "as soon as you can name the thing you love about the other you no longer love them". Or "it falls out of the realm of whatever kind of love this is if you can name it" …

RM: Well, then you have a separation between the object and the other at that point. So, the illusion then that the other is the object is broken once you name it.

MK: Françoise, it's taken us about two years to read these 77 pages!

[*ALL laughter*]

BB: But we have awesome discussions and wonder about all sorts of things! [*More laughter*]

FD: Yes, I was present at this seminar and took notes at this seminar because I started in 1969, and this is in 1972, and I remember. But I could not tell you right now what this means! [*ALL laughter*]

RM: Not that it was easy to follow him when he was there in the room!

FD: It was easy to follow him because he used to speak very slowly and to repeat himself, and to contradict himself. And so it was easy to understand him while he was speaking. But, after the seminars had been published, they have been crushed and now are so dense that you don't have time [to unpack them] … it was easy to write while he was speaking … and he was joking and people were laughing, and many of these jokes are not in the text unfortunately.

RM: That's the nice thing about the oral tradition.

FD: Exactly, he was an 'oral man'. At first, we had, as I told you, we had nothing that was published. So, what circulated were versions of smuggled seminars and they were full of contradictions. It was the text, as it had been pronounced, and it was easy to follow. But after you crush it, like in the *Écrits*, it's really one year [condensed] into 30 pages. But I am very pleased to be in that bath again! [*ALL laughter*]

End of session with Raul

BB [*addressing FD*]: It's so great to hear your experience of having been in the room … I didn't know he was easy to follow in the room …

MK: Even just having a link to and knowing someone who was there makes it come alive in some way!

FD: Yes, I started in 1969, and I remember this one. It was full of people. My first experience of Lacan was being on the roof with Jean Max of the École Normale Supérieure, which at that time was in a different location. This was at the Law school. But, at first, it was in the École Normale Supérieure when Althusser invited him. And, so, we were young and with all those very snobbish people coming, and we were throwing snowballs during the winter! [*ALL laughing*] And, even Jean Max … because at the École Normale Supérieure there were geniuses there among the students, and there was a genius there of mechanics, because you had the scientific and the literary … and his friend, the mechanic (genius), he had put in the microphone [Wagner's operatic music] *Da–da–da–da, da–da–da–da*! So, when Jacques comes out to speak, he comes out with Wagner's charge – *Da–da–da–da*, and so on! So that was joyful, you know! And, you don't have any more of that flavor of wit. Lacan was witty, a very ferocious wit – and that becomes completely expunged from the text. There is no laughing, no wit … so that's why it is so boring! [*ALL laugh*] It was a pleasure … because he used to come with … he was a clown and would say of himself, I am a clown. He used to say, "I am a clown, don't imitate me – do like me, but don't imitate me". And he would come with shoes, green and yellow, and very outrageous, but very well cut. And his cigars … he was speaking without smoking … his cigar [cigarette] completely twisted.

[*End of recording*]

Notes

1 In *Encore, Seminar XX*, see pages 60 and 76.
2 In Lacan's text, he uses the word 'coming', which refers to the action or expression of coming and/or going. The accurate English word would be "cumming". This means Lacan generalizes the act of 'coming' as going somewhere or reaching some place. Here, an interesting ambiguity opens up between the two terms – not only between the two terms but between the works of Freud and Jung. Freud would represent the view that sexuality is a generalized phenomenon and sexual orgasm is a particular function of it. Jung instead would say that there is a generalized nonsexual universal activity of coming and going and the sexual orgasm is the particular instance of that. The generalization is sexual for Freud while nonsexual for Jung. The function or the instance is the same in both.
3 https://www.merriam-webster.com/dictionary/jaculation

Supplemental References

Freud, Sigmund. (1920). *Beyond the Pleasure Principle*. SE 18.

Kierkegaard, S. 1813–1855. (1985). *Fear and Trembling*. Harmondsworth, Middlesex, England: New York: Penguin Books; Viking Penguin.

Lacan, J. (2007). *Écrits* (B. Fink, Trans.). WW Norton, New York.

Lacan, J. (1955–1956). *Psychoses. The Seminar of Jacques Lacan, III*. New York: Norton, 1995.

Lacan, J. (1972–1973). *Encore. The Seminar of Jacques Lacan, XX*. New York: Norton, 1998.

Moncayo, R. (2018). *Knowing, Not-Knowing, and Jouissance: Levels, Symbols, and Codes of Experience in Psychoanalysis*. London: Routledge.

Žižek, S. (1989). *The Sublime Object of Ideology*. London: Verso.

Chapter 15

The Different Meanings of S_2, the Signifier as Semblance

Moncayo Seminar, February 6, 2018, *Encore, Seminar XX*, pg. 122

RM: … but the one that I really like is the sign theory of Jacob von Uexküll. He was a Dutch biologist and he had this notion of the *umwelt*. He influenced Heidegger and other people. And, he has a really interesting way of thinking about signs within the body, the physiology of the body, and in how it may relate to the signifier. So, it's a useful field [semiotics] because actually it could help with psychosomatic breaks and other somatic phenomena, which is so difficult in our field – so, it has that promise. But the interesting thing is that we have signifier and signified, right? Can I bore you with this for five minutes?

BB: You never bore us! Unfortunately, you can never bore us – that's the trouble! You can talk but you cannot bore us! [*Laughing*]

RM: Yeah, you're so funny! Okay, so we have the signifier/signified relation, right? But von Uexküll talks about the 'meaning carrier' and the 'meaning utilizer'. So, the meaning carrier is like a physical object, or it could be a mental object like air is a physical object and sound is a mental object. And then, we have the human signifiers. And, then we have the nonhuman signs, in animal bodies, and how these interact. So, because of the meaning carrier … and I still like the concept of the signifier better because it encapsulates the signifier as a meaning carrier. It's a unit of signification. And, the meaning utilizer is the organism, where it's a subject or it's a self, and signs are signified of the organism. Here's where the signified is in the organism, which in Lacanian theory would say it's the signifier in the Real. But, then, it also duplicates into the 'sensor' and the 'effector' for the sensory motor. So, the sensor is the signifier and the effector, the motor response, is the signified. And then, it also duplicates in communication with 'sender' and 'receiver'. You have a sender, you have a receiver, you have a signifier and signified, and you have a self and other. Then you have a message and code, which is the message that we give, and then the code that is needed to interpret the message. So, I thought that all those categories are kind of

DOI: 10.4324/9781003424581-15

related. But I kind of like – no surprise – the signifier/signified as a category that is kind of an umbrella for all these terms. But, then it's good to be able to develop connections between the signifier and the signified, and all these different categories that semioticians use not only to describe physiological or physical signs. And, you know, how we talk about the analogy between the chain of signifiers as a mental unit, and then the chain of neurons as a biological unit? And then we ask, are these two in an analogous relationship which would lead us perhaps astray because they need to be analyzed separately? … because they're in different domains? And yet, there is an analogy between them. There's an analogy between them and then von Uexküll says, "… is the analogy merely the result of a romantic anthropomorphic interpretation of nature or are we confronted here with a case of homomorphy, a fundamental principle that recurs in different levels of complexity, in different ways? It always is basically the same form. A principle which perhaps involves a hidden genetic correlation". So, the homomorphism is more than an analogy, right? It's a principle that's governing how the sign or the signifier appears in these different domains – in a cultural domain, or physical domain, or biological domain, animal domain, et cetera. So, I thought that was really cool.

GF: Yes, it makes me think about the pursuits of computational psychiatry, where there is this idea of identifying and coding biological aspects of neurology into symbolic representations or schemas.

RM: Right, but the problem is that the concept of representation in computer science is very simplistic and a kind of a poor concept because it's divorced from the history of Western thought, unlike psychoanalysis, which can be traced back to the Greeks, both in experience and knowledge. So, the computer model doesn't have the relationship to jouissance – that's the problem, there's no jouissance in a computer model. Therefore, you would have a psychiatry without the human experience … which would be a real, lamentable condition because then it would be psychiatry becoming just like a machine and something that a computer could do. The computer will replace the psychiatrist, the human psychiatrist, because the computer will be able to read all the signs and give the right medicine and better diagnosis than a human being – better prescriptions than a human being since a computer can review all the literature and all the side effects which psychiatrists cannot keep track of … you know, the most recent literature. So, the computer would be a better psychiatrist, but that wouldn't be psychiatry anymore, because psychiatry means the healing of the psyche. I will raise my objection to that, so that we put this computer psychiatry model in its place as a necessary and important tool to use, perhaps. But psychiatry will have to be regulated by humans as a human discipline … not as something that could be replaced by computer programming.

GF: I guess the principle that computational psychiatry is based on is the idea that the brain is like a computer of symbols, like a 'symbolic computer'. And that it does that in a biological fashion. It has its biological hard drive!

RM: Yes but thought and the symbolic need other levels of reason that the computer will never have. So, there will always be a divide between the human and the computer as far as we know. Computers can provide a good service to the human, but not a lot more than that. And otherwise, we're going to have this kind of awful dystopia ... who was that American writer?

BB: Aldous Huxley?

RM: Yes! Huxley! So, we have to support that and at the same time criticize it.

GF: Well, there is a kind of a calculation of representations that happen when I think, when you think, when we think. It's probably a little different, but ...

RM: Sure, it is the aspect of the brain that is like a machine. But the mind is more than the brain ... that's the thing! The mind is a lot more than the brain.

GF: Right, but they're both one side of the same coin? The brain and the mind, one coin, two sides?

RM: Yes, but the mind needs to regulate the brain. That's how we are self-made because the mind controls the wiring of the brain. So, we have some agency in creating a culture that comes through levels of humanity that are not fully accounted for just by the reduction to the brain.

GF: That's a compelling argument. I'm just trying to think about Lacan now, in terms of how the mind controls the brain, and thinking about the 'mirror stage' and that whole complex where the infant is beginning to distinguish the Imaginary and the Symbolic. In that whole process, I believe you are right with respect to the mind always being the one that gives the brain the food, the impetus ... you know ... the direction of intent.

RM: And there's also the question of jouissance, the question of passion – we've covered this in the seminar – compassion, dispassion, and all those transformations of jouissance that are part of the human experience that are not present in a computer. The computer can follow a program, you know, like the Nazis. The computer program has no qualms about executing its operations. So, I think this is the importance of psychoanalysis ... to hold the line on the question of the mind ... nature gave us these brilliant psychiatrists who are psychoanalysts you know, not for nothing. We have Freud, we have Bion, we have Winnicott, we have Lacan. We have these great psychiatrists who are pushing psychiatry in a different direction than just simply biological computational psychiatry, thank goodness! So, we have to tow that line – not be against the machine and the symbolics of the machine. And maybe I should send my recent chapter devoted to that that we covered in my other seminar, where I look at ... because, in the seminar, there's a lady who's a computer scientist who's training as a psychoanalyst. So, she wrote something developing Freud and Lacan ... and Lacan already developed models for the Symbolic as a cybernetic machine at the time of c. 1955–1960. Sheryl Brahnam, who has her PhD in computer science, wrote a paper that mathematically was more intricate than Lacan but ignored that Lacan later abandoned cybernetics as a model for psychoanalysis. So, she picked it up, and I was asked to review her paper[1]; her mathematical understanding is much more intricate than Lacan's. But she follows basically Lacan's model for a cybernetic or mechanistic way of defining the Symbolic order. This is not that different from the computational models of mind, really, but, you know, 20 years earlier. And that's why I wrote a response … I was asked to review her work and I wrote a response that became the basis for a chapter. And that's the argument, on the one hand, saying, yes, the machine is a good representation of the Symbolic order. But, actually, that's Lacan of 1955, and he moves past that. Then he brings the Real and jouissance … and the Real and jouissance were no longer in the cybernetic model. The editor of the journal was not sure if the paper had literary or linguistic importance, or if it could be applied to literary criticism. In literary studies, mathematics is a weakness of understanding social and literary phenomena. Since I work analytically in the social world and with social facts, mathematical abstraction, that is only relevant for robots, may not be accurate for human beings.

BB: Thank you for explaining that. So, where are we in the text?

GF: Starting Section 4, page 129?

TEXT: It is not enough to have found a general solution to the problem of Borromean knots, for an infinite number of Borromean knots. We must find a way to demonstrate that it is the only solution. But as of our point in time today, there is no theory of knots. Currently, there is no mathematical formalization applicable to knots, apart from a few little constructions like those I showed you, that allows us to foresee that a solution like the one I just gave is not simply ex-sistent, but necessary, in other words, that it doesn't stop – as I define the necessary – being written. I'm going to show it to you right away. It suffices for me to do this (refer to Figure 3).

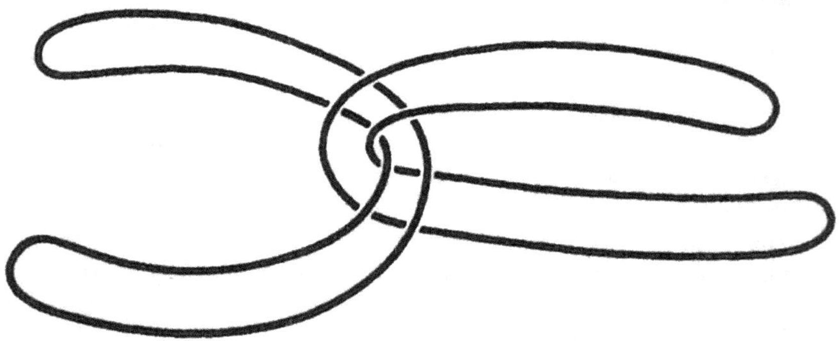

I just passed one of these rings around the other in such a way that they form not the kind of bending I showed you earlier, but simply a sailor's knot. You immediately see that I can, without any difficulty, pursue the operation on either side by making as many sailor's knots as I like, with all the rings of string in the world.

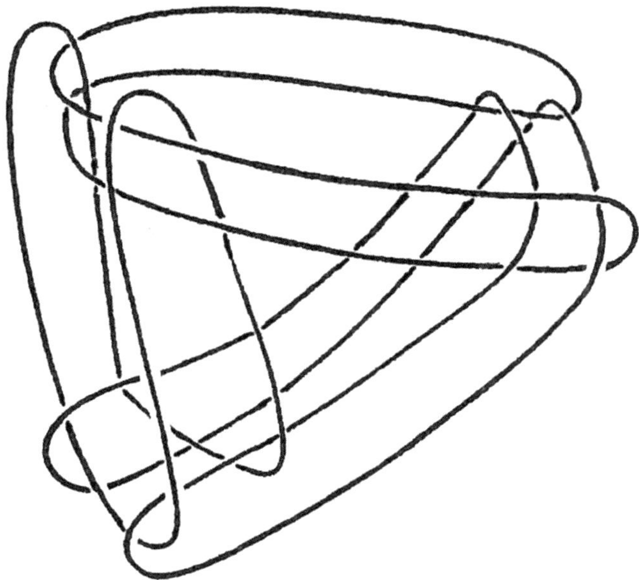

Here too I can close the chain, thereby eliminating the separability these elements had hitherto retained. I use a third ring to join the two ends of the chain (see Figure 4). Here, without any doubt, we have a solution which is just as valid as the first. The knot enjoys the Borromean property that if I cut any one of the rings that I have arranged in this way, all the others are set free.

None of the rings here is any different from the others. There is no privileged point and the chain is strictly homogeneous. You realize that there is no topological analogy between the two ways of knotting the rings of string I showed you. In the case of the sailor's knots, there is what might be called a topology of twisting compared to the preceding one, which is simply one of bending. But it wouldn't be contradictory to use bent rings in a sailor's knot.

Hence you see that the question arises of knowing how to set a limit to the solutions of the Borromean problem. I will leave the question open.

What is at stake for us, as you have realized, is to obtain a model of mathematical formalization. Formalization is nothing other than the substitution of what is called a letter for any number of ones. What does it mean when we write that inertia is, $mv^2/2$, if not that, whatever the number of ones you place under each of those letters, you are subject to a certain number of laws – laws of grouping, addition, multiplication, and so on.

RM: So, there he's aware of what formalization means in mathematics. The problem is that it leads some people to say that Lacan formalized psychoanalysis – you know, like Freud invented it and Lacan formalized it. But mathematicians criticize that because Lacan didn't really formalize it and it's not translatable into arithmetic. So, in this case, Lacan got it right that these letters have to be replaced with numbers. And that's why they're somewhat formalized because they function within the *Principia Mathematica*. When you have letters that function within numbers, as in the *Principia Mathematica*, then it is formalized. But, since Lacan's theory cannot be translated into numbers, it is strictly speaking formal in a logical sense, but not in a mathematical sense. I say this because I once went to Barcelona and presented there, and there was this one analyst who was initially so enthusiastic about Lacan's use of mathematics that he went to get a doctorate in mathematics and logic. And so he knew a lot about logic and mathematics, and he told me that he had changed his mind and that at this point, he did not like the idea of formalization for psychoanalysis, because they pretend to know something about mathematics that they don't. I mean Lacan did, but a lot of Lacanians don't. And, strictly speaking, he didn't formalize it in the sense that his theory can be translated into numbers – at least, so far.

GF: But it's formal in the sense of using the elements of topological geometry?

RM: Right, so he's using different mathematical models. He's using nonempirical mathematical models, but they're not translatable into number computation.

GF: Well, yeah, because it really doesn't matter, because any of these could be scaled. I mean, they sort of have this character which can undergo infinite scaling.

RM: What do you mean by that?

GF: What I mean is that you could have small rings of string, or large rings of string, or multiple numbers of string. But, whatever the size, the shape is always there. So, the numbers that could be represented are of an infinite variety.

BB: Oh, I see, that's interesting. That makes sense, right?

RM: So, you could translate it into numbers when you scale them?

GF: Well, it doesn't matter because if it was scaled you would still never have a key [standard] for the scaling. So, it's formalized by the shape itself, but the shape and the shape configuration could be changed into any infinitude of numbers. It could be scaled – we could have a big ring, we could have a small ring, we could bend it this way, we could bend it that way. It would always be a relative number, based on how it is that you formulated the shape.

BB: That makes sense to me in the way of formalizing it, but the math has to add up. This is not presumed to have an equal sign. It's formalizing it in a way that could have substance to it, there's still a great number of varieties. Does that make sense?

RM: It does, but I want to be convinced! [*Laughing*]

GF: Did you follow me about what I was saying about these shapes?

RM: Yes, because the shapes could be in any kind of form and the form itself is always there. However, they could always be different if you were actually to calculate the measurements in numbers. Okay. It's just that the bar, as far as empiricism is concerned, is to be able to transform things into the *Principia Mathematica* system, right?

GF: Right. And you wouldn't ultimately be able to in the end.

RM: Right, the way they do it in psychology today is that they have questionnaires and assign Likert scale values to the answers and the questions, you know, and that kind of thing, but I don't know how we would do that because ... anyway, let's not go there.

GF: No problem. But I think that is a considerable possibility suggested by Lacan's use of the topology.

RM: Yes, and he uses topology, he uses graphs, he uses mathemes. So, all these different mathematical models that he uses, which sort of feels like Plato saying that all the sciences have to be modeled after mathematics, right? So, it's modeled after mathematics, but it's not computational.

GF: That's the perfect way to put it because it's computationally indefinite. And, yet, what is indefinite and what is finite is the particular shape, the bend – the bend this way, or the bend that way? Or the fact that you have just the ring of string, which, of course, is an analogy for symbolic representation.

RM: Well, psychoanalysis uses 'consciousness', 'mind', and 'subjectivity', right? And these are terms that empirical psychology doesn't use. And Peirce is kind of right in there because sometimes he defines semiosis in terms of phenomenology along with mind and consciousness. And other times he says that these signs have nothing to do with consciousness or phenomenology or the mind, right, which then seems to put it more in the camp of the so-called scientific model. But it's interesting that he tries it both ways and doesn't reconcile it.

GF: Right. So, from what I understand about Peirce, he was very interested in metaphysics early on in his career and was writing essays, like 'A Guess at the Riddle', where he took these stabs at speculative philosophy, creation theory, and how it is that things exist, generally speaking. And, I believe, before he gets into a full-blown system of semiosis, he's got this basic idea that creation is just a matter of 'ones', 'twos', and 'threes'. And the 'ones' are kind of like indeterminate forms or ideas that stem out of the creative mind of the universe. And, these are forms like whiteness, or hardness, largeness – all of these kinds of principles that only can be recognized when they're in contrast against one another. And those contrasts are the 'twos'. So, the world is made up of the 'ones', which you never can fully know or experience (things-in-themselves). But they represent a kind of principle or law that's underneath (or within) all determinate things. And, then the 'twos' emerge from contrast, which you can get a sense of when you, for instance, juxtapose pure colors in relation to one another and qualify their difference. And, finally, once you interpret or give representation to say 'redness' and contrasting 'greenness', the signs of 'red' and 'green' emerge as the 'threes' or the thirds just because they are representing (commonly agreed upon) signs designating these particular colors. So, the sign representations, 'red' and 'green' are 'thirds', but red and green as qualities (or qualia) are 'firsts' … and when they are contrasted with one another, they are 'seconds'. And then underneath red and green as forms of quality, you have 'color' and 'light spectrum', and these are deeper abstractions that we infer. And so [for Peirce] semiotics comes out of that, and it mirrors that idea in Peirce's development of the concepts of the icon, the index, and the symbol. So, some people try to point out that Lacan's understanding of the Real is similar to Peirce's 'one[s]'. And then, Lacan's Symbolic register like the realm of 'the thirds' and 'the seconds' are the Imaginary.

RM: Because they are differentiated by a code?

GF: It could be, but I don't know if it totally plays out. Peirce was not thinking about such possibilities, of course, in the same way as later semioticians. He was thinking more in terms of signs emerging causally from metaphysical creation.

RM: How did he define metaphysics?

GF: Just as the study of the relation of things that are at hand – worldly phenomenon. You know, it's like the de facto ground of the very presence of signs ….

RM: But why is that metaphysics?

GF: I understand Western tradition to define ontology as the study of Being-Itself and metaphysics as the study of the relations of things in Being. And cosmology is the study of space and time in relation to all those determinate relative things in the world, which also depends on there being something there as Being.

RM: Okay, because people often think that metaphysics refers to something beyond the physical but, in that sense, metaphysics is just, you know, the Platonic world of ideas. But, in terms of the embedded relations between things – how things are woven together – it is the structure basically.

GF: Yes, and that is how Aristotle perceives things, as structures. So, again, it means the study of how things are related to one another.

RM: But that word [metaphysics] is a misnomer, right?

GF: Yes, of course.

RM: It is a misnomer because people use it in so many different ways, so that you never know when people are advancing metaphysics or criticizing metaphysics! You don't know what they're advancing or what they're criticizing, because it could mean so many different things.

GF: Right, especially when you go to a place like Sedona, Arizona, you know, where metaphysics is associated with how the crystals shine forth and heal folks, and so on.

RM: But Derrida, for example, criticizes the 'metaphysics of presence'. And, when you read the definition of it, it's sort of very pedestrian, because by presence I think he means how the signified defines reality. Are you familiar with his notion?

GF: Yes.

RM: How do you understand what he means by 'metaphysics of presence'?

GF: Well, I believe he was criticizing Enlightenment thought, which believed its signifiers and classifications to be honing in on accessing full knowledge and understanding of Being. But Derrida's criticism was that what was concealed underneath that kind of knowledge was a power structure. It was a power structure that was formed by using the language a certain way, by using the knowledge structure a certain way to marginalize people that don't have access to that kind of knowledge. And, and so the 'metaphysics of presence' is a critique on what we've actually figured out about what Being is through either science or philosophy, pointing out that these knowledge classifications ultimately don't totally reveal the whole picture, because there's always that power structure of knowledge underneath that which is marginalizing something obscured.

RM: Right, but isn't that more of a definition of the ontic rather than the ontological, like mistaking the idea for the reality?

GF: I think Heidegger would say that, since he said most of the time, we are dealing with the ontical even when we think we're dealing with the ontological. And that was his criticism of the same issue. For Heidegger, the underlying fact is that there's always an 'Understanding' of Dasein that precedes how it is that we understand, or how we label our world and talk about our world.

RM: All right. So that would be the Heideggerian critique of Derrida, right? That's nice, confusing the ontic with the ontological. And the ontological is defined by the deontic, right? That which stands outside the immediate experience of how we experience the world based on our concepts. So, Heidegger's position is that you never really can place an absolute identification (signification) on Being-Itself. You, moreover, can never get to Dasein's core. And Derrida used Heidegger to say, well, not only can we not get to the core of Dasein, but we don't even know what the hell 'Dasein' is, for that whole idea of being able to have 'Dasein' as some kind of knowable structure is confusing and entails problems which indicate that even Heidegger operated out of an Enlightenment mentality, as he's always referring back to Descartes and Aristotle, right? So, even Heidegger is guilty of the 'metaphysics of presence' because he was relying on these traditional language systems. And the thing with Being is that you can't think of Being without non-Being, or emptiness. That's the undefinable quality, the non-being of the One.

GF: Yes, and I believe that really was Derrida's contribution to Heidegger's work … essentially putting the bar across Being by critiquing the concept of the copula, the "is" … for Derrida, this is represented by a crossed-out copula to create an indication of Being (is).

RM: That's Derrida. Okay, but I don't think Derrida had much of a written understanding of non-Being or emptiness, which is sort of what's undefinable about Being or experience – which is the Real.

GF: I think Derrida spent more time working with the concept of the trace.

RM: Right, but for him, there's nothing outside the text, right? That's what puts deconstruction together with hermeneutics, so there's nothing outside the text.

GF: Yes, and that was the criticism of Derrida, that he privileged the text.

RM: Right, whereas Lacan has the Real.

GF: That's why Lacan is so slippery!

RM: Yes, so it's an alternative between either, an objective reality, as in logical empiricism, where you begin with an objective reality, or the hermeneutic deconstructionist view that is just the text with nothing outside the text. Or, the Lacanian version, which is where you have an objective reality, but within the Symbolic. And then you also have this notion of the Symbolic as a limit on the Real, too, because it's not like the Real exists outside the Borromean knot. So, he agrees with Heidegger there that the 'house of language' indicates the 'beyond language' also.

GF: Yes, I agree.

RM: But, without falling into a symbolic determinism.

GF: Yes. And I think that's why Heidegger always emphasized poetry as being 'the way of thinking' and 'way of Being' because poetry opens to that position where there can be more that is spoken outside of language. In other words, there's more to it than what language reveals, but we don't get outside or beyond [the text] to find out.

RM: Well, actually, the question is, how do we get outside? Free association is a way in psychoanalysis. And, the listening of the analyst, where there's also jouissance, you know, on both sides – on the side of the analyst and on your side the analysand – that's the way that psychoanalysis is interacting with something that is not just the Symbolic. And then, in Buddhist meditation, you access the Real through meditation, because in meditation, you have thinking, but you also have non-thinking. And non-thinking is a state of mind that is not linguistic.

GF: I like that interpretation. I'd never thought of free association working therapeutically in that way.

RM: It's like what Heidegger calls thinking at the 'origin of Being' – it's a different kind of thinking. That's the kind of Western way of thinking of meditation, thinking of the origin of Being. And, Zen adds the 'non-thinking'. Dōgen is the foremost Japanese thinker and was a Buddhist Master. Have you heard of him? He plays with thinking, not-thinking and 'non-thinking'. So that's the meditation – 'thinking/'not-thinking' or 'non-thinking' – thinking is just the stream of consciousness. And not-thinking is when you try to not get caught in the stream of consciousness so that your thoughts don't define your experience. But not-thinking can also be repression, where people try to suppress their feelings or their thoughts in meditation and focus on their posture or on the breath and focus on the body. So, the ideal was non-thinking that alternates between thinking and not-thinking, where neither thinking nor not-thinking is privileged.

GF: I like the way that idea maintains openness.

RM: And not-thinking can lead to anti-intellectualism, so Dōgen was very critical of the Rinzai school in Zen where they reject thinking, and you express meaning through shouting, and hitting, and gestures, and not in language.

GF: And getting struck by sticks!

RM: Yes. But Dōgen was critical of that kind of Zen because he thought that you could also express Zen in language, which would be like poetry. So, his writing is poetic and philosophical.

GF: I'd like to learn more.

RM: There's a new translation of the Shōbōgenzō. So that's his main work, the *Shōbōgenzō* – "The Eye and Treasury of the True Law (Dharma)". There's a new translation by Kazuaki Tanahashi, who translated it into one volume, although traditionally it was in four volumes. The nice thing about Dōgen is it is difficult stuff, you know, but they're all short essays!

GF: Well, thank you so much. I unfortunately have to depart.

RM: Okay, me too, but thanks.

[*End of recording*]

Note

1 Primordia of après-coup, fractal memory, and hidden letters: Working the exercises in Lacan's seminar on "The purloined letter" by Sheryl Brahnam. In S: *Journal of the Circle for Lacanian Ideology Critique*, vol. 10 & 11, 202–244. 2017–2018.

Supplemental References

Aristotle. (2009). *The Nicomachean Ethics*. Oxford World Classics. Cambridge: Oxford University Press.

Derrida, J. (1998). *Of Grammatology*. Baltimore, MD: Johns Hopkins University Press.

Dōgen, E. (1241). *Shōbōgenzō*. London and Tokyo: Windmill Publications, 1998.

Heidegger, M. (1927). *Being and Time: A Translation of Sein und Zeit*. Albany: State University of New York Press, 1996.

Heidegger, M. (1969). "The End of Philosophy and the Task of Thinking". *Basic Writings* (Revised and Expanded Edition. Translated by D. F. Krell. London: Harper Perennial, 2008.

Huxley, A. (1932). *Brave New World*. New York: Harper Collins, 2006.

Lacan, J. (1972–1973). *Encore. The Seminar of Jacques Lacan, XX*. New York: Norton, 1998.

Peirce, Charles S. (1867, 2009). *The Essential Peirce: Selected Philosophical Writings. Volumes 1 and 2*. Peirce Edition Project (Ed.). Bloomington & Indianapolis: Indiana University.

von Uexküll, T. (1987). *The Sign Theory of Jakob von Uexküll*. In: Krampen et al. Classics of Semiotics. New York: Plenum.

Whitehead, A.N. and Russell, B. (1962). *Principia Mathematica*. Cambridge: Cambridge University Press. (First and Second Editions, 1910–1913; 1925–1927).

Chapter 16

Significance, Knotting, and 'Naughting'

Moncayo Seminar, February 27, 2018, *Encore, Seminar XX*, pg. 137

A note about the translation: Fink translates Lalangue as Llalangue. In respect to his translation, we keep both 'Lalangue' for Lacan's text and 'lalangue' for ours.

RM: Right, "to get right to the point, knowledge is an enigma" …

TEXT: To get right to the point – knowledge is an enigma. That enigma is presented to us by the unconscious, as it is revealed by analytic discourse. That enigma is enunciated as follows: for the speaking being, knowledge is that which is articulated. People could have noticed that a long time ago, because in tracing out the pathways of knowledge they were doing nothing but articulate things, centering them for a long time on being. Now it is obvious that nothing is, if not insofar as it is said that it is. I call that S_2.

You have to know how to hear that – is it of them-two (*est ce bien d'eux*) that it speaks? It is generally said that language serves to communicate. To communicate about what, one must ask oneself, about which them (*eux*)? Communication implies reference. But one thing is clear – language is merely what scientific discourse elaborates to account for what I call 'llanguage'.

BB: This feels kind of like when God says, "I Am that I Am". To me this feels like this carries all this weight. The enigma is presented to us by the unconscious. "Now it is obvious that nothing is and, so far as it is said, that it is". I mean, it sounds so important, and yet I'm not sure I understand when he calls that S_2 …?

RM: Well, he's also not helping because he's collapsing the difference between *connaissance* and *savoir*. Do you know the difference between these? *Connaissance* is the referential knowledge, the knowledge of science, but savoir is that knowledge in the unconscious – which is an enigma. Scientific knowledge, on the other hand, is not necessarily an enigma. Then he brings in S_2. And, whenever you have S_2, you have the Other of discourse. You could have the Other of scientific discourse, but that's not lalangue. But then he goes back to lalangue. So, there are two that 'it' speaks. So

DOI: 10.4324/9781003424581-16

maybe language serves to communicate, but lalangue is not used to communicate but rather to evoke – to communicate about what one must ask oneself about which of the two. So, are you talking about language? Are we talking about lalangue? Are we talking about S_1, or are we talking about S_2? Those are the terms that are at play here. Communication implies reference, and that's the referential knowledge of science, which would be *connaissance*. "But, one thing is clear, language is merely what scientific discourse elaborates what I call llanguage". So, in a way he's saying language is just science formalizing what otherwise would be the unconscious *savior* of lalangue.

GF: Is it just science, or is it more like the battery of signifiers given by a particular system of language?

RM: Right, that's articulation. But in a way, linguistics would be science for Lacan. And that's the battery of signifiers.

GF: I see, so it's not a particular kind of scientific discourse? It's any kind of linguistics?

RM: I guess people consider linguistics a social science, right?

TEXT: Llanguage serves purposes that are altogether different from that of communication. That is what the experience of the unconscious has shown us, insofar as it is made of llanguage, which, as you know, I write with two l's to designate what each of us deals with, our so-called mother tongue (*lalangue dite maternelle*), which isn't called that by accident.

RM: Lalangue is the mother tongue, so it's related to the mother's desire – as opposed to language where the paternal metaphor, the Name of the Father, is more involved.

GF: When you say the mother's desire, are you saying that it comes from the mother or is it the infant's experience of the mother's desire?

RM: The mother speaks that language, that baby talk, with the baby, right? She plays with words and there's an intonation of desire… *Oh, you're my baby, beautiful baby*, and let's play with this word and that word, and whose little hand is this?… that kind of talk which [Françoise] Dolto says you have to use in the analysis of children.

TEXT: If communication approaches what is effectively at work in the jouissance of llanguage, it is because communication implies a reply, in other words, dialogue. But does llanguage serve, first and foremost, to dialogue? As I have said before, nothing is less certain.

I just got hold of an important book by an author named Bateson about which people had talked my ears off, enough to get on my nerves a bit. I should say that it was given to me by someone who had been touched by the grace of a certain text of mine he translated into his language, adding some commentary to it, and who felt he had found in Bateson's work something that went significantly further than "the unconscious structured like a language".

RM: Yeah, that's not in Bateson. But it was at a time when people were really excited about Gregory Bateson in systems theory, including Andre Patsalides – when he came to the Bay Area, he went to see Bateson and told him about Lacan. Do you know how Bateson fits in here? Bateson is one of the theories of Systems Theory that led to the development of Family Systems Theory. He was an anthropologist, originally married to Margaret Mead; a British guy that lived in America. And he's the one who coined the 'double bind' hypothesis of schizophrenia. I believe his last book was called *Steps to an Ecology of Mind*, where he talks about mental connections in the biosphere. I met him once – he was an amazing guy… I met him in the Esalen Institute and he was this huge, tall guy who looked like a logger! … and he was talking about mental connections in the biosphere. The biosphere is the biological environment, right? It's an ecological term, the biosphere, and then all these poltergeists started happening in the room, like noises and lights going on and off! And then, he started laughing and we were all entranced! He explained that the way to understand poltergeists is all about mental connections in the biosphere, because these are mental connections in the objects in the room that are connecting between what I'm saying in my words and the properties of these physical phenomena, whereby the interaction between the two and the biosphere then produces these phenomena that we call poltergeist [*chuckling*]. I was amazed, also, because my father was very interested in that kind of stuff… he would go and visit the houses that were supposed to be haunted with poltergeists, and he always wanted to take me… and I didn't want to go, because I was scared. Anyway, right there on the spot, Bateson gave a scientific explanation of poltergeist with the phenomena all around us – and we were like, "what's going on, what are these noises, what's going on here?" And the guy was laughing! So, that's Gregory Bateson, and he's now buried at the Green Gulch Farm, which is a very important Zen meeting place here in San Francisco. He was friends with all the Buddhists. And anyway, somebody spoke to Lacan about Bateson in Paris, I think this was Andre Patsalides.

GF: Yes, it says so in the footnote [no. 3].

TEXT: Now Bateson, not realizing that the unconscious is structured like a language, has but a rather mediocre conception of it. But he creates some very nice artifices he calls "metalogues". They're not bad, insofar as they involve, if we take him at his word, some internal, dialectical progress, being produced only by examining the evolution of a term's meaning. As has always been the case in everything that has been called a dialogue, the point is to make the supposed interlocutor say what motivates the speaker's very question, in other words, to incarnate in the other the answer that is already there. It's in that sense that dialogues, classical dialogues – the finest examples of which are represented by the Platonic legacy – are shown not to be dialogues.

RM: That's very interesting. So how do we ordinarily use the word dialogue? For instance, is psychotherapy a dialogue?

BB: I would say it's not a dialogue... but I'm struggling a bit with what he's saying here. I'm not sure I fully understand this statement.

RM: What about an intellectual conversation? Let's say you have a panel with a Jungian, a Lacanian, a Freudian, a Rogerian, a biological psychiatrist... and they're discussing depression. Is that a dialogue?

BB: I guess I'm thinking about it in a more personal way. I expect a dialogue to be a conversation back and forth between two people who are developing or furthering some sort of point of discussion. Sometimes people in these panels just speak 'at' the public or 'to' the audience – they're not really speaking in relationship to someone else. To me, a dialogue involves having to address someone, asking questions, and then taking something from what the other said. But maybe 'discourse' is the better term.

RM: Yes, I agree with you. Thank you. That's a clear differentiation.

BB: And I wouldn't call therapy a dialogue because I'm not trying to speak to the 'I' of the patient and have them speak back to me. It might be a dialogue with the patient's unconscious, if that could be considered a dialogue (if I were in the right position), because I would be trying to listen to you and then respond to you.

RM: Okay, so the thing is that Lacan traces psychoanalysis back to Socrates and the Socratic maieutic, which was a dialogue. And so, Socrates pretended to know nothing, going around town, engaging people in conversations about whatever. But he used that as a way to get to the real questions, and he tried to ask questions to bring out the knowledge that people had embedded within themselves. And that's what Lacan says is similar to psychoanalysis, meaning that you engage people in conversation, apparently, about maybe this or that, but it ends up being about something much more profound that is found within them. So, I guess that's a crossover between your definition of dialogue, which would be, let's say, having an intellectual conversation with somebody directly, as opposed to a panel addressing an audience. So, a dialogue is a personal conversation in your definition?

BB: It would not have to be necessarily personal, but it has to have, in my view, someone with whom I'm dialoguing – not speaking to the universe, or broadly to the public.

RM: But in a panel discussion, the panel presenters are dialoguing, right?

BB: I wish! Most panels I have attended have a bunch of people speaking to themselves pretty much! I haven't been to one of those conferences!

RM: *Touché! Touché!* That's why you don't like to be in panels! [*Laughing*]

GF: Well, where then is there a dialogue?

BB: I mean, to me, this is a dialogue. When we're talking and when you're really asking the question – I thought Raul was really asking me a question and

I positioned myself in a place to try to consider it from my experience – and then he responded. So, it's almost like there's a 'something' that we're throwing back and forth between us that's changing as we go along. And that in my listening, I'm changing what I thought I was listening for in my listening to how Raul responds…

GF: So, a dialogue occurs when two people or more are speaking about the same thing?

BB: Yes, speaking about something… but for me, it has to do more with 'the address'. So, the speech is addressed to someone to consider a question or a statement, and they are asked to respond… not me merely speaking to the general public about my ideas.

GF: But aren't you dialoguing with the general public?

BB: Sure, but the general public can't speak back. So, it seems to me like there's not a dialogue, but rather a lecture. But again, that's my own private definition and it is idiosyncratic. What would you say?

GF: In dialogue, it seems to me that there's more than one speaking about something held or known about in common. For instance, if we're in a dialogue right now, you might be thinking about something completely different than what it is that I'm thinking about. And I might have different objectives and different goals in understanding what you're saying, but somehow, we still connect. And maybe I could say that I am always in dialogue with the Other while speaking with another…

BB: I see. So, dialogue doesn't require listening and being changed by the other that you're speaking to?

GF: No, I think it does… both speaking and listening seem to be elements of a dialogue.

RM: Right, but the definition that Lacan's giving here is closer to the Socratic notion of dialogue, because he says:

As has always been the case, in every everything that has been called a dialogue, the point is to make the supposed interlocutor say what motivates the speaker's very question… in other words, to incarnate in the other the answer that is already there.

So that's getting the person to give the answer, but from their own experience in some way. In that sense, "dialogues, classical dialogues – the finest examples of which are represented by the Platonic legacy – are shown not to be dialogue"… oh wait, so then the Socratic dialogue is not a dialogue. Right, because if you're trying to bring out something that you already know is there in the other … so if the unconscious is at play, you don't know that it is there. So, it can't be a dialogue? Is that what you're saying? Because remember, it's a knowing – Socrates is trying to bring out a knowing that the person doesn't know that they know until Socrates brings it out.

BB: See, I think they would call that a dialogue.

GF: So, you would say it's a dialogue with the other person's unconscious?

BB: I would! It is a dialogue with the other person in the position of unconscious knowing. I think this is because he's really asking them to question things in the dialogue, including asking them to question 'knowledge' itself. I guess it wouldn't be a dialogue if Socrates is trying to get them to understand a 'something' that neither Socrates nor that person he is talking to fully knows. That he is positioned in an address to the unconscious is evidenced by his asking, 'what is love'? I mean, he asks questions. Socrates doesn't tell the other 'this is what love is', but in dialogue with the other, between them, they discover a 'something' that binds us all as people – the feeling of love. I am referencing that feeling of love that is in our experience. We know it, but we have to be changed in order to be able to appreciate it in the here and now, which is a particular type of experiencing and a particular experience of shared knowing.

GF: So, would you say that a dialogue involves a dialectic process or some kind of dialectical movement?

BB: Yes, I think so.

RM: Yes, between the conscious and unconscious subject.

BB: Also, reified words… with words or concepts that get stuck or that are in gridlock… and people have to get moved from their different roles to see the contrast between the words to see or to unlock what's in the words. It's not just subject-object, because words themselves carry so many meanings and they get locked up with them.

RM: Right, subject-object is also S_1 and S_2. It's a relationship between subjects, but it's also a relationship between signifiers.

BB: Oh, see there's an example! I had limited the meaning of 'subject-object' to apply only to an event occurring between one person and another person!

TEXT: If I have said that language is what the unconscious is structured like, that is because language, first of all, doesn't exist. Language is what we tried to know concerning the function of lalangue.

BB: Does he mean language doesn't exist a priori?

RM: So that's the idea of creation, the *creatio ex nihilo* that Lacan refers to, that we create language as we speak. We create both the world and language as we speak. In that sense, it doesn't exist until it manifests.

GF: I am not clear on that because I inherited my language… I didn't originally create it.

RM: No, you didn't. But where is it?

GF: Where is it? Well, language is certainly in the written text.

RM: Right, and that would be language, not speech. Maybe 'speech' is a good example of nonexistence because after you said something, where did language and the words go? The speech either disappears or is transcribed into writing. Speech does exist in written or recorded language. But written language doesn't exist until you pick up and read the book. The book is sitting on the shelf, and, until you read it, it doesn't exist for you. Viewed analogically, that book is yourself. You form your character by reading the book similar to the way a text shapes you without you knowing it or the ego knowing it.

People come to analysis with structured automatic thinking or chaotic thinking about their symptoms. In either case that symptomatic thinking constitutes a form of emotional suffering. Symptomatic thinking leads one to have a chaotic emotional life. So, in analysis, analysands have to structure their chaotic emotional life with symbolic thought and language. But there always remains something beyond thought which constitutes a circular return to jouissance.

For Plato, Peirce, and Freud, the letter had a trace of the reality object. Lacan, following Saussure, talks about the arbitrariness of the sign. This is supposed to be the new social science point of view as distinct from the philosophical perspective of old. So, in the present, the letters don't refer back to the emotional origins of the letters. The letters are emptied out of emotional meaning so that you can refer to new objects with fresh emotional meaning.

We can say that there are four steps in the process of thinking and writing. In general, science doesn't ultimately know what thought is. Therefore, most linguists argue that thought is basically language. You have a concept in language and then you can have a thought. On the other hand, there are people who believe there is thought without language. Lacan resolves this ancient question by saying that the origin of thought is jouissance. The relationship between emotion and thinking is circular, so they mutually determine one another. So, contrary to cognitive psychologists, thought is not the only determinant of emotion and emotion determines thinking. Quine (1960) says the two phenomena are not related – when you and I misunderstand each other, that reflects both of our automatons. Misunderstanding creates an affect associated with a conflict automaton in language. Change in self-awareness leads to a change in affect that leads to a change in thinking. The surprise element that was missing in symbolic thinking is revealed via the misunderstanding. I guess it depends on the definition we have of existence, too.

GF: But if language itself is always somehow concealing lalangue, and if we are always moving from lalangue to language, then language itself is kind of always ambiguous. Even though it appears set and conventional, and I or somebody else can pick up a book and read the language, somebody else might pick up my writing and conceive it to be something entirely different than how I conceived the language to be. So, I get the sense that there's no set convention in language that really locks its meaning into place… so it has a very ambiguous existence.

RM: Well, I like that idea that language doesn't exist, because it just matches with a whole other bunch of stuff. But it needs to be argued – why is it that it doesn't exist? Because Lacan says there are so many things that don't exist – like structure doesn't exist either. You know, structure just manifests. But until it manifests, it doesn't exist. So, that has something to do with the void and form, or structure and event, because the events are the manifestations of structure. But we don't necessarily see the structure, we just see the event that articulates or manifests a particular structure. So, until it manifests, you know, you could say that the structure itself doesn't exist. That's one argument. The other argument is, because language itself is made up of things that do not have intrinsic definition, and the definition only comes from the combination, until you combine [the signifiers] it doesn't exist because the elements of language themselves are insubstantial, or empty. That's another way of saying it doesn't exist.

GF: That's very Buddhist!

RM: Yeah, that's my Buddhist reading of that. But the more phenomenological thing is that when we speak, like we're speaking now, there's a structure manifesting, right? But if we become quiet, and you're not thinking about what you just said, where does thinking and language go? And then, how do they manifest so quickly out of nothing (*ex nihilo*).

GF: Do you mean the grammar?

RM: Well, the grammar and the words! It's like I'm not aware of all the words I know. But, when I speak them, they manifest. Maybe you could say that if language is in the brain, as if the words are in different cells or connections between cells, they're not obstructing anything when they are not existing, right? I mean, if the memories are there, and the language is there, it's not obstructing me right now because I'm not thinking about it. And, in fact, if I don't think about it, you can say, "well, my mind is empty right now". Until you engage me in a conversation, and then we start talking, and then it manifests again. But, until then, where was it? So that's the *creatio ex nihilo*. That's the way that Lacan interprets that concept, although otherwise he's not a creationist. He is rather a creationist in the here and now… it's how we construct the world in the here and now, for until we spoke of the world, the world didn't exist.

BB: I would say we need some really good German words to be very specific about what kind of existence we need. English is not good enough alone since what it seems we are talking about is only one kind of existence. And there are other kinds, for example, memories or words are latent or not latent. I mean, there's an existence in their latency because of certain implications of structures and experiences. Perhaps there are some good old German words to discern the difference between these different kinds of existence, like *Ungrund*? Something like that can begin to differentiate between 'existences'.

RM: For Lacan, existence is Symbolic.

BB: Yes, Symbolic, but I still think you have to go beyond that. There are many kinds of existence that I can think of: existence that informs my speech, or existence that I've actually already picked up unconsciously. But one way or another, things in my environment are already making links and connections because I was exposed to those links and connections three or four times recently either in the media or in something else that I'm seeing. So, my mind, thinking faster than I can sense, has already begun putting bits of existence together. My mind is reading the environment and reading depends on things, ideas, and words already latent in both reading and the environment that is the context for and object of my perception.

RM: So, when we say 'latent', isn't that a way of speaking? Because we say latent, but where is it? That's why people can challenge the unconscious. Where is it?

BB: For me, that is not so hard. Just like I can't see everything that goes into a computer, but I know things exist in it because I can see their traces. We can see the latent stuff. For example, do you know about the experiment in which a video of people playing ball is shown to people and they get distracted by the task of counting the number of balls so they don't consciously register the gorillas that cross the stage? You can ask questions that elicit their knowledge of the gorillas, even though they do not consciously recall having seen the gorillas.

RM: Okay, so we could say that we still don't know exactly how the unconscious operates. I mean there are layers of the mind that constitute memory. And we could say those layers are 'there', but they're not always present. That's why memory is unconscious in a descriptive sense. So, you could say that memory is registered somewhere even though we don't know where that is – it's just an assumption. Or, you can have a biological theory and think that memory is in the connections between cells.

BB: Yes, I agree, but I just want to refine it. Even with the unconscious as one speaks, I feel like we need more terms. Depending on what purpose that organizes my 'looking', I will pick up aspects of my environment that answer that purpose – some I will mark in my physical body and some I will mark with conscious thought or symbols. This registration of my purpose is part of a symbolic chain that's linking me to a distant memory of patterns/experiences that link to that purpose. That process is a different type of unconscious. We are talking about at least two 'somethings' that we can call unconscious, but to say they are the same and that there is only one depletes the concept of the unconscious. They're really different. And part of me thinks that there is a similar problem in how we are talking about the concepts of 'exist' and 'not exist', that they are the same thing. We could have a much subtler conversation if we could better refine our understanding of the different 'kinds' of existence and be more precise in our speaking.

RM: So, you can 'be' and 'not exist' when using these words in a Lacanian sense, right? Because you can 'be', but if you don't have signifiers for the being, then in the Lacanian framework, it wouldn't exist because 'exist' is predicated by the signifier. Anyway, new German terms may help us as suggested!

GF: I understand that I would be a 'willing desire to be' before I speak. I would be a 'desire to speak' and so I would be a form of 'will waiting to become'…

RM: So, in becoming there is existence?

GF: Well, my existence would be manifest as a desire to potentially be something in the signifying realm when I am not speaking. But this is all hard to say! And I mentioned Buddhism before because of the idea that there's no way of locating an originating starting point for existence. So, it's kind of like turtles all the way down, and there is no way to isolate or designate something as 'being itself' or the 'ground of Being' (aside from, perhaps, 'no ground'). There is only becoming since nothing '*ex*-sists' aside from loosely structured events that arise and dissipate. In other words, there's no doctrine of substance in Buddhism.

RM: And, yet there's structure… it's just that you don't necessarily or always see the structure. And, in Buddhism, there also is no becoming because becoming is understood as part of the chain of dependent origination. And so you want to disrupt the chain by trying to become somebody. "I want to be somebody, you know… I want to be recognized as somebody, I want to do 'this' in order to gain or to achieve 'that'". That's becoming, and that's considered to be in the realm of karma or in the chain of dependent origination. So, you would rather do things without trying to become anything! And so what Buddhism says is that things are always emerging out of nothing and disappearing into nothing, so the universe is constantly emerging at every place.

So, it's like what I'm trying to do now to break loose from the becoming chain – I recently finished my book, I sent it and forgot about it! [*Congratulations from others and laughter*]. I don't even want to think about it! I don't want to read it! [*Laughter*] I don't want to think, you know, what am I going to become with this book? Are people going to like it, or are they not going like it… you know, all that stuff that is totally human! But it's all in the Imaginary! So, I just put this book out, and that's it! I don't know anything about it anymore.

GF: What's the title? Do you remember the title? [*Joking*]

RM: No, I don't remember the title! [*Laughing*] If somebody asks me, I hope I'll be able to say something about it! It's a good defense, because then, either way, success, or failure, they're all the same. The important thing is just to pour your heart into it, and to make the big effort, and then offer that to the universe. And then the rest is, you know… may the chips fall where they may. And if people like it, good, and if they don't like it, good too!

GF: But, no, seriously, what's the title?

RM: *Knowing, Not-Knowing, and Jouissance.* And the subtitle is *Levels, Symbols and Codes of Experience in Freud, Lacan, and Psychoanalysis*. But anyway, let's go back to the text.

TEXT: Certainly, it is thus that scientific discourse itself approaches language, except that it is difficult for scientific discourse to fully actualize language, since it misrecognizes the unconscious. The unconscious evinces knowledge that, for the most part, escapes the speaking being. That being provides the occasion to realize just how far the effects of llanguage go, in that it presents all sorts of affects that remain enigmatic.

RM: Ah! This is where he said it! Because Colette Soler refers to this in a book called *The Lacanian Affects*... and this is where Lacan mentions affects that remain enigmatic.

TEXT: Those affects are what result from the presence of llanguage insofar as it articulates things by way of knowledge (*de savoir*) that go much further than what the speaking being sustains (*supporte*) by way of enunciated knowledge.

RM: So, you see the bottom footnote? Fink notes that the French *savior* could also be translated as 'knowing' – that's how I translate it. But Lacan is using knowledge here, so it's confusing. You see what I'm saying? So, *savoir* can be translated as 'knowing' or 'unknown knowing' or 'unconscious knowing', as distinct from knowledge or *connaissance*. So lalangue articulates things by way of knowing – unconscious knowing – and it goes much further than what the speaking being sustains by way of enunciated knowledge, by knowledge statements. So, in that sense, the knowing that emerges in the analytic situation regarding the person's unconscious is better than whatever psychoanalysis can say about the unconscious mind as a scientific statement. That's interesting!

TEXT: Language is, no doubt, made up of llanguage. It is knowledge's hare-brained lucubration (*élucubration*) about llanguage. But the unconscious is knowledge, a knowing how to do things (*savoir faire* or know-how) with llanguage. And what we know how to do with llanguage goes well beyond what we can account for under the heading of language.

Language affects us first of all by everything it brings with it by way of effects that are affects. If we can say that the unconscious is structured like a language, it is in the sense that the effects of llanguage, already there qua knowledge, go well beyond anything the being who speaks is capable of enunciating.

RM: Okay, so that's a different way of differentiating the two – meaning that llanguage has effects that are affects and the effects go well beyond whatever you can say... whatever you're going to either say or enunciate.

TEXT: It is in that regard that the unconscious, insofar as I base it on its deciphering, can only be structured like a language, a language that is always hypothetical with respect to what supports it, namely llanguage. Llanguage is what allowed me to turn my S_2 into a question earlier and ask – is it truly a question of them-two (*d'eux*) in language?

RM: Again, that's interesting – lalangue supports language. So, if we think about that as the paternal metaphor, then you would have the language as numerator and lalangue as denominator, right? The Name of the Father would be the numerator and denominator is the Desire of the Mother. And so, lalangue is the root language of desire that functions as signified for the Name of the Father as the structuring element for regular language.

BB: So "them two" is referring to lalangue and language or the paternal and maternal metaphor?

RM: Yes, lalangue and language.

BB: And that's also the paternal and maternal metaphors?

RM: Well, I'm just saying that would be an interesting way to think about it, because the Name of the Father is the key organizing metaphor for Lacan for language. But the Desire of the Mother is what gives meaning to the Name of the Father. And, if lalangue is the language of Mother, of the mother's desire, then that's what gives meaning to the Name of the Father within language or in the use of language. So, in some ways, the signified for language would also always be in lalangue, which would be how language is rooted in our emotional childhood experience.

TEXT: Stated otherwise, it has become clear, thanks to analytic discourse, that language is not simply communication. Misrecognizing that fact, a grimace has emerged in the lowest depths of science that consists in asking how being can know anything whatsoever. My question today regarding knowledge will hinge on that.

RM: So, there's the contrast between language and lalangue, *connaissance* and *savoir*, and between communication and evocation.

Supplemental References

Bateson, G. (1979). *Mind and Nature*. New York: Bantam Books, 1980.

Lacan, J. (1972–1973). *Encore. The Seminar of Jacques Lacan, XX.* New York: Norton, 1998.

Moncayo, R. (2018). *Knowing, Not-Knowing, and Jouissance: Levels, Symbols, and Codes of Experience in Psychoanalysis*. London: Routledge.

Quine, Willard Van Orman (2013) [1960]. *Word and Object*. (New ed.). Cambridge: MIT Press.

Soler, C. (2015). *Lacanian Affects: The Function of Affect in Lacan's Work.* New York: Routledge.

Chapter 17

Formalization, Scaling, and Measurement

Moncayo Seminar, May 11, 2018, *Encore, Seminar XX*, pg. 58

TEXT: That brings me back to what I myself earlier raised by way of objections to myself, all by myself, namely that there was a male way of botching (*rater*) the sexual relationship and then another.

BB: I am lost already!
RM: Well, 'botching' is ruining, right? And, I guess in French, it is *rater or ratage* and that's the male way of ruining the sexual relationship. Okay, shall we keep going?

TEXT: This botching (*ratage*) is the only way of realizing that relationship if, as I posit, there's no such thing as a sexual relationship. To say thus that everything succeeds does not stop us from saying "not everything succeeds" (*pas tout réussit*), for it is in the same manner – it fails (*ca rate*). It's not a matter of analyzing how it succeeds. It's a matter of repeating until you're blue in the face why it fails.

RM: Right, so then he says 'it fails', its objective. What do you think about that, because I guess people could say that is a matter of opinion. Or is it a fact that relationships between the sexes fail?
MK: Fail in what way?
RM: Yes, and does failure mean that the relationship fails, like in separation and divorce, or does it mean that even if there is no separation or divorce, it fails in that there is a kind of rapport that both sexes would like to have with each other that fails? And, Lacan is very brutal in the way he talks about this topic, but we kind of need that voice nowadays. I mean the statistics go up and down, right, in terms of whether people now get divorced more or if marriages fail more than before. We certainly, in our field, deal with people coming into therapy and analysis talking about the failure of their parental relationships – failure between their parents, and so on. So, we see the sequelae of that. But I don't know if that would have been any much different than the sequelae of a bad marriage or people coming to talk about "yeah,

DOI: 10.4324/9781003424581-17

my parents stayed together, but I'd wish they would have gotten a divorce" – we also certainly hear that, too, almost as much as the other one. But I think there is a consensus, and some people step forward and say, "yes, there is a crisis in relationships, and there is a crisis in marriage". And, of course, the moral Right is saying that the failure of the family, which is producing all these sequelae, is due to modernity, and modernity not accepting the tenets of religion with respect to the family. And the way we need to get out of this crisis is to go back to the traditional values. That's the Tea Party, and the right-wing movement in the US is one response to it. But then, of course, they're faced with dealing with, "yeah, we are moral, and we are following the traditional thing", and then how does that work for our families? And the answer there would be mixed. [*ALL agreement*]

GF: The question of what the traditional values are would be mixed, too.

RM: Do you want to say more about that?

GF: Well, I feel the more you seek to go back to some form of fundamentalism, or traditional belief system, or traditional custom, you find that too has its ambiguities. In other words, there are no pure or true roots to return back to … for instance, you cannot easily say today that we should go back to sacrificing animals as Leviticus tells us we should in order to sanctify ourselves or appease G-d.

RM: Right, but what the Christian church wants to go back to is the Middle Age teaching of St. Augustine, or the other one, what's his name?

GF: Aquinas?

RM: Thomas of Aquinas!… that the order should be that God is in charge, the father represents God and then the mother represents the father, and the child doesn't have authority until he or she grows up. And the only way for them to grow up is for them to accept the authority of the mother and the father. And, both the mother and the father have to accept the authority of God, period, simple, and that's the end of the story, right? That's what we had in the Middle Ages, but, somehow, that didn't work so well for us. So, we had to come up with modernity. So, that's part of the problem. Going back to what Lacan is saying, because this can become very vague, there is a value in having modern people choose their love objects on the basis of imaginary or romantic love. But I guess there is a lack of sexual rapport … that doesn't mean that people have to leave their relationships because of that, but to be able to recognize that there is going to be a lack – there is no ideal relationship. There is going to be a lack in the relationship, and how do we negotiate that. And, whether the negotiation leads in the direction of staying in a relationship or whether the negotiation goes in the direction of leaving and trying to find another one. But the other one will also have some limitations built into it as well.

MK: Does Lacan ever talk about deprivation? Like I am thinking more of a paranoid-schizoid kind of an idea where people are so preoccupied with deprivation that they can't actually grow desire because there is so much hate involved. Like if there is some sort of process that is transforming deprivation into lack, so that you could actually grow desire.

RM: Right, so is it privation or deprivation? Lacan does talk about privation, of course. But he uses it more in a structural way – of different ways of relating to the object in the present rather than putting it in a developmental line where privation can be linked to the breast, where frustration can be linked to the anal phase, and castration can be linked to the genital phase. Yet, I think that is also possible to do. So, the question there … he [Lacan] says privation is the real lack of a symbolic object, as opposed to the way people usually think of deprivation in object relations as the real lack of a real object. Meaning that it is a deficit that shouldn't happen, so that you are deprived of something, and traumatized by something in the environment that shouldn't have taken place. And, if the adequate environment had been in place, then this trauma and this defect wouldn't have taken place. The schizoid-paranoid position[1] in Kleinian theory which refers to the absence of the breast … if you don't have a "good breast" then you have a more radical absence than if you have a good breast and sometimes the 'good breast' is going to be a 'bad breast' because the breast is not going to be there. Otherwise, we have this fantasy of a mother who is a slave to her nursing infant and has to be continuously available. And then, if she fails to be available one time when the baby cries, and she didn't run to give the breast because she had some awfully selfish thing to do – you know, like doing her job or working with another kid or spending time with her partner … and she feels horribly guilty that she damaged her poor child because she wasn't there one-hundred percent of the time – then, there, we have a problematic notion of privation. We should review Lacan's chart on this sometime, because he has a complicated rendering of the different types of lack – Real lack, Symbolic lack, and Imaginary lack – which correlates the three types of lack with the different types of mothers. I should look at that, so that I can give you an intelligible…

MK: What's that chart called or where does he write about this?

RM: This is in the seminar on object relation, which is *Seminar IV*. It's the seminar that comes after *Seminar III* on psychosis. And there he is trying to grapple with these questions. So, if there is an absence – no bottle, no good breast or bad breast – then, what do we have there? We have failure to thrive. We have an actual, real deficit or defect. So, we can't completely eliminate that dimension because that happens. But then, when kids are given everything they need and they are not deprived, like in the studies of hospitalism by René Spitz (1945) where there are these nurses who were doing everything right. So, they were doing all the necessary caretaking behavior and were good caretakers, but there was no desire… no maternal desire there. They were being responsible childcare workers, but with no desire, those kids failed to thrive. So, they weren't deprived of 'human caretaking', I guess you could say, but they didn't experience this sense of being the object of the joy of the mother's desire and the mother speaking lalangue to them. Dany [Nobus][2] recently wrote to me, suggesting a different translation for lalangue – he called it 'lalation'. 'Lalation' technically is when you cannot pronounce the 'r' or the 'l' in one language or another, so you make up different sounds for the words. But he is referring to using that to have a word in English that translates lalangue, instead of keeping it in French, to designate this quality language between the mother and her infant that expresses desire – this Desire of the Mother that is necessary for the child to thrive… and which is going to be messy, and there's going to be narcissistic stuff there… but, it is fundamental. And, if that gets deprived, then that's more damaging than if there is no other adult present there who is caring for the child. So, we have these different levels of privation, but the bottom line from the Lacanian point of view is that privation, or deprivation, is also necessary. Like, "*you are going to have to do without the breast for a while, kiddo. I love you, you are the joy of my desire, but mommy now is tired, and she needs to rest*" (or she needs to go to work, or she needs to talk to her friends, or your brother and sister). Or "*I need to talk to my partner right now, and you are going to have to tolerate the privation of the breast – it's not going to be there for you right now*".

RM: So, those are the two different forms of privation – one is that it is necessary and not all bad, and the other one can be very damaging and traumatizing. The schizoid-paranoid position in Klein just refers not just to the absence of the good breast, but just the alternation between the 'good' and the 'bad' breast.

MK: Thank you for this detour!

GF: So, you mentioned earlier the notion of lalangue being expressive of desire. Could you say something more about that?

RM: Yeah, we can say like all the terms of endearments that mothers or parents use with their infants. They play with different words or with their name, you know, using a diminutive … like they called me 'Raulito' instead of Raul. It's not based on sounds of diminution, but it's a kind of language that is different from the ordinary way of speaking, and it has a stronger quality of affect – and a positive effect. It's the mirroring play, right … "*oh my beautiful baby, and this, this, and that*" … all kinds of combinations can be used. It's the same way lovers talk in the romantic period, and they call each other by different names and maybe using different words in different languages – like, "my little this and this and that". The same thing with a teddy bear, which is also what Françoise Dolto thought, that that language was more important in the treatment of children than free association (which, of course, with children is hard to do). Melanie Klein was doing the play therapy, so Dolto is saying, yes, play therapy but also using this kind of lalangue to speak with them, and to let them address you with lalangue as well.

TEXT: It fails. That is objective. I have already stressed that. Indeed, it is so plain that it is objective that one must center the question of the object in analytic discourse thereupon. The failure is the object.

I already said long ago in what respect the good and the bad object differ. There is the good, there is the bad, oh la la! Today I am trying to begin with that, with what is related to what's good (*le bon*), the good (*le bien*), and to what Freud enunciates. The object is a failure (*un raté*). The essence of the object is failure.

BB: Should I keep reading or is there something to conclude?
RM: Do you understand what he means by the 'object is a failure'?
BB: Maybe failure is the lack and that's what we are actually interested in? That's what I would take it to mean.
RM: Right, that the *objet a* is lost, right? So, it's a failure in that sense – that it has been lost and we have to deal with this loss of the object. And this loss of the object is constitutive of subjectivity. You can't have a subject with a subject that has to deal with this loss of this object or the failure of the object.
BB: So, when he is making the differentiation between what's good (*le bon*) and the good (*le bien*) and what Freud enunciates …
RM: So, I think there, what's good (*le bon*) would be like what feels good … "does that feel good? … does that feel good to you?" And the 'goods' are the 'goods' that are considered 'good' in society, like, you know, having a house; having a car, or having an education; having a good job. And the exchange of goods in society.
BB: Okay. And what Freud enunciates is the third term? What does that refer to?
RM: Yes, what is Freud telling us about what the ethical good is. What value a desirable object is, and what the experience of pleasure and unpleasure or pain is.
BB: What does Freud say about those things in particular?
RM: Well, he tells us about pleasure and pain, because he has the pleasure principle as a key concept and it's related to the question of the drive. But also its a quality associated with feelings – the affective component of the psyche is organized around the pleasure principle. Then, what does he tell us about 'the good'? He tells us something about the superego and the ego ideal, and so 'the good' is what it means to be a 'good boy' or a 'bad boy' or a 'good girl' or a 'bad girl'. Or a 'good dog' and a 'bad dog'!
BB: But is that different from 'a good' (*le bon*) or is that an example of 'the good' (*le bien*) for Freud?
RM: Lacan, because he studied anthropology and with Levi-Strauss, relates it more to the objects of exchange in society – the goods that I exchange in the economy. Freud doesn't quite interpret it that way, but he does discuss the good in terms of a sense of morality and ethics. And, ultimately, he says, this idea of 'the good' and 'the bad' is something irrational and something unconscious that is associated with the superego and identifications with the feelings of love and hate and what not – and, ultimately, the ideal of ethics that Freud aspires to is a kind of rational ethics.

TEXT: You will notice that I spoke of essence, just like Aristotle. So? That means that such old words are entirely usable. At a time when I dragged my feet less than today, that is what I turned to right after Aristotle. I said that, if something freshened the air a bit after all this Greek foot-dragging around Eudemonism,[3] it was certainly the discovery of utilitarianism.

That didn't faze my audience at the time because they'd never heard of utilitarianism – the result being that they couldn't make the mistake of believing that it meant resorting to the useful (*utilitaire*). I explained to them what utilitarianism was in Bentham's work, which is not at all what people think it is. In order to understand it, one must read *The Theory of Fictions*.

Utilitarianism means nothing but the following – we must think about the purpose served by the old words, those that already serve us. Nothing more. We must not be surprised by what results when we use them. We know what they are used for – they are used so that there may be the jouissance that should be (*qu'il faut*). With the caveat that given the equivocation between *faillir* and *falloir*, the jouissance that should be must be translated as the jouissance that shouldn't be/never fails (*qu'il ne faut pas*).

RM: Okay, alright Lacan! [*ALL laughter*]
RM: Okay, let's read footnote #20 …

FOOTNOTE: *Falloir*, used in all the tenses, but only in the third person singular, *il faut*, *il faudrait*, and so on, means "one must", "one should", "one has to", "it is necessary", and so on. Faillir means to "fail", "falter", "default", "miss", or "come up short"; in certain contexts, for example, *j'ai failli faire une gaffe*, "I almost made a blunder," it means to be on the verge of doing something. Both *faillir* and *fallior* are written faut in the third person singular, present tense. Hence, *la jouissance qu'il ne faut pas* is the jouissance that mustn't be, shouldn't be, but can't fail to be or never fails anyway. (*Faillir* also formerly meant to sin [for a girl], to lapse, or to be remiss in one's commitments.) The phrase *la jouissance qu'il faut* works much better with *falloir* than with *faillir*, because the *il* refers to nothing in particular in the case of the former ("the jouissance that is necessary" or "should be"), whereas it refers to a "he" or an "it" in the case of the latter ("the jouissance that it defaults on" or "the jouissance that he doesn't live up to"). Moreover, for *faillir* to work here grammatically, the phrase would have to be recast: *la jouissance à laquelle il faut*.

RM: Okay, so that's a pretty detailed linguistic analysis of the word, but it seems like he is looking at the antithetical meaning of 'primal' words, or the way Freud talked about the antithetical meaning of 'primary' words, meaning that these two words are related – *fallior* and *faillir* – and have opposite meaning because in one "you must", "you should" … it's like the superego and the ego ideal. But then there is the question – is that going to lead to happiness if you do the moral good? Or does it lead to suffering? And which one is better? Some people would say that you have to suffer in your pursuit of the good and you have to do it even though it is painful, because duty is more important than whether you feel happy from the exercise of your duty. That would be the Kantian view. And other people argue from the utilitarian view that you do the good because that's what is going to make you happy. And so he is playing with that ambiguity of whether the good makes you happy or unhappy. And so the *failler* means that the good also makes you fail, or makes you falter, in the sense that maybe you are doing something, but that's going to frustrate your desire and then you are not going to feel so good about it. And you are not going to be sure whether feeling good about it is something necessary or not. Or, it could also mean, yes, we have this ideal, like the superego, that we 'should do this' and we 'should do that', but yet we always fail to satisfy the superego imperative.

Then the question of essence … I would say that it is a good question, in the sense that for Aristotle (and this may be more familiar for you Greg, so please feel free to say something about it) the essence of a dog is the fact that it is a dog. If there is a thing, both a human being and a dog are both there, they are both things, but the essence of a dog is to be a dog. The dog has four legs and a certain kind of shape and behaves in a certain way and barks and whatever … so that's the essence of a dog. Now there is the question, does that essence come with a kind of jouissance? And then there is the essence of a human being, and let's say the essence of being a human being is to be a 'speaking being'. Now, is there a jouissance associated with that? But, in a way, that's kind of a Platonic doctrine in the sense, and Aristotle brings it down to earth so that you have a concrete dog and a concrete human being. Plato would say these two different forms are simply responding to the archetype. The essence of the dog then would be the archetype (or the eternal ideal) of the dog and the essence of a human being is the archetype of a human being … so that's metaphysics [for Plato]. Then there is the question whether the essence has nothing to do with either one of those and the essence refers more to Das Ding – to this question of the thing or the no thing that we are, which would be common to both dogs and human beings. That would explain why dogs and human beings can have this kind of close relationship, because they are both linked to this *Das Ding* that is bigger than either one of them … and that's the essence and the source of jouissance and the Real. So, those are kind of two different ways of thinking about 'essence'. One is more Aristotelian, and one is more Heideggerian and Eastern in the way of thinking about it.

GF: I believe you are on the right track in speaking about causality and the causal structure regarding Aristotle. With Aristotle, you don't want to somehow interfere with all the types of things you should be doing as you develop when you are a dog, meaning the dog moves toward the efficient and final causes of dog[ness] while also maintaining the formal causal structure of a dog. Whereas Plato is more interested in the ingressed nature of the form as a set archetype or ideal in things, and not so much with the characteristics of a thing's causal structure.

RM: I see. That's helpful, thank you.

TEXT: Yes, I am teaching something positive here. Except that it is expressed by a negation. But why shouldn't it be as positive as anything else?

The necessary – what I propose to accentuate for you with this mode – is that which doesn't stop (*ne cesse pas*) what? – being written (*de s'écrire*).

RM: Right, so it's sort of the repetition of the failure that keeps being written, because it's trying to write about something that can't be written. Lacan always says, it doesn't stop from 'being written', and does not stop from 'not being written'. It doesn't stop from being written because we are all trying to circle around and write about this enigmatic thing. And, since the enigmatic thing eludes us, we keep writing and adding more words to it. So, it doesn't stop from being written. But, on the other hand, since it is something enigmatic that is beyond words, then it doesn't stop from not being written ... because it can't be written. So, he plays with both of those paradoxes.

TEXT: That is a very fine way in which to divide up at least four modal categories. I will explain that to you another time, but I will give you a bit more of a taste this time anyway.

BB: Is he still speaking about Aristotle there?

RM: I think he is talking about the modal logic – the categories of the possible, the impossible, the necessary, and the contingent.

TEXT: "What doesn't stop not being written" is a modal category, and it's not the one you might have expected to be opposed to the necessary, which would have been the contingent. Can you imagine? The necessary is linked (*conjugué*) to the impossible, and this "doesn't stop not being written" is the articulation thereof. What is produced is the jouissance that shouldn't be/could never fail (*qu'il ne faudrait pas*). That is the correlate of the fact that there's no such thing as a sexual relationship, and it is the substantial aspect (*le substantiel*) of the phallic function.

BB: So, the substantial aspect of the phallic function is the lack?

RM: So, when he says, "what is produced is the jouissance that shouldn't be" – that's one side ... and the other side is, "could never fail". Meaning, the surplus of jouissance is at work both in the jouissance of the Other and in the phallic jouissance. In the jouissance of the Other one is always trying to reach this ideal romantic fusion with the Other, and you can never stop yourself from trying to achieve that – and, yet it will always fail. So, you will have the experience of both the pleasure of it and the pain of the failure of it at some point. And, in phallic jouissance there's also that question of how satisfying phallic jouissance can be, and yet, how frustrating, and difficult it can be to negotiate phallic jouissance in the sexual act. And, so, that is the jouissance that 'shouldn't be', meaning you shouldn't try to reach for this kind of oneness with the Other because it's going to fail; and yet, even though you shouldn't, we all do anyway and it always fails within relative degrees, right? Relative failure and relative success. The failure here doesn't mean it will not succeed ... rather, that we like it to completely succeed, but it never does. And, so he says, "the correlate of the fact that there's no such thing as a sexual relationship" – okay – "and it is the substantial aspect of the phallic function" – in the sense that the phallic function is to break that attempt to fuse with the mother … and, to kind of tranquilize the child, saying "okay, okay, okay, enough, enough. You have had enough of the breast and if you keep trying to go for it, you are going to drive both of us crazy"! That's already the phallic function, although it's just in relation to the breast. But it's the same thing, because the phallic function of castration here is being interpreted as the intervention that separates the dyad, although the dyad in reality is necessary. The dyad, again, is the same example … it's something necessary, but, at the same time, problematic if it just stays at the level of fusion.

TEXT: Let me now return to the textual level. It is the jouissance that shouldn't be/could never fail (*qu'il ne faudrait pas*) – in the conditional tense. That suggests to me that to use it we could employ protasis and apodosis.

FOOTNOTE: Lacan introduces these terms in his early article, "Logical Time and the Assertion of Anticipated Certainty", where the protasis takes on the meaning of an "if" clause in an if-then type proposition, and the apodosis takes on the meaning of the "then" clause.

RM: So, it's the fancy words for "if" and "then", which creates the logical construction. "If this", "then that".

TEXT: If it weren't for that, things would go better (*ça irait mieux*) – that's a conditional tense · the second part. That is the material implication, the implication the Stoics realized was perhaps what was most solid in logic.

How are we thus going to express what shouldn't be could never fail with respect to jouissance if not by the following? Were there another jouissance than phallic jouissance, it shouldn't be/could never fail to be that one.

RM: So, if there was another jouissance, it shouldn't be that one. So, it means that the Third jouissance is a way to address the problems with phallic jouissance. The problem of phallic jouissance is that it is always a question of who is or is not the phallus/or who has or does not have the phallus. The Third jouissance addresses this problem because it does not measure other subjects in terms of being or having.

And, yet, at the same time, the Third jouissance cannot be divested of the problems of the Imaginary phallus. The Third jouissance is beyond phallic jouissance, but the phallic function remains a prerequisite for the Third jouissance. So, even though the Third jouissance is beyond phallic jouissance, it still requires the phallic function to be installed in order to get at a femininity that is neither phallic nor a regression to a fusion with the Other.

[*ALL thanks and goodbyes – end of session*]

Notes

1 First described in 1946 when Melanie Klein presented her paper, "Notes on Some Schizoid Mechanisms", before the British Psychoanalytic Society.
2 In 2020, Dany Nobus suggested in a personal conversation that the French term 'lalangue' could be translated as the term 'lalation'. Lalation refers to the mother's voice when singing lullabies to a child.
3 Eudemonism is the doctrine that the basis of moral obligations is found in the tendency of "right actions, to produce happiness".

Supplemental References

Aristotle. (2009). *The Nicomachean Ethics*. Oxford World Classics. Cambridge: Oxford University Press.

Bentham, J. 1748–1832. (1843). The Works of Jeremy Bentham. Edinburgh: W. Tait.

Dolto, F. (1982). *Seminario de Psicoanalisis de Ninos*. Buenos Aires: Siglo Veinteuno, 1984.

Freud, Sigmund. (1920). *Beyond the Pleasure Principle*. SE 18.

Lacan, J. (1955–1956). *Psychoses. The Seminar of Jacques Lacan, III*. New York: Norton, 1995.

Lacan, J. (1956–1957). *The Object Relation. The Seminar of Jacques Lacan, IV*. Trans. by A. R. Price. New York: Polity, 2020.

Lacan, J. (1972–1973). *Encore. The Seminar of Jacques Lacan, XX*. New York: Norton, 1998.

Spitz, René A. (1945). 'Hospitalism: An Inquiry into the Genesis of Psychiatric Conditions in Early Childhood', *The Psychoanalytic Study of the Child*, 1, 53–74.

Chapter 18

Gender Discourse, the Phallus, and the *Objet a*

Moncayo Seminar, February 13, 2018, *Encore, Seminar XX*, pg. 131

TEXT: Those are the questions that I am opening up that are designed to announce to you what I hope to transmit to you concerning that which is written.

That which is written – what would that be in the end? The conditions of jouissance. And that which is counted – what would that be? The residues of jouissance. Isn't it by joining that a-sexual up with what she has by way of surplus jouissance – being, as she is, the Other, since she can only be said to be Other – that woman offers it to man in the guise of object a?

RM: So, the text reads "isn't it by joining that *a*-sexual up with what she has by way of surplus jouissance"… which would be feminine jouissance, right? Because women have a supplementary jouissance which is feminine jouissance. I guess that's what he means here. And then being a "she", she is the Other. And then, he connects this other with the *objet a.* So why is woman Other?

BB: I don't know.

RM: Alright, so in gender discourse, the feminist gender discourse, women are Other in the sense that they represent what's not contained within the system – within the phallocentric system or the patriarchal system. Translated into Lacanian theory, the Other here would mean that she's in the Real and she's a mystery. And so, in that sense, she's Other… like sexual gender difference, class difference, race difference. So, the Other would always be the minority. And, in that sense, 'woman' would also fall into that category and 'the self' would be the masculine self, right? But this is a little bit subtler than that kind of gender theory in that this Other – first of all, in Lacanian psychoanalysis, the Other is not an "us" and "them" kind of thing – the Other is the generalized social Other of society. So, society is always Other in relation to the subject. But the society that is Other to the subject is the Symbolic. Whereas femininity is rooted in the Real, so she would be Other because we don't have any categories by which to think of the Real. Then it [she] appears as Other. And that's why then he involves the *objet a* in that because the *objet*

DOI: 10.4324/9781003424581-18

a either is something irrational or is something in the Real that is beyond rationality. So, that would be how I interpret that. Your thoughts?

GF: Well, that makes sense to me, but I get confused about the *objet a*, which, in general, still seems somewhat ambiguous to me. I understand that it's the seven different objects in the Imaginary[1] … but does an *objet a* ultimately refer to any symbolic representation as well? Or any signifier?

RM: So, when you translate an *objet a* to a signifier, it usually tends to acquire a phallic signification. Urine, for instance, is one of the *objet a's* in the Imaginary, and, of course, saying 'urine' sounds like 'you're in'. This has the phallic metaphor in it, but not necessarily. You can go there, or you don't have to go there – whether you are in or out in relation to urine … but I am just playing with the words now to give you an example. Urine is one of the *objet a's*, but urine as an *objet a* is more of an image. Whether girls pee standing up and/or the boys pee sitting down, it's a societal issue. So, people in analysis, they talk about that, right? They say, "Well, you know, I am a girl, but I wanted to pee standing up". Or I'm a boy, but I was a sitter, and so they called me a 'sitter'. And my father called me a 'sitter'. So, here you see where the urine has a direct relationship to sexual difference. And that's why Freud said that he didn't want to separate the urinary flow from the phallic signification.

GF: That's helpful! So, if all signifiers are in the phallic system, how is it that the woman offers to a man supplemental jouissance?

RM: Well, a woman partakes of phallic jouissance, and so partakes of the relationship to the phallic signifier, but additionally has a dimension that's outside of it. A different jouissance. So, according to Lacan, women have both the phallic jouissance and the feminine jouissance, so that's why it's a supplemental jouissance. Because theoretically, and we don't know if this is an idealization, women possess an extra jouissance (minus or plus phi) in the sense that they potentially can experience both at once, phallic jouissance and feminine jouissance. Masculinity, instead, is restricted to phallic jouissance.

Then the *objet a* is also in the Real, right? – that's a different aspect of the *objet a*. In Lacan's work, femininity is considered to have a reach beyond the phallic signifier, and the *objet a* in general differs from the phallic signifier. However, they are also related, and it was never for Lacan a question of an alternative between the two. However, the *objet a*, Lacan said, was his only invention, and is the concept that led him to his later work. Of course, he never abandoned Freud or the concept of the phallus, although several of his early disciples wanted to concentrate on the middle period of his work where he gave an original presentation of Freud's work. Instead, Lacan was too brilliant to be held back by his students, and his early students left him.

We know that Lacan gave us two lists of *objet a* in his work, one in the *Écrits* and one in his early seminars. Freud spoke of the object in terms of a lost object. The *objet a* also has the quality of being lost and separated from the subject.

The breast is lost in weaning, feces with sphincter control, and the phallus with symbolic castration. In the two lists of *objet a*, one features the Imaginary phallus as one of the *objet a's*, and in the other, the Imaginary phallus is not listed but instead becomes the term of an equation. All the *objet a's* are the numerators in an equation where the $-\varphi$ (minus phi: the Imaginary phallus) is the denominator. So, all the *objet a's* have a relationship to the phallus. In that sense, the *objet a* in the Imaginary is determined by the Imaginary phallus. That's in one list. But if you don't like the phallus for some reason, then he (Lacan) gives you another list! In the second list, the phallus becomes just one of the *objet a's*. So, there the ascendancy is on the '*objet a*' rather than the phallus. In the other list, the phallus is in the ascendancy over the *objet a*. So, whichever one you prefer… if you prefer the feminine, you have a list for that, and if you prefer the masculine, you have a list for that! So, Lacan is egalitarian in that way!

The signifier of the Lack in the Other is the signifier of the phallus as a lack. So, the phallus, like the *objet a*, is also missing. The phallus is a signifier, while the *objet a* is not a signifier but an object. The object is mostly Imaginary but also Real. When the *objet a* approaches the Real, it vanishes. Is the *objet a* beyond symbolization as well? There are signifiers for it, and it could not be beyond symbolization because the entire analytic enterprise depends on the symbolization of the Imaginary *objet a*. The *objet a* in the Real that is beyond the signifier is the agalma – that which pleases the gods and that Alcibiades believed that Socrates possessed. But the wisdom of the agalma is not simply a projection or a fantasy. Alcibiades thought the agalma was a phallus. However, Socrates reminded him that there where he saw a phallus, Socrates was nothing. This 'no thing' or emptiness is the agalma, and therefore it is not without imperfections. The jewel is a nothing which is priceless. Lacan said that his analysands had to pay a high price for nothing or for this 'no thing'.

So that's the signifier of the Lack in the Other. And sometimes the matheme appears with an A and sometimes it appears with an O (for 'Other'). In the earlier Graph of Desire, it appears with an A, because it's authored in French. But sometimes he uses the O, not because he wants to be nice to English speakers where we would find the O instead of the A there, but because the O also means the null set. So when he writes it with the O, it's because the null set is implied. So the Other is barred – it has something missing, and what the Other has lost is the *objet a*. One meaning of the bar on the Other is that the Other lost something – that would be the signifier of a lack. And the other meaning of the bar is the lack of a signifier, meaning that what's barred there is representation itself (not that there's a particular representation barred or a particular object) but that representation itself is barred. And that would be the lack of a signifier instead of the signifier of a lack. That would fit more with a null set, because the null set means that the set has no elements that you can define it with, not even the empty set, because with the empty set at least you have an empty parenthesis, right? But with the null set, you have nothing other than the symbol.

TEXT: Man believes he creates - he believes believes believes, he creates creates creates. He creates creates creates woman. In reality, he puts her to work – to the work of the One. And it is in that respect that the Other – the Other insofar as the articulation of language, that is, the truth, is inscribed therein – the Other must be barred, barred on the basis of (*de*) what I earlier qualified as the One missing. That is what S(A) means.

GF: So, this is how the S(A) is? How man creates woman?

RM: It is kind of biblical, right? I mean, he's kind of like… so God created Adam. And then God said, "Well, it's not good that human beings should be alone". So, then, God creates Eve out of one of Adam's ribs. Adam loses a rib and the bone stands in for the Symbolic phallus. But what I think the theory of castration intends to explain is that the Symbolic phallus is missing. And the Lack in the Other appears – or the Symbolic phallus appears – in the place of the Lack in the Other. It is simply a function, but it doesn't have an image. It's both the Symbolic phallus and the phallic function of castration. So, the function of castration is to castrate the Imaginary phallus. And that produces Symbolic masculinity, meaning for men, that in order to "use it", they have to "lose it" so to speak. But it also generates femininity, which you could read as, on one level, the absence of the Imaginary power attributed culturally to the penis… which would be like saying, "Well, women don't have a penis". However, when you say, women don't have the Imaginary phallus, it is more at the psychic level that sexual difference produces an effect, because castration is a function of loss of the imaginary phallus – whereas, at the phenomenological level, castration is a structural loss that is experienced in the Imaginary as something bad that's done to you. But that's in the Imaginary because the phallic function of castration is necessary… it's inevitable to construe subjectivity. So, in that sense, you could say women don't have the Imaginary phallus, but they aspire to be the Imaginary phallus. But also, they have access to the Symbolic phallus, and the phallus is established as something missing. Both phallus and the *objet a* represent something missing. In set theory this is known as the empty set. The empty set links the Symbolic to the second Real. Consequently, we can use the Symbolic phallus to access the Real, too. On the other hand, because of the link to the Symbolic phallus and the phallic function of castration, access is also available to women in the form of the Other jouissance.

GF: I'm intrigued now because I'm thinking about this whole notion of creation in general. And I'm kind of getting the feeling that Lacan is working out of a doctrine of creation, where 'in the beginning' there was unbridled jouissance and then this kind of emergence of the Imaginary arrived whereby objects got sexed according to these particular imaginary phenomena that were then labeled or represented symbolically. And, you know, that was kind of this castration – this biblical Fall of Adam…

RM: Yes, the Fall is the Symbolic castration, but the thing is that Lacan reads the Genesis with Joyce, meaning that we wouldn't have had a human species if we hadn't had the Fall, right? If Adam and Eve hadn't eaten from the apple, and from the Tree of Life, there would be no need for knowledge, or for history, or for the human species. They would just live in Paradise, and you don't need knowledge in paradise. So, if the Fall hadn't happened, there wouldn't be a human species. And, given that, we could say if you believe in a Creator, the Creator was expecting to create not only a universe – a world and Earth where people [human beings] could live along with created species. G-d had to anticipate the Fall as a surprise, but it was no surprise to G-d. If G-d could have anticipated the Fall as part of the structure, then there wouldn't be any original sin or guilt, right? Because, what else were they going to do?! So, to fall was expected of them in the same way that the crucifixion was expected, right? I mean, if you strictly follow the theological argument, and you don't want to blame anybody, we only want to blame God who ordered the death of his Son as a necessary act. In any case, this is one way to understand the Fall without falling into the notion: "yeah, so women are being oppressed, and defined, and given an identity within a patriarchal order… and they need to be freed and emancipated for that in order to find their own separate identity from the dominant masculine order". So, what this is saying in some way is, yes, there is something related to the loss of the phallus that has something to do with this the sexual difference, and with creation of sexual difference in that sense, but once constituted, once femininity is constituted, then she has her own realm. So, it's not like women have to just depend on living in the masculine realm, although they do also have to live there … but, they have their own realm of feminine jouissance. And the Real is, you know, kind of more important in some ways than the Symbolic. We say that the Real is more important than the Symbolic because the Symbolic is like a container without energy of its own, and the energy needs to be provided. The Real is pure energy. The energy can be constructive or destructive. The first Real is the destructive aspect of material energy, while the second Real is the constructive aspect of the Real.

TEXT: That is what S(A) means. It is in that respect that we arrive at the point of raising the question how to make the One into something that holds up, that is, that is counted without being.

RM: Do you understand that? – The text reads: "how to make the One into something that holds up, that is, that is counted without being"? So, what he's trying to say is that this One … that the being of the One is 'nonbeing'. The own being of the One is nonbeing … that's the paradox. And that's consistent with philosophy, with theology, whatever you want.

GF: That's right. And Nonbeing only arises in contrast to Being. Otherwise, there is nothing.

RM: Right, but you remember that this is without being, 'small b', not "capital B". So, the being of the One is non-Being, but not being is the 'small b', meaning the one doesn't have any of the phenomena that otherwise are words and images. So, it's not even in the Torah and not even in the Gospel, because with the Torah, with the Gospel, you have a revelation in language. That would be 'beings' – it's all the words that are said in the Bible, they're all beings, but they're all 'small b' beings that somehow are supposed to invoke this other being, the One that doesn't have its own being because it is without description – so that's the One. And 'it holds up' ... so 'the One into something that holds up'. It's true ... it holds up ... meaning, emptiness is form, or the emptiness can be counted. The zero can be counted as One.

GF: This relates to an essay written by Slavoj Žižek on Friedrich von Schelling. He wrote an introductory essay called "The Abyss of Freedom" (1997), where he speculates along with Schelling that nonbeing, that meontic nonbeing that 'is there' before there were any created 'beings' [small case b], is desire – it's 'a desire to be'.

RM: Yes, well that's pure desire, right? That's like the desire of the analyst – it's a pure desire without object. Because usually desire is conditioned by the *objet a*, but when the *objet a* dissipates, as it reaches the Real, then you end up with a pure desire without a specific object.

GF: And is that what Lacan believes love is or is love a kind of failed desire?

RM: Remember we talked about love in the three registers? Shall I quiz you on that?

BB: Not me today! You get to tell me!

GF: Well, there's love for the Other ... [*chuckling*]

RM: Okay, so Imaginary love is infatuation with the Other. But what you see in the Other is your own object. It always happens, and that's part of romantic love; namely Imaginary love. Yet it covers over all the differences. So, when that romantic love dissipates, then you're left with the differences. And then, how do you work with differences? – that's where the Symbolic love comes in, because the Symbolic love has to do with all the agreements, the clear communications, the commitments, all the papers one signs, the promises one gives... all that is part of Symbolic love. And, then, love in the Real or Real love is that what you love in the other – which is something that is not easily found in Lacan's work, although I found it in a couple of places in Lacan – because the agalma, you know, like when Socrates says to Alcibiades who was in love with him and I paraphrase... "there where you think I'm something, where you see me as something, I am nothing". That's the agalma – the nothing is not an absence, but a presence. And, ultimately, the agalma is what men are also drawn to in women, even though there's the Imaginary object and Imaginary fantasy... but, behind the Imaginary, the *objet a*, is the second Real, which is this kind of emptiness. And that's like 'something in the way she moves that attracts me like no other lover'. That 'something' could be – oh, she's got great 'this' or great 'that', or she's 'smart as a whip' or she's whatever, right? Or it's something undefinable, beyond that – that's the emptiness.

So then Lacan says… you find yourself or your own emptiness in the emptiness of the Other (or something like that)… as if it were your own emptiness. Because, ultimately, even with the phallus, Lacan says that what desire looks for is not the phallus, but the 'lack'.

There's a 'signifier of a lack' and then 'the lack of a signifier', right? So the lack of a signifier is that aspect of the Real, the emptiness … which is counterintuitive because you wouldn't think it's totally anti-romantic… like, 'oh, you love my emptiness? *WTF? What are you talking about? That sounds crazy! Stop talking like that'!* But it's true! That's the mystery! … the mystery of love! And that's the selflessness of it, too, because the emptiness is the no self.

So, I remember when my kids were small. I had the fantasy that I would sacrifice for them… like if something happened or if there was some life and death situation, and one of us had to live and one of us had to die, then I would go for them so they could live. And I was thinking, why am I having this fantasy? Is this some kind of savior fantasy?… What is this? Now, it could be sort of like when people do acts of heroism for a loved one, but that's because the loved one is special to them. So, even though it's altruistic, on a mental level it has an egoistic aspect to it, because would you do that for any child or just for your own child? Well, probably not, but maybe. So that's where, if you do it just for your own children and your child is the special object, it still has a narcissistic component to it because it's your extension that you're saving. So ultimately, you could say you're just saving yourself, right? But there's that aspect I think of 'no self' … and the emptiness of it … that is more profound than that am I sacrificing for the other. What does love your neighbor as yourself mean? Which self is it? Love your neighbor as yourself for the Jews meant love your fellow Jew and not love the goyim as yourself. You're not going to love the goyim as yourself, because they don't have the soul that you have – you only love your fellow Jew as yourself. So Christianity is supposed to improve on that by universalizing that ethic.

GF: This reminds me of St. Augustine's argument for prevenient grace, where he argues that if a child was about to fall into a well, you and perhaps everybody else would be somehow moved to save the child. And really, there's 'nothing' there that is compelling that action. There is nothing there in particular that moves you and you might become nothing by trying to save the child since you may have to give up your life to save the child. But it's interesting that there's really nothing there aside from perhaps the value of the child?

RM: It's more than that, because when you have a little child like that, I remember, you feel this kind of strong feeling of grace or this kind of very pure parental love… but it's also a kind of empty feeling. You know, it's a beautiful feeling but it's also kind of insubstantial. So maybe it's something like that, which is deeper than the Symbolic love, as in when, "well, I'm your parent, and I am responsible for you and I have to send you to school, I have to save money for college"… that's all Symbolic love, right? And then Imaginary love is, "oh, I need to have a child that's going to improve me… are you going to be, you know, a great dancer, or you're going to be, you know, this or that?" That's Imaginary, although it has a Symbolic component to it. But this other feeling, of just this kind of state of transparent, translucent kindness… there's something really wonderful about it. And I think it comes from the emptiness of the Real.

GF: Yes, and it's so powerful, too! I don't know how many people would act on it, especially today, like if a child was about to fall in front of the subway train, or something like that … how many would reach out and save that child? I think there would be many that would do it, but then again, there will be some that would not…

RM: Well, that makes me think of the horrible opposite, which is – I can't take it anymore, I just can't stand all these kids getting shot! I just can't and I don't know how people can live with it! I mean people should be demonstrating *en masse*!… something has to be done!

GF: We should be applying the brakes for sure!

RM: Big time! There should be a scandal! Every three days or every week there's some shootings in schools – unacceptable! Somebody *do* something! And the politicians are just sitting there, trying to save their position to get enough votes. It's complicated. Sorry. That's a distraction. But it's been on my mind. I can't stand it! I don't know how we can limit it!

GF: I don't how we live with it – I hate it – I can't stand it.

RM: I know. But somehow there's a kind of resignation, isn't there? I guess the gun lobby and the politicians don't think they can go against guns all the way. But you know the gun lobby… I guess their solution is to arm everybody! Anyway, sorry. That's a distraction.

GF: It's finitude, and I think we are too bound up in our Imaginary and Symbolic relationships… like, "I've got to go to work today… I can't take time to go lobby down in Washington, I have to keep my work commitments," you know.

RM: Reputation is something… but people should be saying I refuse to live in a country where children are being murdered with impunity.

[End of recording]

Note

1 *Objet a's* include breast, urine, feces, phallus, voice, gaze, the nothing, umbilical cord, or *lathouse* (any objects). Latouse is the object by which any *objet a* can be extended to any commodity object in the marketplace.

Supplemental References

Augustine. (2010). *On the Free Choice of the Will, on Grace and Free Choice, and Other Writings* (P. King, Trans.). New York: Cambridge University Press.

Lacan, J. (2007). *Écrits* (B. Fink, Trans.). W.W. Norton & Co., New York.

Lacan, J. (1972–1973). *Encore. The Seminar of Jacques Lacan, XX*. New York: Norton, 1998.
Plato. (1999). *The Symposium*. New York: Penguin Books.
Žižek, S. (1997). *The Abyss of Freedom Ages of the World* (The Body, In Theory: Histories of Cultural Materialism). University of Michigan, Ann Arbor Michigan.

Chapter 19

Connaissance and Savoir (Rings of String, Topology, and Computation)

Moncayo Seminar, August 6, 2018, *Encore, Seminar XX*, pg. 17

TEXT: What is not a sign of love is jouissance of the Other, jouissance of the Other sex, and as I said, of the body that symbolizes it.

A change of discourses – things budge, things traverse you, things traverse us, things are traversed (*ça se traverse*), and no one notices the change (*personnne n'accuse le coup*). I can say until I'm blue in the face that the notion of discourse should be taken as a social link (*lien social*), founded on language, and thus seems not unrelated to what is specified in linguistics as grammar, and yet nothing seems to change.

For it is with those stupidities that we do analysis, and that we enter into the new subject – that of the unconscious. It is precisely to the extent that the guy is willing not to think anymore that we will perhaps learn a little bit more about it, that we will draw certain consequences from his words (*dits*) – words that cannot be taken back (*se dedire*), for that is the rule of the game. (pg. 17)

This way of topologizing language's status is illustrated most admirably by phonology, insofar as phonology incarnates the signifier in phonemes. But the signifier cannot in any way be limited to this phonemic prop. Once again – what is a signifier. (pg. 19)

What is important is not that it's imaginary – after all, if the signifier allowed us to point to the image, we need to be happy, that would be fine and dandy, but it's not the case. At the level of the signifier/signified distinction, what characterizes the relationship between the signified and what serves as the indispensable third party, namely the referent, is precisely that the signified misses the referent. The joiner doesn't work. (pg. 20)

BB: Let me try to walk through this line by line. Lacan says, "What is not a sign of love"… Do I read him correctly: he suggests that the sign of love is found in the act of changing reasons, in other words, changing discourses? Then he says, "What is not a sign of love is the jouissance of the Other, the jouissance of the other sex, and the body that symbolizes it". Then he suggests that "discourse should be taken as a social link".

So, love as a social link is a discourse, a changing of discourse. And that then puts us in a position to understand that what we're talking about is that there is a 'something borrowed' that must be crossed-over (because it is barred) in this game of love… which is that "changing of discourses", I suppose. When Lacan says this is a

DOI: 10.4324/9781003424581-19

way of topologizing languages, he puts us in the position to say that reason does not pin down or label things in an absolute or universal sense. Instead, reason is linked to a particular context of discourse. It doesn't exist outside of these discourses.

We do not enter into the new subject via reason, but instead, it is with 'stupidities' that we do analysis and enter into the new subject. So, in a certain way, the rule of the game, he says, is: 'I am willing to not think anymore words that can't be taken back and a speaking that does not ex-sist with respect to words spoken'. This is a radical disconnection. Love is the sign of changing discourses and a social link, and it is only with stupidities that we can enter into an analysis of this love. Does the thinking in poetry work this way?

RM: It's the '*ex*-sist'? That means the thinking that is a form of jouissance that doesn't have signifiers… that's outside the Symbolic.

BB: So, is the following correct? First, do we enter into the new subject through the stupidities? Second, is Lacan suggesting that stupidity isn't the "wrong reason"? And third, does stupidity instead mean "I am willing to not think anymore words that can't be taken back"?

RM: Thinking there means secondary process thinking like, "I'm not going to listen to rational reasons why I shouldn't be in love, or I should be in love, or whether I should do this or I shouldn't do that", right? And there's importance in the way he is using 'stupidity'. First there is this stupidity of the lover who's blind to anything but love. And then there's the analytical stupidity, meaning that you have to be willing in analysis to say anything foolish and not be worried about saying something stupid. With the lover, in that sense, there is one who is willing to say something stupid because of love. And, also, it's a kind of 'not knowing' – stupidity in the sense of not knowing exactly under what conditions you're falling in love.

BB: So, it's kind of like 'I'm willing to not think anymore'.

RM: Right, I'm not going to be rational anymore.

BB: So, how does the analysand answer the question 'Who am I?' if, as Lacan says, "the subject is not the one (*celui*), who thinks. The subject is precisely the one we encourage, not to say it all (*tout dire*), as we tell him in order to charm him – one cannot say it all – but rather to utter stupidities". [*Encore, Seminar XX*, pg. 21–22]

RM: Yes, so the stupidities are 'the one who thinks'. 'I think where I am not' – that's where he's playing with the Cartesian permutations of the "I think, therefore I am. I think where I'm not, and I am where I don't think. So, there he is talking about unconscious thinking and the unconscious that is speaking. When I give voice to the unconscious, I'm speaking stupidities.

BB: So, then, we get back to this third party. The third party refers to the position that the poet is in or the position occupied by 'someone' who can't notice love – love representing the changing of discourses and, hence, the changing of reasons. So, at the level of the signifier/signified distinction, what characterizes the relationship between the indispensable third party, that is, the

> referent, and the signified when the signified misses the referent? Is that what Lacan calls '*meconnaissance*' or a misrecognition? Is that what characterizes the relation between the signifier and the signified – when it comes to love – that there's always a misrecognition because the signified always misses the referent similar to the way that in poetry there's also a significant change in discourses or a significant missing?

And it's a little bit like… I'm thinking about Giorgio Agamben, who talks about ways the poet evokes an experience of meaning before you have the words to describe it. Poetry does this by creating a contradiction between discourses. Do you remember being a kid… you have an experience, but you don't know the words for it yet. And then you find the word and have that aha feeling and find yourself saying, "oh, that's love!", or "oh, that's what good means!", or "oh, that's red!" Agamben, I believe, calls it the "infancy of experience".

I fell in love with language this way: I feel confusion, then I feel something, but I don't know the words for it, then comes the feeling "Oh, you mean this!" and then the feelings of oneness with other people and the world follows. Learning about language this way is different from the learning that's top-down or the learning where you get slapped down with "that's not it" every time you don't reproduce the expected language… or the kind of learning that's trying to mimic, "well, I'll just say what he says and see if that's it". It's really different going from the infancy of experience to that of "Aha!"

RM: The infancy of experience refers to one of the types of primary repression.

BB: Who's your reference? Agamben, Lacan, or Freud?

RM: According to me!

BB: Okay, what do you mean by 'infancy of experience'?

RM: Well, I mean that the primary repression is one way to think about it. There's the first signifier of the mother's desire that gets repressed under primary repression, and that would be the false hole. The true hole is where it looks like there's nothing there, but that's only because there are no signifiers. So, the child at first doesn't have any signifying reference. There's something that they're experiencing in their lived experience which isn't the Real and it's not signified yet. There's nothing repressed there, but it's just that there's no reference by which to account for it except when you come up with this 'aha' experience – "oh, this is what this is!". But that's also an approximation.

BB: Of course, but in the self there's a moment when one forges a link to language and the social. In the moment when you join with good faith in the language game, you do so because there's this internal experience that makes you feel joined with others and that the link that joins you is real – that it is not made up, not random.

I remember in supervision with Françoise Davoine, she talked about a specific shift in the treatment of psychosis that occurs when the analysand joins the analyst in the language game. It requires good faith. In psychosis, this good faith has sometimes been lost and must be reestablished in the analysis. I have seen this occur in the treatment of psychosis. These patients in a psychotic state begin by throwing words as if words were objects meant to smash things or meant to make waves. There is a turning point that follows engaging the patient around the game of language which leads him or her to occupy a new position in relation to language and speaking. In this new position words can carry meaning according to a shared code in a context of sincerity and good faith.

RM: Right, but remember, also, what falls under primary repression is the first signifier of the drive, meaning the question of what is the object of my mother's desire? What is it that my mother wants from my father or from the Other, and the first signifier will function as a signified for the Name of the Father.

BB: When I fall in love with a poem, is it because certain words become meaningful to me because they recognize and represent the Desire of the Mother that is embedded in this poem and the representation of the Desire of the Mother takes me to formative places in my unconscious that I wish to rejoin. For example, a word in the poem evokes an image that I associate with my mother's red fingernail polish that in turn leads me to feel love?

RM: Right, you could write a poem, an 'Ode to the Love Object,' where the color red represents the object of desire. So, that would be one type of poetry. But then there's the poetry that also is a form of the jouissance of meaning.

BB: Let me know if this what you're saying. Are you saying when one falls in love with a word that represents mother, one falls in love with words/language – with the saying of things – as a result.

RM: Words capture the object of desire. It is as if the word captured your love object or your object of desire in some way. So, right, but the Name of the Father is the key organizer of language, in Lacanian theory at least. So, there's no way of separating the love for the Father from the love for language. They're related. Or maybe is it possible to say that there's a way of knitting together the love of the mother, and wishing to be the object of the mother's desire as it becomes transmuted into a language game in which these examples of the mother, or this maternal desire, are this relationship to the paternal in the form of a poem – which is different than the form of a discourse. It's different from the Master's Discourse. We would then have to go back and differentiate between speech, language, and discourse, because we throw these terms around and sometimes, they mean the same thing (and sometimes they don't). But we can go back and look to see what Lacan means by the 'changing of discourses'. Is he talking strictly about the four discourses? Is he talking about how we 'change our tune' about the Other or about the object when we're in love? Are we saying that we sing a different song, that we speak different words? – is that what he means by the 'changing of discourses'? Or is he talking about the transformation between the four discourses?

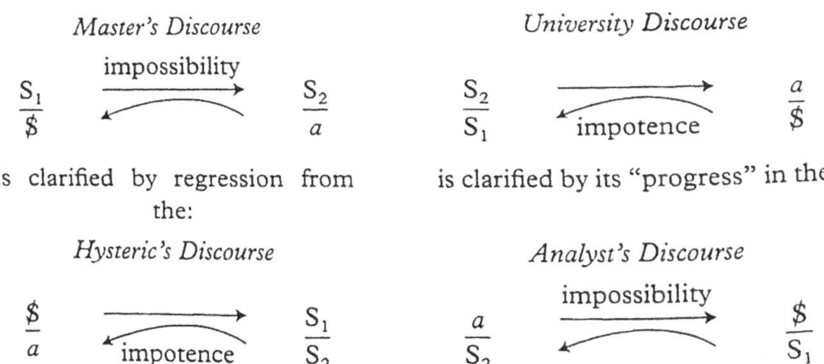

BB: I think he means the four discourses, because that's what he's working with. If we can, let's look at the diagram for a minute on the top of page 17: he refers to 'agent' over 'truth' and 'the Other' over 'production'. So, in the Master's Discourse, the agent [S_1] is the master signifier and it has an impossible relationship to knowledge [S_2]. It [S_1] seeks knowledge [S_2]. The agent tries to do this, but it's impossible. And the production of effort is surplus as first jouissance. So, in the relationship between production and relative truth in the Master's Discourse, "production is a surplus jouissance, and the truth that it is related to is the split subject" [*Encore, Seminar XX*, pgs. 16–17], meaning that the master acts like a cocky master, but he's really or she's really a divided subject. That's the truth. Okay, so let's talk about the line that refers to the impossibility of it. What's the difference between the line that represents S_1 and S_2 in the Master's Discourse and the other line that's curved?

RM: There's an impossibility where S_1 is the master and S_2 is the slave. The curved line refers to the impossibility before which the master becomes a caricature. In the University Discourse, the curved line going left refers to the impotence of the university to produce true speech. In the Hysteric's Discourse, the master is impotent before the woman [S_1]. In the Analyst's Discourse the impossibility refers to what is unknowable about the Real. The impossible remains the source of possibility.

There are two types of S1. One is the master as social ego. And the other is a spiritual master who is the mouthpiece to the master signifier. The social master does not have access to wisdom.

BB: S_2 here is knowledge? What is the relation to the Other?

RM: In the Analyst's Discourse, S_2 is knowledge. In the Master's Discourse, S_2 is the servant, because he's referring here to Hegel's master-slave dialectic.

So, the master can never get enough recognition from the slave that they are a master of... so that's the impossibility. The master is always trying to get recognized as the best... you know like some politicians who say, "it's never been like this" or "you've never seen anything like this", et cetera. So, the politicians can't get the recognition they want so they keep trying to say how great they are as a master and that the recognition from the Other is just not coming.

BB: So, can you explain the small 'a' that's underneath the S_1 in the Master's Discourse. What is the relationship between the Other and production?

RM: The small 'a' in that diagram represents the analyst being in the place of unconscious knowledge. Unconscious knowledge is Symbolic. But the knowledge of the object through the senses is Imaginary. Finally, the *objet a* is Real because the object dissolves in the encounter with the Real. Your second question – the Other makes us work. The slave is the one that produces in response to the demand of the Other.

BB: Does that mean that in the Master's Discourse, the production is surplus jouissance and that surplus jouissance has a relationship to the split subject?

RM: So, he's throwing around Marxist concepts here. The surplus jouissance is from the surplus value that the capitalist obtains from the worker. But here, the slave is the one producing the *objet a*, or producing the goods, and somehow this production meets a kind of infinitude in which you can never produce enough goods or where the goods will never be completely satisfying. So, you end up in a position of divided subject without an object of desire. The subject can also give up this metonymic imaginary search for completion. The subject absorbs the lack, becomes the lack, and becomes whole full thanks to the lack in the Real.

BB: So, this is how I came to terms with this talk about love. When I'm trying to talk about love, and an act of love which is a social link ... that in the Master's Discourse, love looks like this: the agent is a master signifier (i.e., I know the truth, and it's the only truth), and it relates to [an] Other, which is knowledge. However, it's an alienated relationship to knowledge. And as a result of that, it's really what's leftover, the surplus jouissance, that is informing the split subject. Then the split subject is more dependent, or in its love, it's in touch with the surplus jouissance because the other relationships are superficial and because of the impossibility of the master signifier capturing knowledge. So, love in this form is going to take the form of a constant never-ending trying to get S_1 and S_2 to match ... and they're never going to do it! And the dissatisfaction of love will look a particular way in this discourse. With regard to University Discourse, it's going to be a different kind of love. In this one, the agent of love is knowledge and knowledge, as agent, is seeking through surplus jouissance. Yes, knowledge is seeking the *objet a* which is surplus jouissance.

RM: And it never hits the target. Therefore, what it produces is the division and the impotence of the divided subject.

BB: Yes. The impotence of the divided subject is related to the frustration created by the master signifier. How does the master signifier work? Does it always start with the agent seeking knowledge, and then move from knowledge to that something knowledge doesn't gain? Does the split subject form when the effort to seek the master signifier never succeeds?

RM: The academic would like to have the master signifier, but instead, they just reproduce division.

BB: That's nice. I like that way of summing that up!

RM: That's like when you go to those academic conferences where everybody's giving 15-minute presentations and nobody says anything or nobody hears anything, and then, you know, they spend three days doing that [*chuckling*].

BB: In the Master's Discourse, the master signifier (S_1) is the agent? What is it always reproducing?

RM: Yes, it's reproducing this attempt to get recognition from the underling (the servant or slave).

BB: The Master's Discourse is reproducing the attempt to get knowledge so as to recognize what? Is it to get the servant to recognize the master as having knowledge? The master wants to be recognized as a 'master'. But you have taught us that instead, the omnipotent master is simply an impotent, divided subject and that the University Discourse represents a bureaucratic superego that measures with tools like multiple choice exams. You said that the personal relationship to knowledge is a form of subjective unconscious intuition – the unknowing that knows.

RM: Yes. Lacan speaks about the Master's Discourse as an intersubjective discourse. There are social links, but the University Discourse in particular is more difficult because it is the site of angry, unpleasant, disputation.

BB: If Lacan defines 'a' as surplus jouissance, what do you mean that 'a' is the purpose of science?

RM: No, no, no! The surplus jouissance, it's like, for example, the people who can't get enough phallic jouissance. Like with sexual addiction – that's a surplus jouissance because you're always trying to determine who has the phallus or who is the phallus. And so the surplus jouissance is a place where people get stuck. The same with the jouissance of the Other, where there is a wanting of a fusion with the Other that's impossible. So that's also surplus jouissance, and that's different from the *objet a* as the object of science or science as its object. I think that's what the 'a' is doing there in the University Discourse as opposed to the scientist trying to get a surplus jouissance from the object.

BB: Okay, I'll come back to that maybe. So, if we go then to the Hysteric's Discourse, we have the agent as the split subject and the split subject is relating to an Other, which is the master signifier.

RM: Right, and that's easy to see both as intrapsychic and interpersonal …

BB: And then the S_2 is equivalent to knowledge, whereas, for the hysteric, knowledge can never translate back into surplus jouissance. So, the product of the Hysteric's Discourse is an effort at knowledge?

RM: Well, Lacan says the hysteric is the one who wants a master to govern over. So, this structural relation has the complexity of both wanting a master or master signifier for the Other to give the subject the phallus. The hysteric seeks to identify who the master is, and then proceeds to castrate or undo the master. And that's why the master ends up impotent.

BB: Why doesn't the University Discourse end up in impotence instead of impossibility? What's the different significance of those two words? And why is one on the bottom and one on the top?

RM: Well, impotence is at the bottom of the formulation, right? So, it's the relationship between the product and the truth in terms of the positions. And, in the University Discourse, in the search for the object of science, you find division – consider all the struggles that people go through to generate a discovery because they're looking for the unknown. First it looks for the 'a', and the search for the 'a' yields a certain kind of division, because the object is hidden in some way. Then, the scientist wants to find some master signifier that would describe the 'a', but in that process, they experienced impotence. Now, the hysteric… the divided subject… "oh, I'm suffering and I need you to help me because I can't help myself" or whatever, and "I want you to give me some words of wisdom, because I know that you're a subject that knows". Or I assume that you are the subject that is supposed to know – that's the S_2. And "out of that knowledge, give me some words of wisdom"! So, the hysteric wants the analyst to be the *objet a for* the analysand and the truth is that the object of desire doesn't exist or is always missing. So, despite the words of wisdom, despite the knowledge, the analyst doesn't really have the *objet a* that the hysteric wants. Thus, the *objet a* will have to be discovered through castration and through something that's missing for the subject. Does that make sense?

GF: And the missing object of desire always creates the split subject.

RM: Right, because the subject has lost the object of desire. That's the bar on the 'S' of the divided subject.

BB: I thought that in the Analyst's Discourse, what analysis wants to know isn't the 'I' but is that unknown thing? It is surplus jouissance…

RM: Are you talking about the Analyst's Discourse now? So, the analyst is the 'a', the agent, right? And the analysand is the divided subject. But, yet underneath this divided subject, we're trying to generate these signifiers of desire. And then these signifiers of desire represent a form of unconscious *savior* or unconscious knowing… that's S_2 in a position of truth. So, when knowledge is at the position of truth, it is *savior* rather than *connaissance.*

Now, one thing I should tell you, I was reading Lacan's *Seminar XV* on the psychoanalytic act. And there, he makes a distinction based on the difference between words and concepts, which are not the same. So, there's the difference between the two words *connaissance* and *savoir* and then there are two concepts of knowledge. So, Lacan always has two different concepts of knowledge, but sometimes he calls one concept one word, and sometimes he calls the other concept a different word. So, in the psychoanalytic act, he changes the relationship and calls knowledge *savoir* and he calls *connaissance* unconscious knowing. So, he's not always consistent with how he uses these words. But it's always consistent that he has two different conceptions of knowledge – one being '*savoir*' and the other being '*connaissance*'. And *savoir* is the unconscious knowledge which I translate as knowing since we don't have a word for it in English. But, again, he's not always consistent with choosing the arbitrariness of the signifier... sometimes he uses the other signifier for the different concept. So, S_2 here, in the Analyst's Discourse, means unconscious knowing rather than academic knowledge. Whereas in the University Discourse, the agent of S_2 is academic knowledge – its *connaissance.* And what about the S_2 in the Master's and the Hysteric's Discourse? That's technical know-how. It's like I hire a worker for a house, and they know how to repair this and repair that, and so they have all this technical know-how that the master doesn't have.

BB: And, in the Hysteric's Discourse?

RM: Yeah, that's also the expert – "oh, you know, I'm going to my analyst or my therapist, and my psychiatrist is an expert". So that's expertise there. And the S_2 in the Hysteric's Discourse is also like the University Discourse because an expertise is expected. And you have to remove yourself from the position of expertise in order to occupy the analyst's position when faced by the hysteric's desire for a master. First, you use it, and you don't deny it, but then you have to remove yourself from the position of the expert to give ground to their own unconscious knowledge rather than your expert knowledge.

[End of recording]

Supplemental References

Agamben, G. (1993). *Infancy and History: The Destruction of Experience*. Verso; 1st Edition. London and New York.

Descartes, R. (2008). *Meditations on First Philosophy* (M. Moriarty, Trans.). Oxford University Press. London.

Lacan, J. (1972–1973). *Encore. The Seminar of Jacques Lacan, XX.* New York: Norton, 1998.

Lacan, J. (1967–1968). *The Psychoanalytic Act. The Seminar of Jacques Lacan, XV*. UK: Karnac, 2002.

Marx, K. (1818). *The German Ideology*. New York: Prometheus Books, 1998.

Chapter 20

Does a Rat Have Being? The Being of the Subject as a Necessary Hypothesis (Experienced or Supposed)

Moncayo Seminar, March 6, 2018 *Encore, Seminar XX*, p. 139

TEXT: How can being know? It's amusing to see how this question is supposedly answered. Since the limit, as I have posited it, is constituted by the fact that there are beings who speak, people wonder what the knowledge of those who do not speak could be. They wonder about it. They don't know why they wonder about it. But they wonder about it all the same. So, they build a little maze (*labyrinthe*) for rats.

They hope thereby to be on the right track by which to determine what knowledge is. They believe a rat is going to show the capacity it has to learn (*apprendre*). To learn (*a-prendre*) to do what? What interests it, of course. And what do they assume interests it?

They do not take the rat as a being, but rather as a body, which means that they view it as a unit, a rat unit. Now what thus sustains the rat's being? They don't wonder about that at all. Or rather, they identify its being with its body.

People have always imagined that being had to contain a sort of fullness that is characteristic of it. Being is a body. That is where people began in first approaching being, and they laboriously concocted (*élucubré*) a whole hierarchy of beings. Ultimately, they began with the notion that each one should know what keeps it in being (*maintenait à l'être*) – that had to be its good, in other words, what gives it pleasure.

RM: Do you want to read note 6?

TEXT: Lacan's French here is quite idiosyncratic, since *maintenir* is a transitive verb. Lacan seems to construct his phraseology here along the lines of the expression *se tenir à quelque chose* (to hold onto or cleave to something); a more idiomatic translation would be "everyone should know what keeps him going (or alive)". Alternatively, the phrase could be understood as "everyone should know what keeps him alive as a body", for l'être could be taken as "to be it," it referring to the body.

RM: It's interesting that he is using the category of 'being' as opposed to 'instinct' to speak about the rat.

GF: Is that because it would have been better to use instinct, given the scientific discourse?

DOI: 10.4324/9781003424581-20

RM: Well, it's interesting that he's raising this question for us, which would be … I guess we would have to differentiate between lowercase 'b' and capital case 'B' in Heidegger, which is where Lacan borrows these from, or from Sartre against existentialism. So, there's something more than just the stimulus and the response, or the conditioned behavior, or the hunger being the stimulus and then the behavior being the response that he thinks of being. Now, I don't know if he's going toward capital "Being" or lowercase "being", but this reminds me of the Buddha's saying that all beings have the Buddha Nature – so there's a famous koan called Mu: "Does a dog have Buddha nature or not?" Here the question is, does the rat have Buddha Nature or not? Does the rat have being or not?! … being the translation into secular language. But that would be my question to Lacan at this point – does the rat have being or not? Let's see what he argues!

BB: Part of me wants to say that to have being you have to have being for someone and have the 'mirror stage' in mind in some way. The rat, in just following his pleasure, is acting from instinct. In so doing, he does not have being for someone. Maybe, our position of being for someone who has "cares" about us is working within its own Imaginary register in some rudimentary way.

RM: That's very good! So, it's like being for another would be equivalent to interdependence among human's activity, or something like that, right?

BB: Yes, and it engages the Imaginary somewhat …

RM: Right, however, the only thing is that in interdependence or, you know, self and other relations, you have small case 'beings' – but do you have capital case 'Being'? And then, you're saying it requires interaction. In Buddhism, being is something more than interdependence … or interdependence is emptiness, because all beings have no self. So, because we don't have a substantial self, then our self is made by the interactions. But, once you have all the interactions, you can think of the interactions among signifiers, too. If you only consider the Symbolic dimension, once you have yourself as a metaphor – that is as an interaction with somebody else, as an interaction with another in recognition – something about yourself that is not defined by the interaction is lost. So, what's lost in the interaction is the Real (both first and second Real). The Real doesn't depend on interaction. And yet, it's something that we're made of, too, at the same time that we are made by these interactions and relationships.

TEXT: What change thus came about in discourse in order for people to suddenly question that being regarding the means it might have to go beyond itself, that is, to learn more than it needs to know in its being to survive as a body?

The maze leads not only to nourishment but to a button or flap that the supposed subject of this being must figure out how to use to obtain nourishment. Or it has to recognize a feature, a lit or colored feature, to which the being is capable of reacting. What is important is that the question of knowledge is transformed here into that of learning. If, after a series of trials and errors – "trials and errors" was left in English (in the translation) considering the people who carved out this approach to knowledge – the rate diminishes sufficiently, they note that the rat unit is capable of learning something.

The question that is only secondarily raised – the one that interests me – is whether the rat unit can learn how to learn. Therein lies the true mainspring of the experiment. Once it has taken one of these tests, will a rat, faced with another test of the same kind, learn more quickly? That can be easily attested to by a decrease in the number of trials necessary for it to know how it must behave in such a montage – let us call the maze, taken in conjunction with the flaps and buttons that function here, a "montage."

The question has been so rarely raised, though it has been raised, that people haven't even dreamt of investigating the differential effect of having the themes one proposes to the rat – by which it demonstrates its ability to learn – come from the same source or from two different sources, and of having the experimenter who teaches the rat to learn be the same or different. Now, the experimenter is the one who knows something in this business, and it is with what he knows that he invents this montage consisting of the maze, buttons, and flaps. If he were not someone whose relation to knowledge is grounded in a relation to llanguage, in the inhabiting of llanguage or the cohabitation with llanguage, there would be no montage.

BB: So, it sounds like he is asking what is the rat? A rat unit? Is that what its being is? And then, he introduces this question of knowledge versus language. And if a rat can learn, which is different than what a rat knows …

RM: Which is knowledge versus learning …

BB: Right, so if a rat can learn instead of not having knowledge, then it sounds like that has meaning for the rat. And we know that the rat can learn, because he says he can figure out how to get the flaps and doors open better the second time, but we don't know whether he would be able to learn differently with different people. And it's the different person that's going to bring him along – like one experimenter versus another would have a different lalangue. So, it seems he's raising a question of whether the rat is responding to the particular lalangue of the experimenter when it's learning something about how to learn. Or is it responding to something else?

GF: I think that is a great summary because it highlights the kind of relation that the rat might have with the experimenter, whereas the experimenter is setting up a certain domain – a 'montage' – in which the rat is going to respond one way or the other by whatever signifiers are there. So, it's hard to discern if the rat is learning or merely reacting.

BB: Would the rat be able to learn how to do the task quicker having done it once, if it were repeated with a different experimenter. Is the rat picking up, learning, the logic of a particular experimenter? Would he not be able to repeat the next test faster because the thing he's learning is idiosyncratic to the lalangue of the current experimenter, not the experiment? Or are we talking about cognitive developmental stages as outlined by Piaget – what kind of learning is the rat doing?

GF: Yes, any experimenter can copy the next experimenter, so there wouldn't be a whole lot of difference. But, given the fact that it started out with some kind of unconscious lalangue in the background ... I think what's being teased out here is the difference between knowledge and jouissance – a theme prevalent throughout this seminar; namely this assertion that you cannot have one without the other (although they usually get conflated). Lacan seems to always be trying to recognize the jouissance that is hidden, for instance, between the identified scientific reality and the Real that is always in the background determining the montage.

BB: So, is that knowledge that you're describing, or learning?

GF: Well, learning seems to have both elements, knowledge and jouissance ... it always involves some response to jouissance. That's a specific kind of learning. And the rat responds to the jouissance of the lalangue and the montage, and we cannot discern the difference of whether the rat is merely responding instinctually to signifiers in the maze.

BB: So, if I were to repeat back what you said: Lacan notices again and again that there's an element of jouissance in knowledge and learning that science doesn't always give credit to.

RM: Right, which is different from a computer. A rat is not a computer, nor does the rat have language. So, if with the montage of the experiment he's equating language ... and it is equitable with language, given that you could say the montage is just a bunch of levers and food.

GF: Right. Some semioticians would say that's part of the *Umwelt* and its particular significations.

RM: Yes, but that's semiotic, not symbolic. They're semiotic exchanges, you know, at all levels. It's semiotic changes at the biological level, at the level of the cell, and the relationship between the self and the cell in the environment ... which is kind of like the self and the environment. It even sounds similar, except that with humans you have language.

GF: So, something has to be culturally recognized to be Symbolic? It has to be culturally shared to be a symbol as opposed to a mere sign?

RM: You have to have discrete units of letters and signifiers, but somehow the Symbolic is more just than letters and signifiers in say the machine. And that goes back to the question of Being and *savoir*. *Savior* requires language and jouissance. We don't know if the 'rat experience' truly manifests jouissance, although, obviously, the rat experiences pleasure and pain. But, that's instinctual. And, pleasure and pain are regulated by semiotic codes, if they're not regulated by Symbolic codes. The Symbolic also seems to have a dimension of something acausal or unconditioned in it, too, like Tyche, for example. So, there's something in the Symbolic that cannot be entirely reduced to the body and to the machine. What is beyond the machine has to do with the question of Being. So, I'm not sure how we go back to the question of does the rat have 'being' or not, since the rat, you could argue, doesn't have being and doesn't have language. So, what he's calling language here in the experiment is more of a semiotic montage, just like you find in biological systems or computer systems.

GF: Yes, and I think the clue to that was back in Section 128, when he said, “ultimately, they began with the notion that each one should know what keeps it in being, that it has to be good, in other words, what gives you pleasure”. But he seems to be splitting hairs there, because it’s not about what gives pleasure when we say something is ‘good’, because the ‘good’ possesses a certain valuation beyond pleasure. ‘The Good’ has got all those overtones which Plato had in mind when discussing Being with a capital ‘B’. It’s not just pleasure, but it’s also something different or more than mere pleasure.

RM: Right, the pleasure of the good is different than the goodness of pleasure!

TEXT: The only thing the rat unit learns in this case is to give a sign, a sign of its presence as unit. The flap is recognized only by a sign and pressing its paw on this sign is a sign. It is always by making a sign that the unit accedes to that on the basis of which one concludes that there is learning. But this relation to signs is external. Nothing confirms that the rat grasps the mechanism to which pressing the button leads. That’s why the only thing that counts is to know if the experimenter notes that the rat has not only figured it out but learned (*appris*) how a mechanism is to be grasped (*se prend*), in other words, learned what must be grasped (*à-prendre*). If we take the status of unconscious knowledge into account, we must examine the maze experiment in terms of how the rat unit responds to what has been thought up by the experimenter not on the basis of nothing, but on the basis of llanguage.

This example thus leaves the questions regarding the status of knowledge and the status of learning (*apprentissage*) completely intact and distinct. The status of knowledge raises another question, namely how it is taught.

RM: So, again, it sounds like this distinction between learning and knowledge is holding up for Lacan.

BB: And what is the distinction between learning and knowledge?

RM: It’s holding up for him that knowledge requires learning while learning doesn’t require knowledge … that’s the question, whether the rat grasps the concept.

GF: Right, so it’s really more of a response than it is taking those responses and making some kind of inferred assumption, I guess.

RM: Yes, he’s raising important questions, but he’s not really tightly delineating the differences. But you know, there’s a YouTube video that shows mathematical ability in monkeys. And there’s an experiment where they put the monkey in front of a screen, and they have to press all these different buttons to get results. This was a different variety of monkey than a chimpanzee, and it was so quick in its response that it seemed like no thinking was required. The monkey just saw all the mathematical problems presented to it on the screen and immediately responded almost like a machine – perhaps even faster than what a human being could do. I was completely blown away that an animal could have such an unconscious mathematical ability and respond so automatically.

BB: I would like to see that!

GF: But again, this monkey could just be responding to particular markings, or a particular sign. The animal is not registering the numerical system, although we cannot know that for sure.

RM: Yes, but somehow, they intuitively know all the connections of how things are organized.

BB: Is that the unconscious knowledge that's part of lalangue? This last sentence – "if we take the status of unconscious knowledge into account" …

RM: Right, but it seems to be purely semiotic. So, it's a kind of intelligence of the semiotic system that can detect the interactions without requiring language, knowledge, or concept.

GF: Yes, it's somehow understanding the code without understanding the system of the code, or how the code fits into a specific meaning.

RM: Exactly. And it can do it much faster than a human being! … just like a computer can calculate much faster.

GF: But is that understanding of the system in which the code operates the unconscious knowledge of lalangue?

RM: Well, with lalangue you need language. You need the basic elements of language, which is how the mother engages the child with this blend of jouissance and lalangue – that is the rudiment of language over auralization.[1]

GF: Sure, but human beings understand the code as a language, as part of a language system, because of their familiarity or their operational understanding within language.

BB: And, what about this last sentence, that "a maze experiment is on the basis of lalangue", because if lalangue requires language, it doesn't sound like that's what he's saying in this last sentence …

RM: Yeah, I think this is a place where he collapses the semiotic and the Symbolic. But let's posit the working hypothesis that learning can be semiotic or symbolic, while language is distinctly Symbolic. In this case, knowledge would be associated with language and jouissance, while learning is instinctual and semiotic, and tied to the pleasure principle. Whereas with jouissance, there are different levels – there's an evolution of the pleasure principle to forms of jouissance that are something more distinctly human. That's the best I could approximate it at this point, but we'll see if what he says next clarifies it or not.

GF: In the last sentence we read, "If we take the status of unconscious knowledge into account, we must examine the maze experiment in terms of how the rat unit responds to what has been thought up by the experimenter not on the basis of nothing" … I was thinking that he was saying that the experimenter holds the lalangue – that the experimenter is the one that's framing the montage. Then the rat would be reading the language not as a signifier, but as a sign.

TEXT: It is on the basis of the notion of a kind of knowledge that is transmitted, integrally transmitted, that a sifting occurred in knowledge, thanks to which the discourse called scientific discourse was constituted.

It wasn't constituted without numerous misadventures. Hypotheses non fingo …

GF: I am not sure what '*non fingo*' means?

RM: In Wikipedia,[2] it's defined as 'to fain no hypothesis', or 'I can frame no hypothesis', and 'I can try no hypothesis'. It's a famous phrase used by Newton in an essay 'General Scholium' which was appended to the second edition of the *Principia*.

GF: I just feel that Lacan is going to argue against this!

TEXT: 'Hypotheses non fingo', Newton believed he could say, "I assume nothing". But it was on the basis of a hypothesis that the famous revolution – which wasn't at all Copernican, but rather Newtonian – hinged, substituting "it falls" for "it turns". The Newtonian hypothesis consisted in positing that the astral turning is the same as falling. But in order to observe that – which allows one to eliminate the hypothesis – he first had to make the hypothesis.

To introduce a scientific discourse concerning knowledge, one must investigate knowledge where it is. That knowledge, insofar as it resides in the shelter of llanguage, means the unconscious. I do not enter there, no more than did Newton, without a hypothesis.

My hypothesis is that the individual who is affected by the unconscious is the same individual who constitutes what I call the subject of a signifier. That is what I enunciate in the minimal formulation that a signifier represents a subject to another signifier. That is what I enunciate in the minimal formulation that a signifier represents a subject to another signifier. The signifier in itself is nothing but what can be defined as a difference from another signifier. It is the introduction of difference as such into the field, which allows one to extract from llanguage the nature of the signifier (*ce qu'il en est du signifiant*).

GF: So, is he saying that true knowledge consists in recognizing this difference between signifiers?

RM: The difference between signifiers…

GF: Or, that signifiers are essentially given meaning by other signifiers.

RM: Well, concepts are given meaning by other concepts, right? So, it's the same. In theory, it's a signifying structure. But, then there's the question: Is thinking the same as language? And can you say that a theory is constituted as a language or that language is constituted as a theory? But the thing is that language seems to involve a lot more jouissance than a theory. Although some people get really upset about theories [*chuckling*] and you might have a real brawl if you brought all the theorists together into the same room to work it out! You would have one of these cartoon crowds with legs coming out! [*Laughing*] And I would be in the cloud, too! We're all in it, you know! It's hard to talk about theory without having feelings.

BB: Right, exactly!

RM: So, it seems in that sense that the theory has jouissance as well and can be experienced similarly with language. But a thought has more than language Lacan says, because the thought clearly has jouissance.

GF: If I was a rat moving through a semiotic maze, I feel I would not be determining the difference between 'I took the cheese' or 'I didn't take the cheese' based on the fact, you know, cheese smells good or something like that. Those are signifiers, right? So, there's really no 'understanding' the difference between signifiers for the rat … it's just a response.

BB: Or my mother said that I should not eat cheese, but I am going to eat it anyway! I took the cheese because my mother told me not to!

GF: Yes, precisely! [*Laughing*] Therefore, I recollect that every time I enter the maze!

TEXT: Stated otherwise, I reduce the hypothesis, according to the very formulation that lends it substance, to the following: it is necessary to the functioning of llanguage. To say that there is a subject is nothing other than to say that there is a hypothesis. The only proof we have that the subject coincides with this hypothesis, and that it is the speaking individual on whom it is based, is that the signifier becomes a sign.

RM: A sign, right. There he defines a sign as an object that represents something for someone – as opposed to the signifiers that represent a subject to another signifier. So, the 'someone there' that the sign means something to is this supposition of a hypothesis of a subject. But, at the same time, the subject is supplanted by the signifier and the subject falls to the level of the Real.

[End of session]

Notes

1 Auralization is a procedure designed to model and simulate the experience of acoustic phenomena rendered as a sound field in a virtualized space. From Wikipedia, the free encyclopedia – https://en.wikipedia.org/wiki/Auralization

2 Wikipedia – https://en.wikipedia.org/wiki/Hypotheses_non_fingo

Supplemental References

Lacan, J. (1972–1973). *Encore. The Seminar of Jacques Lacan, XX.* New York: Norton, 1998.

Newton, Sir Isaac. (2016). *Principia Mathematica.* First Edition. University of California Press. Berkeley, CA.

Chapter 21

Lalangue, Unconscious Knowledge, and the Soul

Moncayo Seminar, March 20, 2018, *Encore, Seminar XX*, pg. 142

RM: I think we are in the middle of section 3, on page 142.
BB: Let's start again from the top of section three…

TEXT: It is on the basis of the notion of a kind of knowledge that is transmitted, integrally transmitted, that a sifting occurred in knowledge, thanks to which the discourse called scientific discourse was constituted.

It wasn't constituted without numerous misadventures. Hypotheses *non fingo*, Newton believed he could say, "I assume nothing". But it was on the basis of a hypothesis that the famous revolution – which wasn't at all Copernican, but rather Newtonian – hinged, substituting "it falls" for "it turns".

RM: Do you know the difference between 'it falls' and 'it turns'? Because for Copernicus, the planets were turning around the sun. And with Newton, he's stressing that it's because of gravity. And gravity is what makes things fall.
BB: Did Copernicus have a theory about why planets turned the sun? If he didn't have one, did he think it was just because God made it that way? I'm just taking the metaphor another step.
RM: Right! Well, Copernicus thought that the planets circle around the sun, but he didn't have an explanation for it.
BB: Okay, then!

TEXT: The Newtonian hypothesis consisted in positing that the astral turning is the same as falling. But in order to observe that – which allows one to eliminate the hypothesis – he first had to make the hypothesis.

To introduce a scientific discourse concerning knowledge, one must investigate knowledge where it is. That knowledge, insofar as it resides in the shelter of llanguage, means the unconscious. I do not enter there, no more than did Newton, without a hypothesis.

DOI: 10.4324/9781003424581-21

RM: Just one second there! So, what he's doing there is collapsing the distinction between knowledge and *savoir*, by first recognizing the knowledge in science – the knowledge of Copernicus and Newton – and then, he slips into "that knowledge, as far as that resides in the shelter of llanguage",... that would be *savoir*. It wouldn't be 'knowledge', which is *connaissance. Savoir* means the unconscious in a way. But then he is talking about llanguage and unconscious knowledge, or *savoir*, as if it were the same thing as the knowledge in science. The knowledge in science is objective, whereas the knowledge of llanguage is subjective and singular, right? *Savoir* appears in each person in a singular way, as opposed to a knowledge that is kind of objective and social, and everybody has the same relationship to it.

GF: Is he making the claim that no knowledge is possible without a hypothesis first?

RM: Right, that's the basis for it.

GF: So, then, the hypothesis is made and tested and then we get objectivity?

RM: Right, so he says he doesn't make any assumptions, only hypotheses. And, then in the next sentence...

TEXT: My hypothesis is that the individual who is affected by the unconscious is the same individual who constitutes what I call the subject of a signifier. That is what I enunciate in the minimal formulation that a signifier represents a subject to another signifier. The signifier in itself is nothing but what can be defined as a difference from another signifier. It is the introduction of difference as such into the field, which allows one to extract from llanguage the nature of the signifier (*ce qu'il en est du signficant*).

RM: So, there you have it – that the subject and the signifier are interchangeable.

GF: Could you say a little bit more about that?

RM: Well, the subject is what represents a signifier for another signifier. The signifier is what represents a subject for another signifier. So, in this case the signifiers for representing the subject as a metaphor for another signifier are Barri, Greg, and Raul. So, 'Raul' represents me for another signifier, 'Greg', and for another signifier, 'Barri'. So, in language, then, we are represented by signifiers. And, at the same time that we are signified by signifiers, or represented by signifiers – however, there's a part of us that remains outside the signifier because we've been supplanted by the signifier. If you said 'Raul', for instance, you would initiate a series of determinations about who I am as a subject. But then there would be something about me that would be lost... and that lost bit would be in the Real. And then, there's the Imaginary Ego that creates a wall between the Symbolic and the Real.

GF: Is the imaginary in that sense a distortion?

RM: Well, we represent ourselves to each other through our speech and through our names, and yet we all have our own individual fantasies and desires. So, in the fantasy of the relationship in schema L you see that clearly. Do you remember the schema L? It is the one that looks like an hourglass.

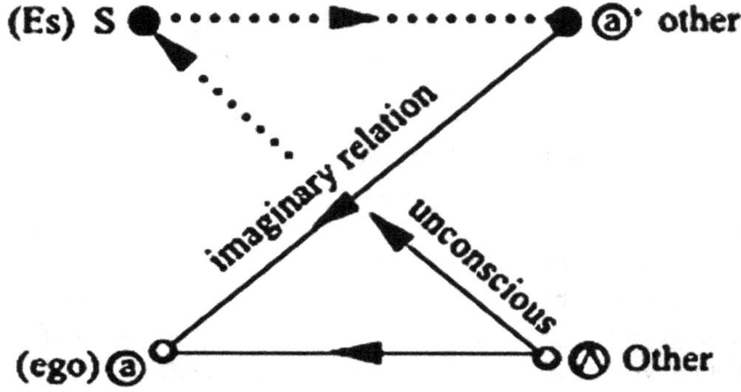

Lacan's 'L Schema'

First, you have the 'pre-subject' or the subject as "it" (not Thou). Then you have the Other as *objet a* and the matheme for the 'ideal Ego'. And then there is the Symbolic Other, or the battery, or the signifiers. In the diagram, the battery of signifiers cannot get to the pre-subject easily because it's blocked by the Imaginary axis – meaning that we're always perceiving the Other through the Ego and the fantasy object. And the signifier is what has to be used to analyze or to work with the Imaginary axis in order to access the Real (depicted also in the diagram). So, when we're saying our names, and we are the interactions of our names, that would be the Symbolic. And because we have a sense of being in this field, we have a sense of what our *objet a* or our fantasy object is or what our ego needs by way of recognition. But we don't let that interfere with the Symbolic discourse, and then that provides an access to the Real.

GF: So, if I was to take a segment of a film where say the camera pans down the street and sets up some scenario, would that segment in its entirety be a signifier? And if it's not spoken, is that a proper form of signification?

RM: That's your *mise-en-scène*. Is there a word for it in English or should we just use the French phrase?

GF: Staging?

RM: Yes, the staging is *mise-en-scène*. So, you are staging an 'other' scene that is composed of both signifiers and objects of fantasy. And you're going to use the signifier to try to delimit or denote, or to point to where the objects of fantasy are. You also would then have an effect of the Real. But the effect of the Real would be something that's obscure or illuminating about the scene. The scene can also give you a sense of what the social reality is, whereby the social reality would be constructed with the signifiers and the objects of fantasy. And the 'reality' that it could give rise could be the aspect of the Real that darkens or obfuscates or renders the scene enigmatic. Or you just watch it, and you are kind of at a loss, confused, or perplexed about the impact that it has on you and not exactly knowing how or where it's hitting you. So that would be the one sense of the Real. The other sense would be if a scene is particularly illuminating and clarifying or revealing something that's more than just the sense of social reality.

BB: Is that the kind of clarifying and revealing like in an 'aha' moment where you see something on a deeper level that allows things to all come together?

RM: Or it evokes a kind of jouissance, a kind of illuminating jouissance, or a jouissance of meaning where you get the meaning as an experience, not just as a dictionary definition. That would be the Real because there's a jouissance there.

BB: Is that like in poetry when you sometimes contrast two things that you wouldn't think go together in a poem and where the contrast of the two are being placed in a way you don't expect, and you have this experience of a jouissance of meaning? And you can do that with images, too. [*RM agrees*]

GF: And the signifier can potentially have a whole range of other signifiers already well established in the horizon of its meaning.

RM: Right, so a signifier can be a nexus of relations and some signifiers have more weight than others because the nexus of relations is greater than any one individual signifier. So, we can think of weights… as a kind of gravity of the signifier.

TEXT: My hypothesis is that the individual who is affected by the unconscious is the same individual who constitutes what I call the subject of a signifier. That is what I enunciate in the minimal formulation that a signifier represents a subject to another signifier. The signifier in itself is nothing but what can be defined as a difference from another signifier. It is the introduction of difference as such into the field, which allows one to extract from llanguage the nature of the signifier (*ce qu'il en est du signifiant*).

RM: "What it has of significance". But, what about it is significant? So there, do you see how he says that signifying itself is nothing but what can be defined as a difference from another signifier. That's an interesting point because the signifier itself, qua nothing – there's an aspect of the signifier in itself qua nothing that is important because that's what allows for the combination to take place. Meaning that each signifier, in itself, has to be empty for it to function as an element of a combination. But the signifier in itself, which is nothing, is in the Real. The signifier in the Real is the signified which refers to a mass of ideas and feelings. And that's similar to how we were discussing before the way subjects interact with the signifiers. There's something in itself about each one of us that is a 'nothing', that is 'nonself'. I think it is interesting that when Socrates was on trial, he offers a speech of defense in which he wants to preserve his soul and he wants to preserve his purity. He doesn't care that he's going to get killed because he'd rather be killed than compromise his beliefs. So, he said, "You can kill me, but even if you kill me, you do nothing to my soul because only I can do something to my soul". It's an interesting formulation: whereas the abuses of the Other on the subject do nothing to the individual soul [however counterintuitive that may sound in terms of how we think of abuse and trauma…]. Because Socrates says something about this soul being nothing, and if he can keep it as nothing, then dying doesn't matter (or something like that). The way he keeps it as 'a nothing' is to be consistent with what he thinks and with his beliefs, and so on. So, in all of the signifying networking that was going on there in Greece, with the trial, and did he do this or that, or did he reject the gods and so forth… he was representing a fierce kind of individuality at a time when the society expected you to be bound by guilt and shame, under obligation to the other, and to honor of your family, et cetera. So, it was all about being defined as a kind of social subject, but he stressed the importance of the individual – and his way of going about dying was his way of manifesting that.

GF: So, the distinction that Lacan is making here, is that a difference that can be traced back to jouissance?

RM: Right, because the subject in the Real is a jouissance, the signifying net itself is nothing – and, because of jouissance, there's not much you can say about the beyond signifier. That is at the level of the Real. Then, at the level of Symbolic, you're talking about the relations between the differences between signifiers which establish meaning. The other thing I was going to say earlier is that a signifier can function as an element of a system, but a signifier can also function as a code. And, when it functions as a code it has a different function, because when it functions as a code, it regulates the relationship of other signifiers. Whereas when it's functioning simply as an element of a battery of signifiers, it is just a placeholder in the interactions regulated by the code. But the code is symbolized also by a signifier. So, all we have to do for Socrates is one's own self-care, because we only hurt ourselves if we don't do our own self-care, regardless of what the Other is doing to you. So, he says it doesn't matter what others are doing to you, because, ultimately, they cannot destroy your soul. Only you can destroy your soul. All you have to be careful of is to take care of yourself and to be attuned with your individual soul. We're using his language here – but your individuality, your singularity as a subject, is what you are responsible to care for.

BB: I would like to flesh out the idea of soul. For me, the soul for Socrates is his relationship to the gods in the ideal. It's his relationship to what it is to be a man or what it is to be happy or what is love. That's something that the gods know, and he seeks to know something about that.

RM: It's a moral virtue, right? You have to act according to moral virtue, ethical virtue, and that's how you take care of your soul, regardless of how the other treats you. So here, they're trying to kill him. They're trying to tell him he is doing this, he's doing that, he's corrupting the youth, he's rejecting the gods… he's providing a critical critique of society. So, they are unhappy, and they accuse him, and then he is condemned to death… and he's fine with it, because he feels that he's acting in accordance with his virtue.

BB: But could I suggest that he is doing something that's more Symbolic, in that his relationship to the gods is a "one of a kind of discourse" that he had to get from somewhere. Throughout the years, there's a discourse that goes on between generations about our place in relationship to the gods, the ancestors, and our posterity. So, to me, virtue as lived in a life is something that neither we nor Socrates could make up on our or his own – taking care of oneself is taking care of that place, that Symbolic place that's an intergenerational gift and a Symbolic gift. And he is actually providing that understanding to those others in a position to represent that Symbolic gift who are not in the polis of Athens. When people collapse the space of this gift into something narcissistic and egotistical, then it is no longer Symbolic in the sense of an open place wherein each person, like Heidegger or Socrates suggest, works to realize some meaning. Those Socrates criticized, those speaking fallacies, are collapsing this gift of language within discourse.

RM: Right, but there was a conflict. He was disagreeing with Greek gods in how the polis was organized around the worship of the gods. And, while he didn't have a monotheistic God, he had a sense of a deity or god that perhaps would be attuned with rationality. And he was rejecting the gods of his time, and for that, they wanted to kill them. That was one reason... the other one is because he was teaching the young people to think independently, and they didn't want the young people thinking independently. They wanted the young people to think according to what the society thought at the time.

BB: Of course. I'm just saying that when you read Socrates, he's always talking about the ideal that the gods know about that he doesn't. And even though he doesn't agree with the religion of the time, I would say that he believes the religion is lacking the virtue that the gods really represent. This is a virtue that a person can't control in the way those who put Socrates on trial meant to do.

RM: Yes, he is trying to stress that virtue is connected to reason more than to the gods, although he doesn't reject the gods entirely.

BB: When I read through Plato, my understanding is that he represents the gods as that which man cannot know completely. So, you couldn't merely have priests say, "this is what God wants you to do". Rather, what's in the realm of the gods isn't something that men can fully understand – one can only 'approach' it. But I think some of the people who were religious then didn't think of it that way. They thought that they could define what the gods want and then they would tell the citizens to do it... which collapses things into a kind of power relationship where there's a demand for coercive mirroring or a demand that you 'do what I say you do' and not think as an independent person. So, a particular authority is established.

GF: I find it interesting that Socrates abided by the law, and he abides by all the rationality of the society at the time – the intergenerational discourse. But he does so at the stake of his body. So, he has to give up his body to arrive at that 'no self' of the soul. So, those two things are not the same for him, apparently.

RM: Right, because the body was the prison of the soul. Because he thought he would do more damage to his soul by adapting to what they wanted from him.

He thought he would kill his soul if he did that. In order to save it, he had to die. But that goes with the philosophy of duality of body and soul.

GF: It seems that way, although if you're trying to care for yourself, you're probably not trying to get yourself executed!

BB: This is my own interpretation, but I felt like he was saying that his wish to be a member of the Athenian polis required that he act according to that law which was consistent with his beliefs and teachings. He did not want to leave the world and not be an Athenian. He wanted to be an Athenian in the sense that he knew it to be, which meant that he had to give these people the power to kill his body.

GF: And the law is a signifying code that is standing behind everything. Nobody in particular 'is' the Law which metes out our justice.

BB: Some people have tried to be the Law.

GF: Yes, people act as representatives of it. A judge interprets the Law or represents the Law but isn't the Law in itself.

TEXT: Stated otherwise, I reduce the hypothesis, according to the very formulation that lends it substance, to the following: it is necessary to the functioning of llanguage. So does this have to do with free association in some way? That, really, in order to have hypotheses, you have to have free association which is the closest thing to lalangue... because otherwise, one is speaking in this kind of language that people speak in that is maybe more prefabricated or just what everyone says.

RM: It's the narratives and the storytelling, which is more at the level of the social discourse. So, it's almost as if the play of differences with the signifier – let's say the *fort da* of Freud, is right at the beginning of vocalization. So, the child is using the phonemes which are also *objet a*, because the phoneme is an *objet a* used to describe the presence and absence of the mother and the control that the symbol gives the child over the presence and absence (which otherwise he can't control). And, from those plays of difference – between "here", "gone", "mother present", "mother absent" – from that lalangue, it allows one to extract from llanguage the nature of the signifier. So, from then on, this lalangue *fort da* will help construct language around this dimension of presence and absence, by this "you are here" or "you are gone"; "are you self?" or "Other?"; "do I love you?" or "do I hate you?"; and, so on and so forth.

TEXT: To say that there is a subject is nothing other than to say that there is a hypothesis. The only proof we have that the subject coincides with this hypothesis, and that it is the speaking individual on whom it is based, is that the signifier becomes a sign.

RM: Okay, so how does the signifier become a sign? Basically, Lacan is defining the subject as a hypothesis, given that we could say we don't know anything about the subject in the Real. So, it would be a hypothesis of the subject that you expect the subject to behave in certain ways. So and so is going to do this or that, right? So, that hypothesis is how you construct the subject in your mind. The only proof we have that the subject coincides with this hypothesis is the speech of the one on whom it is based – then the signifier becomes a sign... a sign of 'someone'.

GF: Yes, the sign recognized by some other signifier in the battery. So, a signifier in a certain way is not yet the objective sign...

RM: Yes. Well, that's the confusion in the use of all these terms, because 'sign', if you use it in terms of the semiotics of Peirce, represents an object to someone. But then sometimes the 'sign', like in the theory of the signifier in Saussure, is described by the equation in which the signified is over the signifier and that whole relation is called the sign. So, there are different uses of the word 'sign'. And, of course, a sign can be semiotic and not symbolic at all, and it doesn't even have to be in language. The telegraph transmits signs – the dots and dashes are signs even though they're not letters.

GF: I'm fascinated by the idea of the hypothesis [of the subject] in terms of the Imaginary, and I am assuming that a good hypothesis would entail the 'good Imaginary'. The alternative would be a 'distorted Imaginary'. So, if the subject is recognized in a hypothesis, it seems the starting place would always be from the Imaginary as it is signified in speech. And then somebody recognizes that and potentially offers correction if it is distorted ...

RM: Right, that's more the 'imagination'. That would be like imagining along the lines of Einstein's thought experiment which is also a hypothesis. So, he imagines himself flying or riding on a beam of light, and then does the calculations to show that at a certain point, the speed of light comes to zero... something like that. Here he is using the image to construct his formulas which then gives him something of the Real of how light operates in the universe. Using this thought experiment, which is really an image, triggers his mathematical mind... his Symbolic mind. So that's a good example of the three registers at play, but there I would say that's the imagination more than the Imaginary as Lacan conceives it, because it's the imagination at the service of science, not at the service of the Symbolic.

GF: Does the Imaginary always entail distortion?

RM: It blocks access to and supplants the Real by offering the illusion that the Imaginary really is the Real, and it distorts the Symbolic structure because how things appear is not 'what' appears. What appears is the structure, but the structure is Symbolic, and it is distorted by how it appears in the Imaginary in the phenomenal field.

BB: I'm having trouble with the term 'distort'. There can't be just one 'correct way' to take something from the Real and translate it into the Imaginary, or language, or understanding. The Real is made of different stuff than those other categories ...right?

RM: Well, the power of visual perception gives you a strong sense of reality. So, it makes you think that what you see is the Real. In that sense, perception 'supplants' the Real. But the Real, fundamentally, is a form of emptiness or a dimension of reality that's beyond images. The Imaginary gives us the illusion that images are what is real. So, the Real instead has to force the Imaginary and the Symbolic into a different type of relation. That's the change in the Borromean knot. For example, I was talking about giving supervision in a case… Can I talk about that, or would that be a distraction? Or do we have to go?

BB: Unfortunately, we have to go soon, but we have a few minutes. Can you tell us in a few minutes?

RM: Yes, well, this morning, this young couple, they broke up because she wanted to be a go-go dancer and it was making the guy extremely jealous because she thrives on getting all kinds of attention from men – and with him, even though she loved him, she was frigid… which is not an uncommon experience. So, frigidity signaled no apparent desire for him, and although she wanted to be in a relationship with him, she didn't desire him in that way and remained frigid in their sexual relation. But she really thrived on being a go-go dancer! She has a very nice body and all the guys go crazy. And so, then he had a dream that they broke up, because he recognized that he was trying to change her desire to be a go-go dancer which she sees as her independence as a woman. So, finally he said, 'I support you in your go-go dancing, but that's not what I want for a relationship'. And then, she said, 'Okay, I want to go-go dance, so I guess we're done'. And then he has another dream, because they also work together in a restaurant where one of the other waitresses becomes transman. Apparently, in reality, there's a waitress who just cut off her breasts as part of the process of becoming a she-man. And, so, he was threatened in the dream that the ex-girlfriend was going to be more interested in the *she*-man than in him. Which also goes with another dream where he was pregnant and was going to have a child with a girlfriend. But, instead of her being pregnant, he was pregnant. So, there's all these Imaginary formations on the surface of how the structure appears. But the structure seems to be that she wants to be the phallus on the move. She wants to be the object of desire, to be wanted. But she herself doesn't have a desire for anything in particular that she would want from him or he doesn't have anything that he can offer her because she's frigid. So then, he fantasizes that being the phallus is more powerful because he interprets her action of going go-go dancing as a choice of leaving him instead of being with him. He attributes the action to her even though he's the one who said, 'well, if you're going to go-go dance, I bless you on your path but that's not what I want for a partner'. Interesting, right? So, there's all this structure about man, about woman – who is the phallus, who has the phallus, who has desire, who doesn't have the desire, and all that, which is part of the Symbolic structure that appears in this kind of Imaginary form.

BB: That's very helpful. Thank you.

[End of session]

Supplemental References

Lacan, J. (1972–1973). *Encore. The Seminar of Jacques Lacan, XX*. New York: Norton, 1998.

Peirce, Charles S. (1867, 2009). *The Essential Peirce: Selected Philosophical Writings. Volumes 1 and 2*. Peirce Edition Project (Ed.). Bloomington & Indianapolis: Indiana University.

Plato. (1984). *Apology*. In Four Texts on Socrates: Plato's *Euthyphro, Apology, and Crito and Aristophanes' Clouds* (Thomas G. West and Grace Starry West, Trans.). Ithaca, NY: Cornell University Press.

Bibliography

Agamben, Giorgio. (1993). *Infancy and History: The Destruction of Experience*. Verso; 1st Edition, London.
Aquinas, Thomas. (1966). *Summa Theologica*. Edited by Thomas Gilby, OP. 60 vols. Cambridge: Blackfriars.
Aristotle. (2009). *The Nicomachean Ethics*. Oxford World Classics. Cambridge: Oxford University Press.
Augustine. (2010). *On the Free Choice of the Will, On Grace and Free Choice, and Other Writings* (P. King, Trans.). New York: Cambridge University Press.
Bateson, G. (1979). *Mind and Nature*. New York: Bantam Books, 1980.
Bentham, Jeremy, 1748–1832. (1843). *The Works of Jeremy Bentham*. Edinburgh: W. Tait.
Bion, W. (1961). *Experiences in Groups*. London: Routledge.
Dahl, Roald. (1982). *The BFG*. United Kingdom: Penguin Books.
Derrida, Jacques. (1998). *Of Grammatology*. Baltimore, MD: Johns Hopkins University Press.
Derrida, J., Domingo, W., Hulbert, J., Ron, M., & M.-R. L. (1975). 'The Purveyor of Truth', *Yale French Studies*, 52, 31–113.
Descartes, Rene. (2008). *Meditations on First Philosophy* (M. Moriarty, Trans.). London: Oxford University Press.
Dilthey, Wilhelm (1996). *Selected Works, Volume IV: Hermeneutics and the Study of History*. Princeton, NJ: Princeton University Press.
Dōgen, E. (1241). *Shōbōgenzō*. London and Tokyo: Windmill Publications, 1998.
Dolto, F. (1982). *Seminario de Psicoanalisis de Ninos*. Buenos Aires: Siglo Veinteuno, 1984.
Freud, Sigmund. (1895). A Project for a Scientific Psychology. *SE* 1.
Freud, Sigmund. (1900). Interpretation of Dreams. *SE* 4.
Freud, Sigmund. (1915). Instincts and their Vicissitudes. *SE* 14.
Freud, Sigmund. (1915). Repression. *SE* 14.
Freud, Sigmund. (1915). The Unconscious. *SE* 14.
Freud, Sigmund. (1913, 1919). *Totem and Taboo: Resemblances Between the Mental Lives of Savages and Neurotics*. New York: Moffat, Yard and Company.
Freud, Sigmund. (1920). *Beyond the Pleasure Principle*. SE 18.
Freud, Sigmund. (1927). *Essais de Psychanalyse*. Paris: Payot.
Freud, Sigmund. (1930). *Civilization and its Discontents*. SE 21.
Harrison, George. (1969). '*Something*', from the Beatles' album Abbey Road.
Hegel, F. H. (1807) 2018. *The Phenomenology of the Spirit*. Cambridge: Cambridge University Press.

Heidegger, M. (1927). *Being and Time: A Translation of Sein und Zeit*. Albany: State University of New York Press, 1996.

Heidegger, M. (1943). 'On the Essence of Truth', *Basic Writings* (Revised and Expanded Edition) (D. F. Krell, Trans.). London: Routledge, 1993.

Heidegger, M. 2008 (1969). 'The End of Philosophy and the Task of Thinking', *Basic Writings* (Revised and Expanded Edition) (D. F. Krell, Trans.). London: Harper Perennial.

Hurst, A. (2008). *Derrida vis-vis Lacan: Interweaving Deconstruction and Psychoanalysis*. New York: Fordham University Press.

Huxley, A. (1932). *Brave New World*. New York: Harper Collins, 2006.

Jakobson, R. (1990). *On Language*. Cambridge, MA: Harvard University Press.

Jagger, Mick and Richards, Keith. (1965). *('I Can't Get No') Satisfaction*, from the Rolling Stones' album, Out of Our Heads.

Johnson, B. (1977). 'The Frame of Reference: Poe, Lacan, Derrida', *Yale French Studies*, 55/56, 457–505.

Joyce, J. (1976, 1939). *Finnegan's Wake* (Centennial ed.). New York: Penguin Books.

Kant, I. (2004). *Critique of Practical Reason* (T. K. Abbott, Trans.). Dover Publications, London.

Kierkegaard, Søren. 1813–1855. (1985). *Fear and Trembling*. Harmondsworth, Middlesex, England: New York: Penguin Books; Viking Penguin.

Kristeva, J. 1980 (1941). *Desire in Language*. New York: Columbia University Press.

Levi-Strauss, C. (1967). *The Elementary Structures of Kinship*. Boston, MA: Beacon Press.

Levi-Strauss, C. (1978). *Myth and Meaning*. London: Routledge.

Lacan, J. (1954–1955). *The Ego in Freud's Theory and in the Technique of Psychoanalysis. The Seminar of Jacques Lacan, II*. New York: Norton, 1988.

Lacan, J. (1955–1956). *Psychoses. The Seminar of Jacques Lacan, III*. New York: Norton, 1995.

Lacan, J. 2020 (1956–1957). *The Object Relation. The Seminar of Jacques Lacan, IV* (A. R. Price, Trans.). New York: Polity.

Lacan, J. (1959–1960). *The Ethics of Psychoanalysis. The Seminar of Jacques Lacan, VII*. New York: Norton.

Lacan, J. 2001 (1960–1961). *Transference. The Seminar of Jacques Lacan, VIII*. New York: Norton.

Lacan, J. (1961–1962). *Identification. The Seminar of Jacques Lacan, IX*. New York: Norton.

Lacan, J. (1967–1968). *The Psychoanalytic Act. The Seminar of Jacques Lacan, XV*. UK: Karnac, 2002.

Lacan, J. 2007 (1969–1970). *The Other Side of Psychoanalysis. The Seminar of Jacques Lacan, XVII*. New York: Norton.

Lacan, J. (1970–1971). *On a Discourse That Would Not Be Semblance*. London: Karnac.

Lacan, J. 1998 (1972–1973). *Encore. The Seminar of Jacques Lacan, XX*. New York: Norton.

Lacan, J. (1974–1975). *RSI. The Seminar of Jacques Lacan, XXII* (C. Gallagher, Trans.). Retrieved from: http://hdl.handle.net/10788/179

Lacan, J. 2016 (1975–1976). *The Sinthome. The Seminar of Jacques Lacan. Encore, Seminar XXIII*. London: Polity Press.

Lacan, J. (2007). Écrits (B. Fink, Trans.). New York: WW Norton.

Low, Barbara. (1920). *Psycho-Analysis. A Brief Account of the Freudian Theory*. Abingdon-on-Thames: Routledge.

Marcuse, Herbert. (1955). *Eros and Civilization. A Philosophical Inquiry Into Freud*. Boston, MA: Beacon Press.

Marx, K. (1818). *The German Ideology*. New York: Prometheus Books, 1998.

Moncayo, R. (2008). *Evolving Lacanian Perspectives for Clinical Psychoanalysis. On Narcissism, Sexuation, and the Phases/Faces of Analysis in Contemporary Culture*. London: Karnac.

Moncayo, R. (2012). The Emptiness of Oedipus: Identification and Non-identification in Lacanian Psychoanalysis. Routledge/Taylor & Francis Group.

Moncayo, R. (2017). *Jouissance, Lalangue, Sinthome, and Nomination*. London: Routledge.

Moncayo, R. (2018). *Knowing, Not-Knowing, and Jouissance: Levels, Symbols, and Codes of Experience in Psychoanalysis*. London: Routledge.

Muller, J. P. (1996). *Beyond the Psychoanalytic Dyad. Developmental Semiotics in Freud, Peirce, and Lacan*. New York: Routledge.

Newton, Sir Isaac. (2016). *Principia Mathematica*. First Edition. University of California Press. Berkeley, Calif.

Nietzsche, Friedrich Wilhelm. (1995). *The Birth of Tragedy*. New York: Dover Publications.

Peirce, Charles S. (1867, 2009). *The Essential Peirce: Selected Philosophical Writings. Volumes 1 and 2*. Peirce Edition Project (Ed.). Bloomington & Indianapolis: Indiana University.

Peirce, Charles S. (1940). *Philosophical Writings of Peirce*. J. Buchler (Ed.). New York: Dover, 1955.

Plato. (1980). *Cratylus*. Cambridge: Hackett Classics Plato. The Apology. In: Harvard Classics. CT: Grolier Enterprises.

Plato. (1984). *Apology*. In Four Texts on Socrates: Plato's *Euthyphro, Apology, and Crito and Aristophanes' Clouds* (Thomas G. West and Grace Starry West, Trans.). Ithaca, NY: Cornell University Press.

Plato. (1999). *The Symposium*. New York: Penguin Books.

Quine, Willard Van Orman (2013) [1960]. *Word and Object* (New ed.). Cambridge: MIT Press.

Saussure, F. 1966 (1915). *Course in General Linguistics*. New York: Mc-Graw Hill.

Soler, Colette. (2015). *Lacanian Affects: The Function of Affect in Lacan's Work*. Routledge.

Soler, Colette. (2018). *Lacan – The Unconscious Reinvented* (The Center for Freudian Analysis and Research Library (CFAR)). Routledge.

Sophocles. (1993). *Antigone*. New York: Dover Publications.

Spencer-Brown, G. (1969). *Laws of Form*. London: Allen & Unwin.

Spencer-Brown, G. (1969/1979). *Laws of Form*. New York: Dutton.

Spitz, René A. (1945). 'Hospitalism: An Inquiry into the Genesis of Psychiatric Conditions in Early Childhood', *The Psychoanalytic Study of the Child*, 1, 53–74.

von Uexküll, T. (1987). 'The Sign Theory of Jakob von Uexküll', in: Krampen et al. (Eds.). *Classics of Semiotics*. New York: Plenum, pp. 147–179.

Whitehead, A. N. and B. Russell. (1962). Principia Mathematica. Cambridge: Cambridge University Press (First and Second Editions, 1910–1913; 1925–1927).

Wittgenstein, Ludwig. (1953). *Philosophical Investigations*. Oxford: Blackwell.

Žižek, Slavoj. (1989). *The Sublime Object of Ideology*. London: Verso.

Žižek, Slavoj. (1997). *The Abyss of Freedom Ages of the World* (The Body, In Theory: Histories of Cultural Materialism). Ann Arbor: University of Michigan.

Index

Note: Page numbers followed by "n" denote endnotes

For Product Safety Concerns and Information please contact our EU representative GPSR@taylorandfrancis.com
Taylor & Francis Verlag GmbH, Kaufingerstraße 24, 80331 München, Germany

www.ingramcontent.com/pod-product-compliance
Lightning Source LLC
Chambersburg PA
CBHW070324270326
41926CB00017B/3750

* 9 7 8 1 0 3 2 5 4 3 7 7 2 *